824.8P295s 1982
main   Selections.

2 1765 0004 9172 3

D0369877

WITHDRAWN

WITHDRAWN

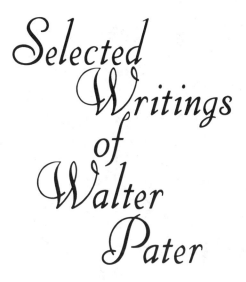

Selected
Writings
of
Walter
Pater

edited with an introduction and notes by

Harold Bloom

Columbia University Press / New York

Copyright © 1974 by Harold Bloom

All rights reserved.

Reprinted by arrangement with The New American Library, New York, N.Y.

Library of Congress Cataloging in Publication Data

Pater, Walter, 1839–1894.
    Selected writings of Walter Pater.

    Reprint. Originally published: New York:
New American Library, 1974.
    Bibliography: p.
    I. Bloom, Harold. II. Title.
PR5131.5.B57 1982   824'.8   81–17099
ISBN 0-231-05480-1   AACR2
ISBN 0-231-05481-5 (pbk.)

Columbia University Press   New York
Columbia University Press Morningside Edition 1982

Clothbound Columbia University Press books are Smyth-sewn and printed
on permanent and durable acid-free paper.

Contents

INTRODUCTION   vii
CHRONOLOGY   xxxiii
BIBLIOGRAPHY   xxxv

The Child in the House   **1**

from **The Renaissance:**
   Studies in Art and Poetry   **17**

Preface   17
Sandro Botticelli   23
Leonardo Da Vinci   31
The School of Giorgione (excerpt)   52
Conclusion   58

from **Imaginary Portraits**   **64**

Sebastian Van Storck   64
Denys l'Auxerrois   85

from **Appreciations**   **103**

Style   103
Wordsworth   125
Coleridge   143
Charles Lamb   170
"Measure for Measure"   181
Aesthetic Poetry   190
Dante Gabriel Rossetti   199
Postscript (Romanticism)   208

from **Plato and Platonism**   **224**

The Genius of Plato   224

from **Greek Studies**   **241**

    Hippolytus Veiled:
        A Study from Euripides   241

from **Sketches and Reviews**   **263**

    A Novel by Mr. Oscar Wilde   263

Introduction

The Crystal Man

... What is this song or picture, this engaging personality presented in life or in a book, to *me*? What effect does it really produce on me? Does it give me pleasure? and if so, what sort or degree of pleasure? How is my nature modified by its presence, and under its influence?

—PATER, Preface to *The Renaissance*

... Why should a poem not change in sense when there is a fluctuation of the whole of appearance? Or why should it not change when we realize that the indifferent experience of life is the unique experience, the item of ecstasy which we have been isolating and reserving for another time and place, loftier and more secluded.

—STEVENS, "Two or Three Ideas"

1. "AESTHETIC" CRITICISM

Pater is a great critic of a kind common enough in the nineteenth century—Coleridge, Lamb, Hazlitt, De Quincey, above all Ruskin—but scarcely to be found in the twentieth. Difficult to define, this sort of critic possesses one salient characteristic. His value inheres neither in his accuracy at the direct interpretation of meaning in texts nor in his judgments of relative eminence of works and authors. Rather, he gives us a vision of art through his own unique sensibility, and so his own writings obscure the supposed distinction between criticism and creation. "Supposed," because who can convince us of that distinction? To adapt Shelley's idea of the relation between poetry and the universe, let us say that criticism creates the poem anew, after the poem has been annihilated in our minds by the recurrence of impressions blunted by reiteration. Ruskin's or Pater's criticism tends to create anew not so much a particular work of art but rather the precisely appropriate consciousness of the perceptive reader or viewer. This does not mean that these great critics are monuments to the Affective Fallacy, or that literary historians with Formalist tendencies are justified in naming Ruskin and Pater as critical Impressionists. Oscar Wilde, who brilliantly vulgarized both his prime precursors, insisted that their work treated "the work of art simply as a starting-point for a new creation." Matthew Arnold had asserted that the "aim of criticism is to see the object as in itself it really is." A few years later, implicitly invoking Ruskin against Arnold, Pater slyly added that "the first step towards seeing one's object as it really is, is to know one's impression as it really is, to discriminate it, to realise it distinctly." Wilde, attempting to complete his master, charmingly amended this to the grand statement that "the primary aim of the critic is to see the object as in itself it really is not." Between Arnold's self-deception and Wilde's wit comes Pater's hesitant and skeptical emphasis upon a peculiar kind of vision, with which he identifies all aesthetic experience.

We owe to Pater our characteristic modern use of "aesthetic," for he emancipated the word from its bondage to philosophy, both when he spoke of the "aesthetic critic" in his "Preface" to *The Renaissance*, and when he named the work of Morris and Rossetti as the "aesthetic poetry" in *Appreciations*. Vulgarized again by his ebullient disciple Wilde, and by the parodies of Wilde as Bunthorne in Gilbert and Sullivan's *Patience*, and of Pater himself as Mr. Rose in W. H. Mallock's *The New Republic*, Pater had to endure the debasement of "aesthete" as a term, and we endure it still. Pater meant us always to remember what mostly we have forgotten, that "aesthete" is from the Greek *aisthetes*, "one who perceives." So the "aesthetic critic" is simply the perceptive critic, or literary critic proper, and "aesthetic poetry" is precisely the contemporary poetry that is most perceptive, that is, in one's judgment most truly poetry.

Pater's key terms as a critic are "perception" and "sensation," which is response to perception. "Vision" for Pater, as for Blake, is a synonym for Coleridge's or Wordsworth's "Imagination," and Pater further emulated Blake by questing after the "spiritual form" of phenomena as against "corporeal form." This is the "form" that: "Every moment . . . grows perfect in hand or face," according to the almost preternaturally eloquent "Conclusion" to *The Renaissance*. In the marvelous "Postscript" (on "Romanticism") to *Appreciations*, Pater traces the genesis of form:

> . . . there are the born romanticists, who start with an original, untried *matter*, still in fusion; who conceive this vividly, and hold by it as the essence of their work; who, by the very vividness and heat of their conception, purge away, sooner or later, all that is not organically appropriate to it, till the whole effect adjusts itself in clear, orderly, proportionate form; which form, after a very little time, becomes classical in its turn.

Vividness and *heat* purge away from the Romantic idea all that is not form, and form is the reward of the aesthete or perceptive man, if he has the strength to persist in his purgation. "In the end, the aesthetic is completely crushed and destroyed by the inability of the observer who has himself been crushed to have any feeling for it left." That dark observation is by Wallace Stevens, an heir (unwilling) of Pater's aestheticism. A more accurate observation of the aesthete's defeat comes from as great an heir, more conscious and willing, who attributed to Pater's influence his poetic generation's doomed attempt "to walk upon a rope, tightly stretched through serene air." Yeats nevertheless got across to the other side of the Nineties, and carried Pater alive into our century in *Per Amica Silentia Lunae* (1917) and *A Vision* (1925, 1937). Pater's vision of form culminates in Yeats's Phase 15: "Now contemplation and desire, united into one, inhabit a world where every beloved image has bodily form, and every bodily form is loved." Pater, for whom the attained form demanded purgation, an *askesis* (to which I shall return), hesitantly held back from this Yeatsian version of a High Romantic Absolute.

To know Pater, and to apprehend his influence not only on Stevens and Yeats, but on Joyce, Eliot, Pound, and many other writers of our century, we need to place Pater in his Oedipal context in the cultural situation of his own time. The pleasures of reading Pater are intense, to me, but the importance of Pater transcends those pleasures, and finally is quite out of proportion to Pater's literary achievement, fairly large as that was. Pater is the heir of a tradition already too wealthy to have required much extension or variation when it reached him. He revised that tradition, turning the Victorian continuation of High Romanticism into the Late Romanticism or "Decadence" that prolonged itself as what variously might be called Modernism, Post-Romanticism or, self-deceivingly, Anti-Romanticism, the art of Pound's Vortex. Though Pater compares oddly, perhaps not wholly adequately, with the great Victorian prose prophets, he did what Carlyle, Ruskin, Newman, Arnold could not do: he fathered the future. Himself wistful and elaborately reserved, renouncing even his own strength, he became the most widely diffused (though more and more hidden) literary influence of the later nineteenth upon the twentieth century. In its diffusion, particularly in America, the Paterian influence was assimilated to strikingly similar elements in Nietzsche and Emerson, a process as indubitable as it is still largely unstudied. When Yeats proclaimed the "profane perfection of mankind" or Pound or Stevens their images of the poet as a crystal man, they combined Pater with Nietzsche and Emerson (both of whom he seems to have neglected). "Just take one step farther," Nietzsche urged, and "love yourself through Grace; then you are no longer in need of your God, and the whole drama of fall and redemption is acted out in yourself." "In the highest moments, we are a vision," is the antinomian counsel of Emerson. Pater's first essay, "Diaphaneite," read to an Oxford literary group in 1864, presented the artist as a transparent or crystal image of more-than-human perfection, an Apollonian hero. How often, in Modern poetry, we have heard these strains mingled, until by now our latest poets alternately intoxicate and eradicate themselves in the inhuman effort that might sustain a vision so exalted. Pater, though a theorist of the Dionysian, evaded the heroic vitalism of a Nietzsche or the quasi-divine self-reliance of an Emerson, declining to present himself either as prophet or as orator. Yet his baroque meditations upon art, hieratic and subdued, touch as firmly upon the ruinous strength of our major Modern poets as any other precursor of our sensibility does.

2. PRIVILEGED MOMENTS

Pater's context begins with his only begetter, Ruskin, whose effect can be read, frequently through negation, throughout Pater's work. Believing, as he says in "Style," that imaginative prose largely took the place of poetry in the modern world, Pater necessarily assumed, consciously I think, the characteristic malady of Post-Enlightenment poetry, the new creator's anxiety-of-influence in regard to his precursor's priority, which becomes a menacing spiritual authority, in a direct transference from the natural to the imaginative world. Ruskin, despite his irrelevant mania for ferocious moralizing, is the major "aesthetic critic," in Pater's sense, of the nineteenth century. Stylistically, Pater owed more to Swinburne, but stance rather than style is the crucial indebtedness of a poet or imaginative prose writer. This is Swinburne, *sounds* like Pater, yet menaced him not at all:

> All mysteries of good and evil, all wonders of life and death, lie in their hands or at their feet. They have known the causes of things, and are not too happy. The fatal labour of the world, the clamour and hunger of the open-mouthed all-summoning grave, all fears and hopes of ephemeral men, are indeed made subject to them, and trodden by them underfoot; but the sorrow and strangeness of things are not lessened because to one or two their secret springs have been laid bare and the courses of their tides made known; refluent evil and good, alternate grief and joy, life inextricable from death, change inevitable and insuperable fate.

Swinburne is speaking of Michelangelo, Aeschylus, Shakespeare; masters of the Sublime, whose mastery does not lessen "sorrow and strangeness." The accent here becomes Pater's (Cecil Lang surmises that Gautier's prose is behind Swinburne's, and Gautier also affected the early Pater), but the attitude, superficially akin to Pater's, is profoundly alien to the Epicurean visionary. Swinburne broods on knowledge and powerlessness, but Pater cared only about perception, about seeing again what Michelangelo, Aeschylus, Shakespeare *saw*. Ruskin's Biblical style was no burden to the Hellenizing Pater, but Ruskin's critical stance was at once initial release yet ultimate burden to his disciple. For this is Pater's Gospel, but it is Ruskin's manifesto: ". . . the greatest thing a human soul ever does in this world is to see something, and tell what it saw in a plain way. Hundreds of people can talk for one who can think, but thousands can think for one who can see. To see clearly is poetry, prophecy and religion all in one." Pater was not concerned to tell what he saw in a plain way, but he was kindled by this exaltation of seeing.

Ruskin himself, though uniquely intense as a prophet of

the eye, belonged to the Spirit of the Age in his emphasis, as Pater well knew. The primal source of later Romantic seeing in England was Wordsworth, who feared the tyranny of the eye, yet who handed on to his disciples not his fear of the visual, nor (until much later) his Sublime visionary sense, but his program for renovation through renewed encounters with visible nature. Carlyle, a necessary link between Wordsworth and Ruskin, equated the heroism of the poet with "the seeing eye." But a trouble, already always present in Wordsworth and Coleridge, developed fully in Ruskin's broodings upon vision. *Modern Painters III* (1856) distinguishes: "the difference between the ordinary, proper, and true appearances of things to us; and the extraordinary, or false appearances, when we are under the influence of emotion, or contemplative fancy; false appearances, I say, as being entirely unconnected with any real power or character in the object, and only imputed to it by us." This imputation of life to the object-world Ruskin called the "pathetic fallacy" and judged as "a falseness in all our impressions of external things." The greatest order of poets, the "Creative" (Shakespeare, Homer, Dante), Ruskin declared free of the pathetic fallacy, finding it endemic in the second order of poets, the "Reflective or Perceptive" (Wordsworth, Keats, Tennyson). Himself a thorough Wordsworthian, Ruskin did not mean to deprecate his Reflective (or Romantic) grouping, but rather to indicate its necessary limitation. Like Pater after him, Ruskin was haunted throughout his life and writings by Wordsworth's "Intimations" Ode, which objectified for both critics their terrible sense of bereavement, of estrangement from the imaginative powers they possessed (or believed themselves to have possessed) as children. Both Ruskin and Pater began as Wordsworthian poets, and turned to imaginative prose partly because of the anxiety-of-influence induced in them by Wordsworth.

Ruskin's formulation of the pathetic fallacy protests the human loss involved in Wordsworth's compensatory imagination. As such, Ruskin's critique prophesies the winter vision of Wallace Stevens, from "The Snow Man" through to "The Course of a Particular." When Stevens reduces to what he calls the First Idea, he returns to "the ordinary, proper, and true appearances of things to us," but then finds it dehumanizing to live only with these appearances. So the later Ruskin found also, in his own elaborate mythicizings in *Sesame and*

Lilies and related books, and in the Wordsworthian autobiography, *Praeterita*, that closed his work. What Wordsworth called "spots of time," periods of particular splendor or privileged moments testifying to the mind's power over the eye, Ruskin had turned from earlier, as being dubious triumphs of the pathetic fallacy. Pater, who subverted Ruskin by going back to their common ancestor, Wordsworth, may be said to have founded his criticism upon privileged moments of vision, or "epiphanies" as Joyce's Stephen, another Paterian disciple, was to term them.

The "epiphany," for us, has been much reduced, yet still prevails as our poets' starting-point for moving from sensation to mastery, or at least to self-acceptance:

> Perhaps there are times of inherent excellence,
>
> .   .   .   .
>
> Perhaps there are moments of awakening,
> Extreme, fortuitous, personal, in which
>
> We more than awaken. . . .

But Stevens's good moments, as here in *Notes Toward a Supreme Fiction*, have receded even from the modified Wordsworthianism that Pater offered as privileged moments, or pathetic fallacies raised to triumphs of perception. For Ruskin's "Perceptive" poets are Pater's "Aesthetic" poets, not a second order but the only poets possible in the universe of death, the Romantic world we have come to inhabit. Joyce's Stephen, recording epiphanies as "the most delicate and evanescent of moments," is recollecting Pater's difficult ecstasy that flares forth "for that moment only." The neo-orthodox, from Hopkins through Eliot to Auden, vainly attempted to restore Pater's "moments" to the religious sphere, yet gave us only what Eliot insisted his poetry would not give, instances of "the intense moment / Isolated, with no before and after," the actual art (such as it is) of *Four Quartets* even as it was of *The Waste Land*. Pater remains the most honest recorder of epiphanies, by asking so little of them, as here in the essay on the poet Joachim Du Bellay in *The Renaissance*:

> A sudden light transfigures a trivial thing, a weathervane, a windmill, a winnowing flail, the dust in the barn door; a moment—and the thing has vanished, because it was pure

effect; but it leaves a relish behind it, a longing that the accident may happen again.

"He had studied the nostalgias," like his descendant in Stevens's more qualified vision, and he did not pretend we could be renovated by happy accidents. Yet he offered a program more genuinely purgative than High Romanticism had ventured:

> . . . painting and poetry . . . can accomplish their function in the choice and development of some special situation, which lifts or glorifies a character, in itself not poetical. To realise this situation, to define, in a chill and empty atmosphere, the focus where rays, in themselves pale and impotent, unite and begin to burn . . .

This, from the early essay on "Winckelmann," presents the embryo of a Paterian epiphany. Here is such an epiphany at its most central, in the crucial chapter, "The Will as Vision," of *Marius the Epicurean*:

> Through some accident to the trappings of his horse at the inn where he rested, Marius had an unexpected delay. He sat down in an olive garden, and, all around him and within still turning to reverie . . . A bird came and sang among the wattled hedgeroses: an animal feeding crept nearer: the child who kept it was gazing quietly: and the scene and the hours still conspiring, he passed from that mere fantasy of a self not himself, beside him in his coming and going, to those divinations of a living and companionable spirit at work in all things . . .

> In this peculiar and privileged hour, his bodily frame, as he could recognize, although just then, in the whole sum of its capacities, so entirely possessed by him—Nay! actually his very self—was yet determined by a far-reaching system of material forces external to it . . . And might not the intellectual frame also, still more intimately himself as in truth it was, after the analogy of the bodily life, be a moment only, an impulse or series of impulses, a single process . . . ? How often had the thought of their brevity spoiled for him the most natural pleasures of life . . . —To-day at least, in the peculiar clearness of one privileged hour, he seemed to have apprehended . . . an abiding place. . . .

> Himself—his sensations and ideas—never fell again precisely into focus as on that day, yet he was the richer by its ex-

perience . . . It gave him a definitely ascertained measure of his moral or intellectual need, of the demand his soul must make upon the powers, whatsoever they might be, which had brought him, as he was, into the world at all . . .

All of Pater is in this passage. Wordsworth lamented the loss of an earlier glory, ultimately because such glory was equal to an actual sense of immortality. He celebrated "spots of time," not because they restored that saving sense, but in the hope they testified to his spirit's strength over a phenomenal world of decay, and so modestly hinted at some mode of survival. Ruskin, until he weakened (on his own terms), insisted on the Homeric strength of gazing upon ocean, and seeing no emblem of continuity but only pure physical nature: "Black or clear, monstrous or violet-coloured, cold salt water it is always, and nothing but that." Pater's Marius has been found by a skeptical but comforting compromise between the natural visions of Wordsworth and Ruskin. "Peculiar and privileged," or "extreme, fortuitous, personal" as Stevens was to call it, the time of reverie abides in Ruskin's "pure physical nature," yet holds together in continuity not only past and present but what was only potential in the past to a sublimity still possible in the future. The self still knows that it reduces to "sensations and ideas" (the subtitle of *Marius the Epicurean*), still knows the brevity of its expectation, knows even more strongly it is joined to no immortal soul, yet now believes also that its own integrity can be at one with the system of forces outside it. Pater's strange achievement is to have assimilated Wordsworth to Lucretius, to have compounded an idealistic naturalism with a corrective materialism. By de-idealizing the epiphany, he makes it available to the coming age, when the mind will know neither itself nor the object but only the dumbfoundering abyss that comes between.

3. HISTORICISMS:
RENAISSANCE AND ROMANTICISM

Pater began to read Ruskin in 1858, when he was just nineteen, eight years before he wrote his first important essay, "Winckelmann." From then until the posthumously published writings, Pater suffered under Ruskin's influence, though from the start he maintained a revisionary stance in regard to his precursor. In place of Ruskin's full, prophetic, even overwhelming rhetoric, Pater evolved a partial, hesitant, insinuating rhetoric, yet the result is a style quite as elaborate as his master's. The overt influence, Pater buried deep. He mentioned Ruskin just once in his letters, and then to claim priority over Ruskin by two years as the English discoverer of Botticelli (as late as 1883, Ruskin still insisted otherwise, but wrongly). Ruskin is ignored, by name, in the books and essays, yet he hovers everywhere in them, and nowhere more strongly than in *The Renaissance* (1873), for Pater's first book is primarily an answer to *The Stones of Venice* (1851, 1853) and to the five volumes of *Modern Painters* (1843–1860). Where Ruskin had deplored the Renaissance (and located it in Italy, between the fourteenth and sixteenth century), elevating instead the High Middle Ages, Pater emulated the main movement of English Romanticism by exalting the Renaissance (and then anticipated later studies by locating its origins in twelfth-century France). Yet the polemic against Ruskin, here as elsewhere, remains implicit. One of Pater's friends reported that once, when talking of Ruskin's strength of perception, Pater burst out: "I cannot believe that Ruskin saw more in the church of St. Mark than I do." Pater's ultimate bitterness, in this area, came in 1885, when Ruskin resigned as Slade Professor of Fine Art at Oxford. Pater offered himself for the professorship, but it went to one Hubert Von Herkomer, and not to the author of the notorious book on the Renaissance, whose largest departure from Ruskin was in opposing a darker and hedonistic humanism to the overtly moral humanism of his aesthetic precursor.

The vision of Pater's *Renaissance* centers upon the hope of what Yeats was to call Unity of Being. Drawing his epigraph from the Book of Psalms, Pater hints at the aesthetic man's salvation from the potsherds of English Christianity in the 1860's: "Though ye have lain among the pots, yet shall ye be as the wings of a dove covered with silver, and her feathers with yellow gold" (Psalms 68:13). The aesthetic man, surrounded by the decaying absolutes inherited from Coleridge-as-theologian, accepts the truths of solipsism and isolation, of mortality and the flux of sensations, and glories in the singularity of his own peculiar kind of contemplative temperament. Pater would teach this man self-reconcilement and self-acceptance, and so Unity of Being. In the great figures of the Renaissance—particularly Botticelli, Michelangelo, Leonardo—Pater presents images of this Unity of aesthetic contemplation. Ruskin, a greater critic than Pater, did not over-idealize the possibilities of aesthetic contemplation, not even in books as phantasmagoric as *The Queen of the Air*. Pater's desperation, both to go beyond Ruskin and to receive more from art, is at once his defining weakness in comparison to Ruskin, and his greater importance for what was to come, not just in the 1880's and 1890's, but throughout our century.

In his vision of the Renaissance, Pater inherits the particular historicism of English Romanticism, which had found its own origins in the English Renaissance, and believed itself a renaissance of that Renaissance. Between the High Romantics and Pater many losses were felt, and of these Darwin compelled the largest. *The Renaissance* is already a Darwinian book, rather in the same way that *The Stones of Venice* was still a Coleridgean book. Pater's moral tentativeness necessarily reflected his own profound repressions, including his aversion to heterosexuality, and the very clear strain of sadomasochism in his psyche. But the intellectual sanction of Pater's skeptical Epicureanism was provided by the prevalent skepticism even of religious apologias in the age of Newman and the Oxford Movement. Evolution, whether as presented by Christian historicisms or by Darwin himself, gave the self-divided Pater a justification for projecting his temperament into a general vision of his age's dilemmas. His later work, considered further on in this Introduction, found a governing dialectic for his skepticism in the Pre-Socratics and Plato, but in *The Renaissance* the personal projection is more direct, and proved more immediately influential.

The "Preface" to *The Renaissance* outlines a cycle in the concept of renaissance, which goes from an early freshness with "the charm of *ascêsis*, of the austere and serious girding of the loins in youth" to "that subtle and delicate sweetness which belongs to a refined and comely decadence." The Greek word *ascêsis* (or *askesis*) originally referred to athleticism, but easily transferred itself, even in ancient time, to an exercise in spiritualizing purgation. Paterian *askesis* is less a sublimation (as it seems when first used in the "Preface") than it is an aesthetic self-curtailment, a giving-up of certain powers so as to help achieve more originality in one's self-

mastery. An Epicurean or hedonistic *askesis* is only superficially a paradox, since it is central in the Lucretian vision
that Pater labored to attain. For Lucretius, truth is always in
appearances, the mind is a flow of sensory patterns, and
moral good is always related directly to pleasurable sensations. But intense pleasure, as Epicurus taught, is grossly
inferior to possessing a tranquil temperament. Pater's Epicureanism, in *The Renaissance*, was more radical, and hesi-
tates subtly at exalting a quasi-homosexual and hedonistic
humanism, particularly in the essays on Leonardo and on
Winckelmann.

In the essay on "Two Early French Stories," Pater identifies
his "medieval Renaissance" with "its antinomianism, its spirit
of rebellion and revolt against the moral and religious ideas
of the time." Pater's own antinomianism is the unifying element in his great first book, as he elaborately intimates "a
strange idolatry, a strange rival religion" in opposition to the
Evangelical faith of Ruskin and the revived orthodoxies of
the Oxford Movement. The extraordinary essay on Botticelli,
a triumphant prose poem, sees in his Madonna "one of those
who are neither for Jehovah nor for His enemies," and hints
at a sadomasochistic sadness with which Botticelli conceives the universe of pleasure he has chosen. In the essay
on Leonardo, which may be Pater's finest poem, the visionary
center is reached in the notorious (and wholly magnificent)
passage on *La Gioconda*, which Yeats brilliantly judged to be
the first Modern poem, but which he proceeded to butcher by
printing in verse form as the first poem in *The Oxford Book
of Modern Verse* (1936). Yeats, in his "Introduction," asked
an insightful and largely rhetorical question: "Did Pater fore-
shadow a poetry, a philosophy, where the individual is nothing, the flux of *The Cantos* of Ezra Pound, objects without
contour . . . , human experience no longer shut into brief
lines, . . . the flux . . . that within our minds enriches itself,
re-dreams itself . . . ?"

Freud, in his study of Leonardo, found in the Mona Lisa
the child's defense against excessive love for his mother, by
means of identifying with her and so proceeding to love boys
in his own image, even as he had been loved. In one of his
most troubling insights, Freud went on to a theory of the
sexual origins of all thought, a theory offering only two ways
out for the gifted; a compulsive, endless brooding in which
all intellectual curiosity remains sexual, or a successful sub-

limation, in which thought, to some extent, is liberated from its sexual past. Is Pater, throughout *The Renaissance*, and particularly in the "Leonardo" and the "Conclusion," merely a fascinating, compulsive brooder, or has he freed his thought from his own over-determined sexual nature? Some recent studies reduce Pater only to the former possibility, but this is to underestimate an immensely subtle mind. Here is the crucial passage, not a purple patch but a paean to the mind's mastery over its own compulsiveness:

> The presence that rose thus so strangely beside the waters, is expressive of what in the ways of a thousand years men had come to desire. Hers is the head upon which all "the ends of the world are come," and the eyelids are a little weary. It is a beauty wrought out from within upon the flesh, the deposit, little cell by cell, of strange thoughts and fantastic reveries and exquisite passions. Set it for a moment beside one of those white Greek goddesses or beautiful women of antiquity, and how would they be troubled by this beauty, into which the soul with all its maladies has passed! All the thoughts and experience of the world have etched and moulded there, in that which they have of power to refine and make expressive the outward form, the animalism of Greece, the lust of Rome, the mysticism of the middle age with its spiritual ambition and imaginative loves, the return of the Pagan world, the sins of the Borgias. She is older than the rocks among which she sits; like the vampire, she has been dead many times, and learned the secrets of the grave; and has been a diver in deep seas, and keeps their fallen day about her; and trafficked for strange webs with Eastern merchants, and, as Leda, was the mother of Helen of Troy, and, as Saint Anne, the mother of Mary; and all this has been to her but as the sound of lyres and flutes, and lives only in the delicacy with which it has moulded the changing lineaments, and tinged the eyelids and the hands. The fancy of a perpetual life, sweeping together ten thousand experiences, is an old one; and modern philosophy has conceived the idea of humanity as wrought upon by, and summing up in itself, all modes of thought and life. Certainly Lady Lisa might stand as the embodiment of the old fancy, the symbol of the modern idea.

Most broadly, this is Pater's comprehensive vision of an equivocal goddess whom Blake called "the Female Will" and the ancient Orphics named *Ananke*, meaning "Necessity." Pater dreads and desires her, or perhaps desires her precisely through his dread. Desire dominates here, for the sight of her is a privileged moment, an epiphany of the only divinity

Pater truly worshipped. In the essay following, on "The School of Giorgione," Pater speaks of "profoundly significant and animated instants, a mere gesture, a look, a smile, perhaps— some brief and wholly concrete moment—into which, however, all the motives, all the interests and effects of a long history, have condensed themselves, and which seem to absorb past and future in an intense consciousness of the present." The Lady Lisa, as an inevitable object of the quest for all which we have lost, is herself a process moving toward a final entropy, summing up all the estrangements we have suffered from the object-world we once held close, whether as children, or in history. She incarnates too much, both for her own good and for ours. The cycles of civilization, the burden our consciousness bears, render us latecomers but the Lady Lisa perpetually carries the seal of a terrible priority. Unity of Being she certainly possesses, yet she seems to mock the rewards Pater hoped for in such Unity. A powerful juxtaposition, of the ancient dream of a literal immortality, of living all lives, and of Darwinianism ("modern philosophy"), ends the passage with an astonishing conceptual image. The Lady Lisa, as no human could hope to do, stands forth as a body risen from death, and also as symbol of modern acceptance of Necessity, the non-divine evolution of our species. She exposes, as Pater is well aware, the hopelessness of the vision sought by *The Renaissance*, and by all Romantic and Post-Romantic art.

Yet, with that hopelessness comes the curious reward of the supreme Paterian epiphany. Rilke remarked of the landscape behind the Madonna Lisa that "it is Nature which came into existence . . . something distant and foreign, something remote and without allure, something entirely self-contained. . . ." Following Rilke, the psychologist J. H. Van den Berg associates this estrangement of an outer landscape with the growth of a more inward, alienated self than mankind had known before:

> The inner life was like a haunted house. But what else could it be? It contained everything. Everything extraneous had been put into it. The entire history of the individual. Everything that had previously belonged to everybody, everything that had been collective property and had existed in the world in which everyone lived, had to be contained by the individual. It could not be expected that things would be quiet in the inner self.

In his way, Van den Berg, like Rilke, sides with Ruskin and not with Pater, for the implicit argument here is that the Romantic inner self cost too much in solipsistic estrangement. But Pater was a divided man, humanly wiser than he could let himself show as a Late Romantic moralist-critic. His vision of the Mona Lisa is as much a warning as it is an ideal. This, he says, is our Muse, mistress of Unity-of-Being. The poets of the Nineties, including the young Yeats, chose to see the ideal and not to heed the warning. The further work of Pater, after *The Renaissance*, shows the Aesthetic Critic accepting his own hint, and turning away from self-destruction.

One cannot leave the "Conclusion" to *The Renaissance* without acknowledging the power which that handful of pages seems to possess even today, a hundred years after their composition. In their own generation, their pungency was overwhelming; not only did Pater withdraw them in the second edition, because he too was alarmed at their effect, but he toned them down when they were restored in the third edition (I have given the changes in this volume's Notes). The skeptical eloquence of the "Conclusion" cost Pater considerable preferment at Oxford. There is a splendidly instructive letter from John Wordsworth (clerical grand-nephew of the poet) to Pater, written in 1873, indignantly summing up the "Conclusion" as asserting: "that no fixed principles either of religion or morality can be regarded as certain, that the only thing worth living for is momentary enjoyment and that probably or certainly the soul dissolves at death into elements which are destined never to reunite." One can oppose to this very minor Wordsworth a reported murmur of Pater's: "I wish they would not call me a hedonist. It gives such a wrong impression to those who do not know Greek."

Early Pater, in all high seriousness, attains a climax in those wonderful pages on the flux-of-sensations, and the necessity of dying with a faith in art, that conclude *The Renaissance*. Written in 1868, they came initially out of a review of William Morris's poetry that became the suppressed essay on "Aesthetic Poetry." They gave Pater himself the problem of how he was to write up to so fierce a demand-of-self: "To burn always with this hard, gemlike flame, to maintain this ecstasy, is success in life."

4. FICTIVE SELVES

Pater's own life, by his early standards, was only ambiguously a success. His work, after *The Renaissance*, is of three kinds, all of them already present in his first book. One is "imaginary portraits," a curious mixed genre, of which the novel *Marius the Epicurean* is the most important, and of which four excellent shorter examples are given in this volume: the semi-autobiographical "The Child in the House," two stories from the book called *Imaginary Portraits*, and a classical example from *Greek Studies*. Another grouping of Pater's work, critical essays, were mostly gathered in *Appreciations*, from which I have selected liberally. The last group, classical studies proper, stand a little apart from the rest of his work, are more lightly represented in this book, and will be considered at the close of this Introduction.

"Imaginary portraits," in Pater's sense, are an almost indescribable genre. Behind them stand the monologues of Browning and of Rossetti, the *Imaginary Conversations* of Landor, perhaps Sainte-Beuve's *Portraits contemporains*. Like *The Renaissance* and *Appreciations*, they are essays or quasi-essays; like "The Child in the House" they are semi-autobiographical; yet it hardly helps to see "Sebastian Van Storck," or "Denys l'Auxerrois" or "Hippolytus Veiled" as being essays or veiled confessions. Nor are they romance-fragments, though closer to that than to short stories. It may be best to call them what Yeats called his Paterian stories, "Mythologies," or "Romantic Mythologies." Or, more commonly, they could be called simply "reveries," for even at their most marmoreal and baroque they are highly disciplined reveries, and even the lengthy *Marius the Epicurean* is more a historicizing reverie than it is a historical novel. "Reverie" comes from the French *rêver*, "to dream," and is already used in music to describe an instrumental composition of a dreamlike character. The power and precariousness alike of Pater's reveries are related to their hovering near the thresholds of wish-fulfillment. I suspect that Pater's nearest ancestor here is Browning, even as Ruskin looms always behind Pater's aesthetic criticism. Just as Browning made fictive selves, to escape his earlier strain of Shelleyan subjectivity in the verse-romances *Pauline, Paracelsus*, and *Sordello*, so Pater turned to "imaginary portraits" to escape the subjective confession that wells up in his "Leonardo da Vinci" and "Conclusion" to *The Renaissance*. On this view, *The Renaissance* is Pater's version of Shelley's *Alastor* or Keats's *Endymion*; it is a prose-poem of highly personal Romantic quest after the image of desire, visualized by Pater in the Mona Lisa. Turning from so deep a self-exposure, Pater arrives at his kind of less personal reverie, a consciously fictive kind.

Pater had no gifts for narrative, or drama, or psychological portrayal, and he knew this well enough. Unlike Browning, he could not make a half-world, let alone the full world of a mythopoeic master like Blake. Pater, who intensely admired both poets, oriented his portraits with more specific reference to the most inescapable of Romantic poets, Wordsworth, concerning whom he wrote the best of his essays in strictly literary criticism. In the nearly-as-distinguished essay on "Coleridge," Pater justly praises Wordsworth as a more instinctual poet than Coleridge. Wordsworth is praised for "that flawless temperament . . . which keeps his conviction of a latent intelligence in nature within the limits of sentiment or instinct, and confines it to those delicate and subdued shades of expression which perfect art allows." Pater, too consciously, seeks in his portraits to be instinctual rather than intellectual, hoping that thus he can avoid drama and self-consciousness. Unfortunately, he cannot sustain the Wordsworthian comparison, as again he knew, for though he shared Wordsworth's early naturalism, he lacked the primordial, Tolstoyan power that sustains poems like "The Ruined Cottage," "Michael," "The Old Cumberland Beggar." Yet he yearned for such power, and would have been a Wordsworthian novelist, like George Eliot and Hardy, if he had found the requisite strength. But this yearning, poignantly felt all through the beautiful Wordsworth essay, was a desperate desire for his opposite. Wordsworth lived in nature, Pater in a dream. Longing for the sanctities of earth, Pater found his true brothers in Rossetti and Morris, poets of phantasmagoria, and his true children in Yeats and the Tragic Generation. The "imaginary portraits" are crucial to our understanding of Pater, but as art they are equivocal achievements, noble but divided against themselves.

5. SORROWS OF INFLUENCE

My own favorite among Pater's books is *Appreciations*, which is more generously represented in this volume than any of his other books, partly because I love it best, but mostly because it is not otherwise available. Pater is not the greatest critic English Romanticism produced—Coleridge and Ruskin vie for that eminence—but he is certainly the most underrated major nineteenth-century critic, in our own time. He is superior to his older rival, Arnold, and to his disciple, Wilde, both of whom receive more approval at this moment. Yet even as a literary critic, he is evasive, and remains more a master of reverie than of description, let alone analysis, which is alien to him. This becomes a curious critical strength in him, which requires both description and analysis to be apprehended.

Appreciations begins with the extraordinary essay on "Style," which is Pater's *credo* as a literary critic. As the essay urges awareness of the root-meanings of words, we need to remember that "style" originally meant an ancient instrument for writing on a waxed tablet, and having one pointed end for incising words, and one blunt end for rubbing out writing, and smoothing the tablet down. We might also remember that "appreciations" originally meant "appraisals." Before appraising Wordsworth, Coleridge, Rossetti, Morris, Lamb, and others, Pater offers us a vision of his stylistic attitude, incisive but also ascetic. Ian Fletcher, Pater's best scholar, reminds us that Pater's idea of style is "as a mode of perception, a total responsive gesture of the whole personality." Since Pater's own style is the most highly colored and self-conscious of all critics who have written in English, there is a puzzle here. Pater attempted to write criticism as though he were style's martyr, another Flaubert, and his insistence upon *askesis*, the exercise of self-curtailment, hardly seems compatible with a whole personality's total response. We do not believe that the style is the man when we read Pater, and a glance at his letters, which are incredibly dull and nonrevelatory, confirm our disbelief. Pater's style, as befits the master of Wilde and Yeats, is a mask, and so Pater's idea of style and his actual style are irreconcilable. As always, Pater anticipates us in knowing this, and the essay "Style" centers upon this division.

Prose, according to Pater, is both music's opposite and capable of transformation into the condition of music, where form and matter seem to dissolve into one another. Pater's subject is always the mystery of utter individuality in the artistic personality; his style strives extravagantly to award himself such individuality. Whether in matter or style, Pater has therefore a necessary horror of literary influence, for to so desperate a quester after individuality *all* influence is over-influence. Pater's subject-matter is also Ruskin's and Arnold's; his style is also Swinburne's, or rather one of Swinburne's styles. Unlike Emerson and Nietzsche, who refused to see themselves as latecomers, Pater's entire vision is that of a latecomer longing for a renaissance, a rebirth into imaginative earliness. The hidden subject of *Appreciations* is the anxiety of influence, for which Pater's remedy is primarily his idea of *askesis*. "Style" urges self-restraint and renunciation, which it calls an economy of means but which in Pater's actual style seems more an economy of ends. Ruskin, threatening precursor, was profuse in means and ends, master of emphasis and of a daemonic, Sublime style, which in his case *was* the man. Swerving from Ruskin, Pater turns to Flaubert in "Style," seeking to invent a father to replace a dominant and dangerous aesthetic parent. But guilt prevails, and Pater's anxiety emerges in the essay's long concluding paragraph, which astonishingly seems to repeal the special emphasis of everything that has come before. "Good art, but not necessarily great art," Pater sadly murmurs, suddenly assuring us that greatness depends not upon style but on the matter, and then listing Dante, Milton, the King James Bible, and Hugo's *Les Misérables*, which seems rather exposed in this sublime company, and hardly rivals Flaubert in its concern with form. By the test of finding a place in the structure of human life, Hugo will receive the palm before Flaubert, Ruskin before Pater, Tennyson (secretly despised by Pater) before Rossetti and Morris. The final *askesis* of the champion of style is to abnegate himself before the burden of the common life he himself cannot bear.

In the essay, "Wordsworth," Pater has the happiness of being able to touch the commonal through the greatest mediating presence of nineteenth-century poetry. The essays on Wordsworth of Arnold and, *contra* Arnold, of A. C. Bradley, have been profoundly influential on rival schools of modern Wordsworthian interpretation, and Pater has not, but a reading of the three essays side by side will show Pater's superiority. His Wordsworth is neither Arnold's poet of Nature nor Bradley's poet of the Sublime, but rather a poet of instinctual pagan religion. Wordsworth would have been outraged by Pater's essay, and most modern scholars agree that Pater's Wordsworth is too much Pater's Marius and too little Wordsworth. Against which, here is Pater's account of Wordsworth's actual religion, *as a poet*:

> Religious sentiment, consecrating the affections and natural regrets of the human heart, above all, that pitiful awe and care for the perishing human clay, of which relic-worship is but the corruption, has always had much to do with localities, with the thoughts which attach themselves to actual scenes and places. Now what is true of it everywhere, is truest of it in those secluded valleys where one generation after another maintains the same abiding place; and it was on this side, that Wordsworth apprehended religion most strongly. Consisting, as it did so much, in the recognition of local sanctities, in the habit of connecting the stones and trees of a particular spot of earth with the great events of life, till the low walls, the green mounds, the half-obliterated epitaphs seemed full of voices, and a sort of natural oracles, the very religion of those people of the dales, appeared but as another link between them and the earth, and was literally a religion of nature.

What is most meaningful for Pater are those voices coming from low walls, green mounds, tombstones. These things remain *things* in Wordsworth, wholly other than ourselves, yet we are deeply affected by what emanates from them. Pater was converted by them to the only religion he ever sincerely held, "literally a religion of nature." Just as the spots of time gave Wordsworth not a sense of the Divine, but precise knowledge to what point and how his own mind displayed a mastery over outward sense, so for Pater the spots of time he located in works of art gave a precise knowledge of the limited efficacy of the great Romantic program for renovation. The Romantics, as Pater understood and Arnold did not, were not nature-poets, but rather exemplars of the power of the mind, a power exerted against the object-world, or mere universe of death. Like Ruskin, and like Yeats and Stevens, Pater is a Romantic critic of Romanticism.

Whether Pater writes on Giorgione or Winckelmann, the myth of Dionysus or Plato and the Doctrine of Change, Rossetti or Wilde, he writes as a conscious post-Wordsworthian, and his true subject is the partial and therefore tragic (because momentary) victory that art wins over the flux of sensations. The step beyond Pater is the one taken by his disciple, Yeats, who insists on the tragic joy of art's defeat, and who in his savage last phase celebrates the flux, exulting in his own doctrine of change.

Pater, withdrawing in *Appreciations* as in *Marius* from hail-ing the Heraclitean flux, is most moved by Wordsworth's quiet and primordial strength, the instinctual power of "impassioned contemplation." The eloquent and compassionate essay on "Coleridge" begins from Pater's recognition that Coleridge lacked this strength, and goes on to reject Coleridge's theological reliance upon outworn Absolutes. More strikingly, Pater pioneers in rejecting the Organic Analogue that Coleridge popularized. The motto of Pater's essay on Coleridge might well come from Nietzsche: "But do I bid thee be either plant or phantom?" Coleridge, Pater suggests, bid us be both, and so "obscured the true interest of art," which is to celebrate and lament our intolerably glorious condition of being mortal gods.

Beyond his steady defense of art's dignity against metaphysical and religious absolutes, Pater's nobility and uniqueness as a nineteenth-century literary critic stem from his insistence that the later nineteenth-century poet "make it new," even as that poet (like Pater himself) remains fully conscious of the inescapable sorrows of influence. Such a poet wanders in the half-lights of being a latecomer, trailing after the massive, fresh legacy of Goethe, Wordsworth, Blake, Hugo, Keats, Shelley, Baudelaire, Browning, even as Pater trailed after De Quincey, Lamb, Hazlitt, Coleridge, Arnold and the inescapable Ruskin, quite aside from Swinburne and the unmentioned Emerson and Nietzsche. Pater is still the best critic Pre-Raphaelite poetry has had, largely because he understood so well the anxiety of influence consciously present in Rossetti and unconsciously at work in Morris. The great essay on Morris, "Aesthetic Poetry," properly close to the "Conclusion" to *The Renaissance* which was quarried from it, presents Pater's most unguarded vision of poetic experience, so that Pater inevitably suppressed it:

> . . . exotic flowers of sentiment expand, among people of a
> remote and unaccustomed beauty, somnambulistic, frail,
> androgynous, the light almost shining through them . . . The
> colouring is intricate and delirious, as of "scarlet lilies." The
> influence of summer is like a poison in one's blood, with a
> sudden bewildered sickening of life and all things . . . A
> passion of which the outlets are sealed, begets a tension of
> nerve, in which the sensible world comes to one with a
> reinforced brilliancy and relief—all redness is turned into
> blood, all water into tears . . . One characteristic of the
> pagan spirit the aesthetic poetry has . . . —the sense of death
> and the desire of beauty: the desire of beauty quickened by
> the sense of death . . .

Remarkably hinting that sadomasochistic yearnings and the
anxiety of being a late representative of a tradition are closely
related, Pater implies also that the heightened intensity of
Morris and Rossetti (and of Pater) compensates for a
destructively excessive sexual self-consciousness. The sensible world becomes phantasmagoria because one's own nature
is baffled. A critic who understands the dialectic of style, as
Pater magnificently did, is in no need of psychoanalytic reduction, as these essays on Morris and Rossetti show. *Appreciations*, which influenced Wilde and Yeats, Joyce and Pound, and
more covertly Santayana and Stevens, has had little influence
upon modern academic criticism, but one can prophesy that
such influence will yet come. In a letter (January 8, 1888)
to the young poet Arthur Symons, Pater recalled the marvelous dictum of Rossetti: "Conception, my boy, FUNDAMENTAL
BRAINWORK, that is what makes the difference in all art."
Pater's apt purpose in this recall was to urge Symons, and the
other poets of his generation—Yeats, Dowson, Lionel Johnson
—to make it new again through the fundamental brainwork
necessary to overcome anxieties-of-influence. Here is the
prophecy, addressed to the Paterian poets of the Tragic Generation, which Pound and his Modernists attempted to fulfill:

> I think the present age an unfavourable one to poets, at least
> in England. The young poet comes into a generation which
> has produced a large amount of first-rate poetry, and an
> enormous amount of good secondary poetry. You know I
> give a high place to the literature of prose as a fine art, and
> therefore hope you won't think me brutal in saying that the
> admirable qualities of your verse are those also of imagina-
> tive prose; as I think is the case also with much of Browning's
> finest verse. . . .

The Poundian dictum, that verse was to be as well written as prose, initially meant Browningesque verse and Paterian prose, as Pound's early verse and prose show. That literary Modernism ever journeyed too far from its Paterian origins we may doubt increasingly, and we may wonder also whether modern criticism as yet has caught up with Pater.

6. CENTRIFUGAL AND CENTRIPETAL

In the important essay on Romanticism that he made the "Postscript" to *Appreciations*, Pater insisted that: "Material for the artist, motives of inspiration, are not yet exhausted . . . ," yet he wondered how "to induce order upon the contorted, proportionless accumulation of our knowledge and experience, our science and history, our hopes and disillusion . . ." To help induce such an order seems to be the motive for *Plato and Platonism* (1893) and the posthumously published *Greek Studies* (1895). The Plato of Walter Pater is Montaigne's Plato (and probably Shelley's), a skeptical evader of systems, including his supposed own, whose idea of order is the dialectic: "Just there, lies the validity of the method—in a dialogue, an endless dialogue, with one's self." Clearly this is Pater more than Plato, and we need not wonder why Pater favored this above his other books. In the chapter, "The Genius of Plato," which I have included, Pater gives us another reverie, an idealized imaginary portrait of what he would have liked the mind of Pater to be. A comparison with Emerson's Plato (also influenced by Montaigne) is instructive, for the Plato of *Representative Men* is criticized for lacking "contact," an Emersonian quality not far removed from "freedom" or wildness. Unlike Plato, the author of the *Dialogues*, Walter Pater's visionary indeed lacks "contact," even as Pater severely made certain he himself lacked it.

Pater gives us the author of *The Republic* as "a seer who has a sort of sensuous love of the unseen," and whose mythological power brings the unseen closer to the seen. This Plato is possible and possibly even more than marginal, yet he does seem more Ficino or Pico della Mirandola than he was Plato, for he is more a poet of ideas than a metaphysician, and more of a solipsistic Realist than an Idealist. Above all, he is Pater's "crystal man," a model for Yeats's vision of an *antithetical* savior, a greater-than-Oedipus who would replace Christ, and herald a greater Renaissance than European man had known.

From reading both Hegel and Darwin, Pater had evolved a curious dialectic of history, expounded more thoroughly in *Greek Studies*, using the terms "centripetal" and "centrifugal" as the thesis and antithesis of a process always stopping short of synthesis:

> All through Greek history we may trace, in every sphere of the activity of the Greek mind, the action of these two opposing tendencies,—the centrifugal and centripetal . . . There is the centrifugal, the Ionian, the Asiatic tendency, flying from the centre . . . throwing itself forth in endless play of undirected imagination; delighting in brightness and colour, in beautiful material, in changeful form everywhere, in poetry, in philosophy . . . its restless versatility drives it towards . . . the development of the individual in that which is most peculiar and individual in him . . . It is this centrifugal tendency which Plato is desirous to cure, by maintaining, over against it, the Dorian influence of a severe simplification everywhere, in society, in culture . . .

The centrifugal is the vision of Heraclitus, the centripetal of Parmenides, or in Pater's more traditional terms from the "Postscript" to *Appreciations*, the centrifugal is the Romantic, and the centripetal the Classic. Pater rather nervously praises his Plato for Classic correctiveness, for a conservative centripetal impulse against his own Heraclitan Romanticism. Reductively, this is still Pater reacting against the excesses of *The Renaissance*, and we do not believe him when he presents himself as a centripetal man, though Yeats was partially persuaded, and relied upon Pater's dialectic when he created his own version of an aesthetic historicism in *A Vision*.

Pater, in his last phase, continued to rationalize his semi-withdrawal from his own earlier vision, but we can doubt that even he trusted his own hesitant rationalizations. We remember him, and read him, as the maker of critical reveries who yielded up the great societal and religious hopes of the major Victorian prose-prophets, and urged us to abide in the mortal truths of perception and sensation. His great achievement, in conjunction with Swinburne and the Pre-Raphaelites, was to empty Ruskin's aestheticism of its moral bias, and so to purify a critical stance appropriate for the apprehension of Romantic art. More than Swinburne, Morris, Rossetti, he became the father of Anglo-American Aestheticism, and subsequently the direct precursor of a Modernism that vainly attempted to be Post-Romantic. I venture the prophecy that he will prove also to be the valued precursor of a Post-Modernism still fated to be another Last Romanticism. We can judge, finally, this ancestor of our own sensibility as he himself judged Plato:

> His aptitude for things visible, with the gift of words, empowers him to express, as if for the eyes, what except to the eye of the mind is strictly invisible, what an acquired asceticism induces him to rank above, and sometimes, in terms of harshest dualism, oppose to, the sensible world. Plato is to be interpreted not merely by his antecedents, by the influence upon him of those who preceded him, but by his successors, by the temper, the intellectual alliances, of those who directly or indirectly have been sympathetic with him.

Chronology

August 4, 1839 Born in Shadwell, East London; soon after birth was moved to Enfield, near London, setting of "The Child in the House."

January 28, 1842 Death of father, Richard Pater.

1853–1858 Attendance at the King's School, Canterbury.

February 25, 1854 Death of mother, Maria Pater.

1858 Entered Queen's College, Oxford, where he read classics, and was greatly influenced by Ruskin's work.

1862 Graduated Queen's College; remained in Oxford instructing private pupils.

1864 Elected Fellow of Brasenose College, Oxford, where he subsequently lived, taught, and wrote.

Summer 1865 Journeyed in Italy, particularly to Florence and Pisa.

1866 First essay in print, early version of "Coleridge."

1869 Rented house in Oxford, with his sisters Hester and Clara; became associated with Burne-Jones, Rossetti, and Swinburne.

1873 First book, *Studies in the History of the Renaissance,* published.

1876 Attacked as the Decadent "Mr. Rose," in W. H. Mallock's satire, *The New Republic.*

1878 "The Child in the House" printed.

1885   *Marius the Epicurean* published.

August, 1885   Moved, with his sisters, to London.

1887   *Imaginary Portraits* published.

1889   *Appreciations* published.

1893   *Plato and Platonism* published.

Summer 1893   Returned to Oxford with his sisters.

July 30, 1894   Death in Oxford.

Bibliography

I. Collected Editions
The Works, 9 vols., London, 1900-1901.
New Library Edition of the Works, 10 vols., London, 1910;
New York, 1967.

II. Separate Works
1. *Studies in the History of the Renaissance,* London, 1873.
———second edition, 1877, re-entitled *The Renaissance: Studies in Art and Poetry,* with the "Conclusion" excluded and the essay "The School of Giorgione" added. In the third edition, the "Conclusion" was revised and restored, 1888. Recent editions are by L. Kronenberger, New York, 1959, and Sir Kenneth Clark, London, 1961.
2. *Marius the Epicurean: His Sensations and Ideas,* 2 vols., London, 1885. Second edition, 1885; third edition with many changes, 1892. The edition by H. Bloom, New York, 1970, reprints the third edition.
3. *Imaginary Portraits,* London, 1887. The edition by Eugene J. Brzenk, New York, 1964, also contains "Diaphaneite," "Apollo in Picardy," and "An English Poet," as well as "The Child in the House" and the four Portraits of the original volume.
4. *Appreciations,* London, 1889. The second edition omits the essay "Aesthetic Poetry."
5. *Plato and Platonism: A Series of Lectures,* London, 1893.
6. *An Imaginary Portrait,* Oxford, 1894. A reprint of "The Child in the House" from its first appearance in *Macmillan's Magazine,* August 1878, and thus remedying its exclusion from *Imaginary Portraits,* 1887. Reprinted again in *Miscellaneous Studies,* 1889.
7. *Greek Studies: A Series of Lectures,* London, 1895.
8. *Miscellaneous Studies: A Series of Essays,* London, 1895.
9. *Gaston De Latour: An Unfinished Romance,* London, 1896.
10. *Essays from "The Guardian,"* London, 1896.
11. *Sketches and Reviews,* New York, 1919.
12. *The Letters of Walter Pater,* ed. L. Evans, Oxford, 1970.

III. Selected Criticism (arranged chronologically)

1. W. H. Mallock, *The New Republic*, London, 1877. Pater is attacked in the satirical portrait of Mr. Rose, the aesthete.
2. Oscar Wilde, review of *Imaginary Portraits, The Pall Mall Gazette*, June 11, 1887.
3. Oscar Wilde, review of *Appreciations, The Speaker*, March 22, 1890.
4. Arthur Symons, *Studies in Two Literatures*, London, 1897.
5. A. C. Benson, *Walter Pater*, London, 1906.
6. George Saintsbury, *History of English Prose Rhythm*, London, 1912.
7. J. S. Harrison, "Pater, Heine, and the Old Gods of Greece," *Publications of the Modern Language Association*, XXXIX, 1924.
8. T. S. Eliot, "The Place of Pater," in *The Eighteen-Eighties*, ed. Walter de la Mare, Cambridge, 1930.
9. R. C. Child, *The Aesthetic of Pater*, New York, 1946.
10. Graham Hough, *The Last Romantics*, London, 1949. Contains a crucial essay on Pater.
11. Frank Kermode, *Romantic Image*, London, 1957. A central study of the Paterian influence upon modern poetry.
12. Rene Wellek, *A History of Modern Criticism*, 1750–1950, New Haven, 1955–1966.
13. R. T. Lenaghan, "Pattern in Pater's Fiction," *Studies in Philology*, XVIII, 1961.
14. A. Ward, *Walter Pater: The Idea in Nature*, London, 1965.
15. G. C. Monsman, *Pater's Portraits*, Baltimore, 1967.
16. G. Levine and W. Madden, eds., *The Art of Victorian Prose*, New York, 1968. See particularly the essays by G. S. Fraser, G. Robert Stange, and A. D. Culler.
17. D. J. deLaura, *Hebrew and Hellene in Victorian England*, Austin, 1969.
18. Richard Ellmann, "Overtures to *Salome*", in *Oscar Wilde: A Collection of Critical Essays*, ed. Ellmann, Englewood Cliffs, N.J., 1969.
19. J. B. Gordon, "The Imaginary Portrait: Fin de Siècle Icon," *The Windsor Magazine*, 1970.
20. H. Bloom, *Yeats*, New York, 1970. Contains a chapter on "Late Victorian Poetry and Pater."
21. H. Bloom, *The Ringers in the Tower: Studies in Romantic Tradition*, Chicago, 1971. Contains a revised version of an "Introduction" to *Marius the Epicurean*.
22. Ian Fletcher, *Walter Pater*, Harlow, Essex, revised edition, 1971. First published in 1959, this monograph is much the most useful and informed criticism Pater has received, and is a necessary starting-point for all future study.

The Child
in the House[1]

As Florian Deleal walked, one hot afternoon, he overtook by
the wayside a poor aged man, and, as he seemed weary with
the road, helped him on with the burden which he carried, a
certain distance. And as the man told his story, it chanced
that he named the place, a little place in the neighbourhood
of a great city, where Florian had passed his earliest years,
but which he had never since seen, and, the story told, went
forward on his journey comforted. And that night, like a
reward for his pity, a dream of that place came to Florian, a
dream which did for him the office of the finer sort of memory, bringing its object to mind with a great clearness, yet,
as sometimes happens in dreams, raised a little above itself,
and above ordinary retrospect. The true aspect of the place,
especially of the house there in which he had lived as a child,
the fashion of its doors, its hearths, its windows, the very
scent upon the air of it, was with him in sleep for a season;
only, with tints more musically blent[2] on wall and floor, and
some finer light and shadow running in and out along its
curves and angles, and with all its little carvings daintier. He
awoke with a sigh at the thought of almost thirty years which
lay between him and that place, yet with a flutter of pleasure
still within him at the fair light, as if it were a smile, upon it.[3]
And it happened that this accident of his dream was just the
thing needed for the beginning of a certain design he then
had in view, the noting, namely, of some things in the story
of his spirit—in that process of brainbuilding by which we
are, each one of us, what we are. With the image of the
place so clear and favourable upon him, he fell to thinking
of himself therein, and how his thoughts had grown up to

him. In that half-spiritualised house he could watch the
better, over again, the gradual expansion of the soul which
had come to be there—of which indeed, through the law
which makes the material objects about them so large an
element in children's lives, it had actually become a part;
inward and outward being woven through and through each
other into one inextricable texture—half, tint and trace and
accident of homely colour and form, from the wood and the
bricks; half, mere soul-stuff, floated thither from who knows
how far. In the house and garden of his dream he saw a
child moving, and could divide the main streams at least of
the winds that had played on him, and study so the
first stage in that mental journey.

The *old house*, as when Florian talked of it afterwards he
always called it, (as all children do, who can recollect a
change of home, soon enough but not too soon to mark a
period in their lives) really was an old house; and an element
of French descent in its inmates—descent from Watteau, the
old court-painter,[4] one of whose gallant pieces still hung in
one of the rooms—might explain, together with some other
things, a noticeable trimness and comely whiteness about
everything there—the curtains, the couches, the paint on the
walls with which the light and shadow played so delicately;
might explain also the tolerance of the great poplar in the
garden, a tree most often despised by English people, but
which French people love, having observed a certain fresh
way its leaves have of dealing with the wind, making it
sound, in never so slight a stirring of the air, like running
water.[5]

The old-fashioned, low wainscoting went round the rooms,
and up the staircase with carved balusters and shadowy
angles, landing half-way up at a broad window, with a swallow's nest below the sill, and the blossom of an old pear-tree
showing across it in late April, against the blue, below which
the perfumed juice of the find of fallen fruit in autumn was
so fresh. At the next turning came the closet which held on
its deep shelves the best china. Little angel faces and reedy
flutings stood out round the fireplace of the children's room.
And on the top of the house, above the large attic, where the
white mice ran in the twilight—an infinite, unexplored won-
derland of childish treasures, glass beads, empty scent-bottles
still sweet, thrum of coloured silks, among its lumber[6]—a
flat space of roof, railed round, gave a view of the neighbour-

ing steeples; for the house, as I said, stood near a great city, which sent up heavenwards, over the twisting weather-vanes, not seldom, its beds of rolling cloud and smoke, touched with storm or sunshine. But the child of whom I am writing did not hate the fog because of the crimson lights which fell from it sometimes upon the chimneys, and the whites which gleamed through its openings, on summer mornings, on turret or pavement. For it is false to suppose that a child's sense of beauty is dependent on any choiceness or special fineness, in the objects which present themselves to it, though this indeed comes to be the rule with most of us in later life; earlier, in some degree, we see inwardly; and the child finds for itself, and with unstinted delight, a difference for the sense, in those whites and reds through the smoke on very homely buildings, and in the gold of the dandelions at the roadside, just beyond the houses, where not a handful of earth is virgin and untouched, in the lack of better ministries to its desire of beauty.

This house then stood not far beyond the gloom and rumours of the town, among high garden-wall, bright all summer-time with Golden-rod, and brown-and-golden Wall-flower—*Flos Parietis*, as the children's Latin-reading father taught them to call it, while he was with them. Tracing back the threads of his complex spiritual habit, as he was used in after years to do, Florian found that he owed to the place many tones of sentiment afterwards customary with him, certain inward lights under which things most naturally presented themselves to him. The coming and going of travellers to the town along the way, the shadow of the streets, the sudden breath of the neighbouring gardens, the singular brightness of bright weather there, its singular darknesses which linked themselves in his mind to certain engraved illustrations in the old big Bible at home, the coolness of the dark, cavernous shops round the great church, with its giddy winding stair up to the pigeons and the bells—a citadel of peace in the heart of the trouble—all this acted on his child-ish fancy, so that ever afterwards the like aspects and incidents never failed to throw him into a well-recognised imaginative mood, seeming actually to have become a part of the texture of his mind. Also, Florian could trace home to this point a pervading preference in himself for a kind of comeliness and dignity, an *urbanity* literally, in modes of life, which he connected with the pale people of towns, and which made him susceptible to a kind of exquisite satisfaction in the trimness and well-considered grace of certain things and persons he afterwards met with, here and there, in his way through the world.

So the child of whom I am writing lived on there quietly; things without thus ministering to him, as he sat daily at the window with the birdcage hanging below it, and his mother taught him to read, wondering at the ease with which he learned, and at the quickness of his memory. The perfume of the little flowers of the lime-tree fell through the air upon them like rain; while time seemed to move ever more slowly to the murmur of the bees in it, till it almost stood still on June afternoons. How insignificant, at the moment, seem the influences of the sensible things which are tossed and fall and lie about us, so, or so, in the environment of early child-hood. How indelibly, as we afterwards discover, they affect us; with what capricious attractions and associations they figure themselves on the white paper,[7] the smooth wax, of our ingenuous souls, as "with lead in the rock for ever,"[8] giving form and feature, and as it were assigned house-room in our memory, to early experiences of feeling and thought, which abide with us ever afterwards, thus, and not otherwise. The realities and passions, the rumours of the greater world without, steal in upon us, each by its own special little pas-sageway, through the wall of custom about us; and never afterwards quite detach themselves from this or that acci-dent, or trick, in the mode of their first entrance to us. Our susceptibilities, the discovery of our powers, manifold experi-ences—our various experiences of the coming and going of bodily pain, for instance—belong to this or the other well-remembered place in the material habitation—that little white room with the window across which the heavy blossoms could beat so peevishly in the wind, with just that particular catch or throb, such a sense of teasing in it, on gusty morn-ings; and the early habitation thus gradually becomes a sort of material shrine or sanctuary of sentiment; a system of visible symbolism interweaves itself through all our thoughts and passions; and irresistibly, little shapes, voices, accidents —the angle at which the sun in the morning fell on the pillow—become parts of the great chain wherewith we are bound.

Thus far, for Florian, what all this had determined was a peculiarly strong sense of home—so forcible a motive with all of us—prompting to us our customary love of the earth, and the larger part of our fear of death, that revulsion we have from it, as from something strange, untried, unfriendly; though life-long imprisonment, they tell you, and final banishment from home is a thing bitterer still; the looking forward to but a short space, a mere childish *goûter*[9] and dessert of it, before the end, being so great a resource of effort to pilgrims and wayfarers, and the soldier in distant quarters, and lending, in lack of that, some power of solace to the thought of sleep in the home churchyard, at least—dead cheek by dead cheek, and with the rain soaking in upon one from above.

So powerful is this instinct, and yet accidents like those I have been speaking of so mechanically determine it; its essence being indeed the early familiar, as constituting our ideal, or typical conception, of rest and security. Out of so many possible conditions, just this for you and that for me, brings ever the unmistakeable realisation of the delightful *chez soi*;[10] this for the Englishman, for me and you, with the closely-drawn white curtain and the shaded lamp; that, quite other, for the wandering Arab, who folds his tent every morning, and makes his sleeping-place among haunted ruins, or in old tombs.

With Florian then the sense of home became singularly intense, his good fortune being that the special character of his home was in itself so essentially home-like. As after many wanderings I have come to fancy that some parts of Surrey and Kent are, for Englishmen, the true landscape, true home-counties, by right, partly, of a certain earthy warmth in the yellow of the sand below their gorse-bushes, and of a certain grey-blue mist after rain, in the hollows of the hills there, welcome to fatigued eyes, and never seen farther south; so I think that the sort of house I have described, with precisely those proportions of red-brick and green, and with a just perceptible monotony in the subdued order of it, for its distinguishing note, is for Englishmen at least typically home-life. And so for Florian that general human instinct was reinforced by this special home-likeness in the place his wandering soul had happened to light on, as, in the second degree, its body and earthly tabernacle; the sense of harmony between his soul and its physical environment became, for a time at least, like perfectly played music, and the life led there singularly tranquil and filled with a curious sense of self-possession. The love of security, of an habitually undisputed standing-ground or sleeping-place, came to count for much in the generation and correcting of his thoughts, and afterwards as a salutary principle of restraint in all his wanderings of spirit. The wistful yearning towards home, in absence from it, as the shadows of evening deepened, and he followed in thought what was doing there from hour to hour, interpreted to him much of a yearning and regret he experienced afterwards, towards he knew not what, out of strange ways of feeling and thought in which, from time to time, his spirit found itself alone; and in the tears shed in such absences there seemed always to be some soul-subduing foretaste of what his last tears might be.

And the sense of security could hardly have been deeper, the quiet of the child's soul being one with the quiet of its home, a place "inclosed" and "sealed." But upon this assured place, upon the child's assured soul which resembled it, there came floating in from the larger world without, as at windows left ajar unknowingly, or over the high garden walls, two streams of impressions, the sentiments of beauty and pain—recognitions of the visible, tangible, audible loveliness of things, as a very real and somewhat tyrannous element in them—and of the sorrow of the world, of grown people and children and animals, as a thing not to be put by in them. From this point he could trace two predominant processes of mental change in him—the growth of an almost diseased sensibility to the spectacle of suffering, and, parallel with this, the rapid growth of a certain capacity of fascination by bright colour and choice form—the sweet curvings, for instance, of the lips of those who seemed to him comely persons, modulated in such delicate unison to the things they said or sang,—marking early the activity in him of a more than customary sensuousness, "the lust of the eye," as the Preacher says;[11] which might lead him, one day, how far! Could he have foreseen the weariness of the way! In music sometimes the two sorts of impressions came together, and he would weep, to the surprise of older people. Tears of joy too the child knew, also to older people's surprise; real tears, once, of relief from long-strung, childish expectation, when he found returned at evening, with new roses in her cheeks, the little sister who had been to a place where there was a wood, and brought back for him a treasure of fallen acorns, and black crow's feathers, and his peace at finding her again near him mingled all night with some intimate sense of the distant forest, the rumour of its breezes, with the glossy blackbirds aslant and the branches lifted in them, and of the perfect nicety of the little cups that fell. So those two elementary apprehensions of the tenderness and of the colour in things grew apace in him, and were seen by him afterwards to send their roots back into the beginnings of life.

Let me note first some of the occasions of his recognition of the element of pain in things—incidents, now and again, which seemed suddenly to awake in him the whole force of that sentiment which Goethe has called the *Weltschmerz*,[12] and in which the concentrated sorrow of the world seemed suddenly to lie heavy upon him. A book lay in an old bookcase, of which he cared to remember one picture—a woman sitting, with hands bound behind her, the dress, the cap, the hair, folded with a simplicity which touched him strangely, as if not by her own hands, but with some ambiguous care at the hands of others—Queen Marie Antoinette, on her way to execution—we all remember David's drawing, meant merely to make her ridiculous.[13] The face that had been so high had learned to be mute and resistless; but out of its very resistlessness, seemed now to call on men to have pity, and forbear; and he took note of that, as he closed the book, as a thing to look at again, if he should at any time find himself tempted to be cruel. Again, he would never quite forget the appeal in the small sister's face, in the garden under the lilacs, terrified at a spider lighted on her sleeve. He could trace back to the look then noted a certain mercy he conceived always for people in fear, even of little things, which seemed to make him, though but for a moment, capable of almost any sacrifice of himself. Impressible, susceptible persons, indeed, who had had their sorrows, lived about him; and this sensibility was due in part to the tacit influence of their presence, enforcing upon him habitually the fact that there are those who pass their days, as a matter of course, in a sort of "going quietly." Most poignantly of all he could recall, in unfading minutest circumstance, the cry on the stair, sounding bitterly through the house, and struck into his soul for ever, of an aged woman, his father's sister, come now to announce his death in distant India; how it seemed to make the aged woman like a child again; and, he knew not why, but this fancy was full of pity to him. There were the little sorrows of the dumb animals too—of the white angora, with a dark tail like an ermine's, and a face like a flower, who fell into a lingering sickness, and became quite delicately human in its valetudinarianism, and came to have a hundred different expressions of voice—how it grew worse and worse, till it began to feel the light too much for it, and at last, after one wild morning of pain, the little soul flickered away from the body, quite worn to death already, and now but feebly retaining it.

So he wanted another pet; and as there were starlings about the place, which could be taught to speak, one of them was caught, and he meant to treat it kindly; but in the night its young ones could be heard crying after it, and the responsive cry of the mother-bird towards them; and at last, with the first light, though not till after some debate with himself, he went down and opened the cage, and saw a sharp bound of the prisoner up to her nestlings; and therewith came the sense of remorse,—that he too was become an accomplice in moving, to the limit of his small power, the springs and handles of that great machine in things, constructed so ingeniously to play pain-fugues on the delicate nerve-work of living creatures.

I have remarked how, in the process of our brainbuilding, as the house of thought in which we live gets itself together, like some airy bird's-nest of floating thistle-down and chance straws, compact at last, little accidents have their consequence; and thus it happened that, as he walked one evening, a garden gate, usually closed, stood open; and lo! within, a great red hawthorn in full flower, embossing heavily the bleached and twisted trunk and branches, so aged that there were but few green leaves thereon—a plumage of tender, crimson fire out of the heart of the dry wood. The perfume of the tree had now and again reached him, in the currents of the wind, over the wall, and he had wondered what might be behind it, and was now allowed to fill his arms with the flowers—flowers enough for all the old blue-china pots along the chimney-piece, making *fête* in the children's room. Was it some periodic moment in the expansion of soul within him, or mere trick of heat in the heavily-laden summer air? But the beauty of the thing struck home to him feverishly; and in dreams all night he loitered along a magic roadway of crimson flowers, which seemed to open ruddily in thick, fresh masses about his feet, and fill softly all the little hollows in the banks on either side. Always afterwards, summer by summer, as the flowers came on, the blossom of the red hawthorn still seemed to him absolutely the reddest of all things; and the goodly crimson, still alive in the works of old Venetian masters or old Flemish tapestries, called out always from afar the recollection of the flame in those perishing little petals, as it pulsed gradually out of them, kept long in the drawers of an old cabinet. Also then, for the first time, he seemed to experience a passionateness in his relation to fair outward objects, an inexplicable excitement in their presence, which disturbed him, and from which he half longed to be free. A touch of regret or desire mingled all night with the remembered presence of the red flowers, and their perfume in the darkness about him; and the longing for some undivined, entire possession of them was the beginning of a revelation to him, growing ever clearer, with the coming of the gracious summer guise of fields and trees and persons in each succeeding year, of a certain, at times seemingly exclusive, predominance in his interests, of beautiful physical things, a kind of tyranny of the senses over him.

In later years he came upon philosophies which occupied him much in the estimate of the proportion of the sensuous and the ideal elements in human knowledge, the relative parts they bear in it; and, in his intellectual scheme, was led to assign very little to the abstract thought, and much to its sensible vehicle or occasion. Such metaphysical speculation did but reinforce what was instinctive in his way of receiving the world, and for him, everywhere, that sensible vehicle or occasion became, perhaps only too surely, the necessary concomitant of any perception of things, real enough to be of any weight or reckoning, in his house of thought. There were times when he could think of the necessity he was under of associating all thoughts to touch and sight, as a sympathetic link between himself and actual, feeling, living objects; a protest in favour of real men and women against mere grey, unreal abstractions; and he remembered gratefully how the Christian religion, hardly less than the religion of the ancient Greeks, translating so much of its spiritual verity into things that may be seen, condescends in part to sanction this infirmity, if so it be, of our human existence, wherein the world of sense is so much with us,[14] and welcomed this thought as a kind of keeper and sentinel over his soul therein. But certainly, he came more and more to be unable to care for, or think of soul but as in an actual body, or of any world but that wherein are water and trees, and where men and women look, so or so, and press actual hands. It was the trick even his pity learned, fastening those who suffered in anywise to his affections by a kind of sensible attachments. He would think of Julian, fallen into incurable sickness, as spoiled in the sweet blossom of his skin like pale amber, and his honey-like hair; of Cecil, early dead, as cut off from the lilies, from golden summer days, from women's voices; and then what comforted him a little was the thought of the turning of the child's flesh to violets in the turf above him. And thinking of the very poor, it was not the things which most men care most for that he yearned to give them; but fairer roses, perhaps, and power to taste quite as they will, at their ease and not task-burdened, a certain desirable, clear light in the new morning, through which sometimes he had noticed them, quite unconscious of it, on their way to their early toil.

So he yielded himself to these things, to be played upon by them like a musical instrument, and began to note with deepening watchfulness, but always with some puzzled, unutterable longing in his enjoyment, the phases of the seasons and of the growing or wandering day, down even to the shadowy changes wrought on bare wall or ceiling—the light cast up from the snow, bringing out their darkest angles; the brown light in the cloud, which meant rain; that almost too austere clearness, in the protracted light of the lengthening day, before warm weather began, as if it lingered but to make a severer workday, with the school-books opened earlier and later; that beam of June sunshine, at last, as he lay awake before the time, a way of gold-dust across the darkness; all the humming, the freshness, the perfume of the garden seemed to lie upon it—and coming in one afternoon in September, along the red gravel walk, to look for a basket of yellow crab-apples left in the cool, old parlour, he remembered it the more, and how the colours struck upon him, because a wasp on one bitten apple stung him, and he felt the passion of sudden, severe pain. For this too brought its curious reflexions; and, in relief from it, he would wonder over it—how it had then been with him—puzzled at the depth of the charm or spell over him, which lay, for a little while at least, in the mere absence of pain; once, especially, when an older boy taught him to make flowers of sealing-wax, and he had burnt his hand badly at the lighted taper, and been unable to sleep. He remembered that also afterwards, as a sort of typical thing— a white vision of heat about him, clinging closely, through the languid scent of the ointments put upon the place to make it well.

Also, as he felt this pressure upon him of the sensible world, then, as often afterwards, there would come another sort of curious questioning how the last impressions of eye and ear might happen to him, how they would find him—the scent of the last flower, the soft yellowness of the last morning, the last recognition of some object of affection, hand or voice; it could not be but that the latest look of the eyes, before their final closing, would be strangely vivid; one would go with the hot tears, the cry, the touch of the wistful bystander, impressed how deeply on one! or would it be, perhaps, a mere frail retiring of all things, great or little, away from one, into a level distance?

For with this desire of physical beauty mingled itself early the fear of death—the fear of death intensified by the desire of beauty. Hitherto he had never gazed upon dead faces, as sometimes, afterwards, at the *Morgue* in Paris, or in that fair cemetery at Munich, where all the dead must go and lie in state before burial, behind glass windows, among the flowers and incense and holy candles—the aged clergy with their sacred ornaments, the young men in their dancing-shoes and spotless white linen—after which visits, those waxen, resistless faces would always live with him for many days, making the broadest sunshine sickly. The child had heard indeed of the death of his father, and how, in the Indian station, a fever had taken him, so that though not in action he had yet died as a soldier; and hearing of the "resurrection of the just,"[15] he could think of him as still abroad in the world, somehow, for his protection—a grand, though perhaps rather terrible figure, in beautiful soldier's things, like the figure in the picture of Joshua's Vision in the Bible[16]—and of that, round which the mourners moved so softly, and afterwards with such solemn singing, as but a worn-out garment left at a deserted lodging. So it was, until on a summer day he walked with his mother through a fair churchyard. In a bright dress he rambled among the graves, in the gay weather, and so came, in one corner, upon an open grave for a child—a dark space on the brilliant grass—the black mould lying heaped up round it, weighing down the little jewelled branches of the dwarf rosebushes in flower. And therewith came, full-grown, never wholly to leave him, with the certainty that even children do sometimes die, the physical horror of death, with its wholly selfish recoil from the association of lower forms of life, and the suffocating weight above. No benign, grave figure in beautiful soldier's things any longer abroad in the world for his protection! only a few poor, piteous bones; and above them, possibly, a certain sort of figure he hoped not to see. For sitting one day in the garden below an open window, he heard people talking, and could not but listen, how, in a sleepless hour, a sick woman had seen one of the dead sitting beside her, come to call her hence; and from the broken talk evolved with much clearness the notion that not all those dead people had really departed to the churchyard, nor were quite so motionless as they looked, but led a secret, half-fugitive life in their old homes, quite free by night, though sometimes visible in the day, dodging from room to room, with no great goodwill towards those who shared the place with them. All night the figure sat beside him in the reveries of his broken sleep, and was not quite gone in the morning—an odd, irreconcileable new member of the household, making the sweet familiar chambers unfriendly and suspect by its uncertain presence. He could have hated the dead he had pitied so, for being thus. Afterwards he came to think of those poor, home-returning ghosts, which all men have fancied to themselves— the *revenants*[17]—pathetically, as crying, or beating with vain hands at the doors, as the wind came, their cries distinguishable in it as a wilder inner note. But, always making death more unfamiliar still, that old experience would ever, from time to time, return to him; even in the living he sometimes caught its likeness; at any time or place, in a moment, the faint atmosphere of the chamber of death would be breathed around him, and the image with the bound chin, the quaint smile, the straight, stiff feet, shed itself across the air upon the bright carpet, amid the gayest company, or happiest communing with himself.

To most children the sombre questionings to which impressions like these attach themselves, if they come at all, are actually suggested by religious books, which therefore they often regard with much secret distaste, and dismiss, as far as possible, from their habitual thoughts as a too depressing element in life. To Florian such impressions, these misgivings as to the ultimate tendency of the years, of the relationship between life and death, had been suggested spontaneously in the natural course of his mental growth by a strong innate sense for the soberer tones in things, further strengthened by actual circumstances; and religious sentiment, that system of biblical ideas in which he had been brought up, presented itself to him as a thing that might soften and dignify, and light up as with a "lively hope,"[18] a melancholy already deeply settled in him. So he yielded himself easily to religious impressions, and with a kind of mystical appetite for sacred things; the more as they came to him through a saintly person who loved him tenderly, and believed that this early preoccupation with them already marked the child out for a saint. He began to love, for their own sakes, church lights, holy days, all that belonged to the comely order of the sanctuary, the secrets of its white linen, and holy vessels, and fonts of pure water; and its hieratic purity and simplicity became the type of something he desired always to have about him in actual life. He pored over the pictures in religious books, and knew by heart the exact mode in which the wrestling angel grasped Jacob,[19] how Jacob looked in his mysterious sleep,[20] how the bells and pomegranates were attached to the hem of Aaron's vestment, sounding sweetly as he glided over the turf of the holy place.[21] His way of conceiving religion came then to be in effect what it ever afterwards remained—a sacred history indeed, but still more a sacred ideal, a transcendent version or representation, under intenser and more expressive light and shade, of human life and its familiar or exceptional incidents, birth, death, marriage, youth, age, tears, joy, rest, sleep, waking—a mirror, towards which men might turn away their eyes from vanity and dullness, and see themselves therein as angels, with their daily meat and drink, even, become a kind of sacred transaction—a complementary strain or burden,[22] applied to our every-day existence, whereby the stray snatches of music in it re-set themselves, and fall into the scheme of some higher and more consistent harmony. A place adumbrated itself in his thoughts, wherein those sacred personalities, which are at once the reflex and the pattern of our nobler phases of life, housed themselves; and this region in his intellectual scheme all subsequent experience did but tend still further to realise and define. Some ideal, hieratic persons he would always need to occupy it and keep a warmth there. And he could hardly understand those who felt no such need at all, finding themselves quite happy without such heavenly companionship, and sacred double of their life, beside them.

Thus a constant substitution of the typical for the actual

took place in his thoughts. Angels might be met by the way, under English elm or beechtree; mere messengers seemed like angels, bound on celestial errands; a deep mysticity brooded over real meetings and partings; marriages were made in heaven; and deaths also, with hands of angels thereupon, to bear soul and body quietly asunder, each to its appointed rest. All the acts and accidents of daily life borrowed a sacred colour and significance; the very colours of things became themselves weighty with meanings like the sacred stuffs of Moses' tabernacle, full of penitence or peace.[23] Sentiment, congruous in the first instance only with those divine transactions, the deep, effusive unction of the House of Bethany,[24] was assumed as the due attitude for the reception of our every-day existence; and for a time he walked through the world in a sustained, not unpleasurable awe, generated by the habitual recognition, beside every circumstance and event of life, or its celestial correspondent.

Sensibility—the desire of physical beauty—a strange biblical awe, which made any reference to the unseen act on him like solemn music—these qualities the child took away with him, when, at about the age of twelve years, he left the old house, and was taken to live in another place. He had never left home before, and, anticipating much from this change, had long dreamed over it, jealously counting the days till the time fixed for departure should come; had been a little careless about others even, in his strong desire for it—when Lewis fell sick, for instance, and they must wait still two days longer. At last the morning came, very fine; and all things—the very pavement with its dust, at the roadside—seemed to have a white, pearl-like lustre in them. They were to travel by a favourite road on which he had often walked a certain distance, and on one of those two prisoner days, when Lewis was sick, had walked farther than ever before, in his great desire to reach the new place. They had started and gone a little way when a pet bird was found to have been left behind, and must even now—so it presented itself to him—have already all the appealing fierceness and wild self-pity at heart of one left by others to perish of hunger in a closed house; and he returned to fetch it, himself in hardly less stormy distress. But as he passed in search of it from room to room, lying so pale, with a look of meekness in their denudation, and at last through that little, stripped white room, the aspect of the place touched him like the face of one dead; and a clinging back towards it came over him, so intense that he knew it would last long, and spoiling all his pleasure in the realisation of a thing so eagerly anticipated. And so, with the bird found, but himself in an agony of homesickness, thus capriciously sprung up within him, he was driven quickly away, far into the rural distance, so fondly speculated on, of that favourite country-road.

NOTES

1. Though first published in book form as part of the posthumous *Miscellaneous Studies* (1895), this Paterian vision of his own childhood first appeared in *Macmillan's Magazine* in August, 1878, with the title "Imaginary Portrait. The Child in the House." I preface it to this volume of *Selected Writings,* out of chronology, because it is Pater's key-signature, the largest clue to his work, criticism and imaginary portraits alike.

2. "More musically blent" suggests Pater's Platonic or Shelleyan use of music as the vision of art's ultimate resting place, or the knowledge of that which pertains to love in harmony and system. See the remark in "The School of Giorgione" that all art constantly aspires to the condition of music, presumably because music *appears* to have overcome the dualism of form and content, or style and substance.

3. The "almost thirty years" hints at the identity of Florian and Pater, since Florian leaves home at twelve, and Pater was forty-one when he wrote "The Child in the House."

4. Jean Antoine Watteau, French painter (1684–1721), taught the painter Jean Baptiste Pater, from whom Walter Pater liked to claim descent. See "A Prince of Court Painters" in the *Imaginary Portraits.*

5. See the poplar tree in Pater's "Denys l'Auxerrois."

6. "Thrum" are fringes or tufts; "lumber" here means household stuff, generally archaic.

7. The "white paper" here is Locke's metaphor for the human mind when it is prereflective, while the "smooth wax" is Aristotle's metaphor for the same state of the mind.

8. "With lead in the rock forever" is quoted from Job 19:23-24.

9. *Goûter:* "lunch."

10. *Chez soi:* "at home."

11. "The lust of the eye" is from I John 2:16.

12. *Weltschmerz:* "world-sorrow," the dark vision of the sentimental Age of Sensibility, in Germany as in England.

13. Jacques Louis David (1748–1825), major French painter.

14. "The world of sense is so much with us" alludes to Wordsworth's sonnet, "The world is too much with us . . ."

15. "Resurrection of the just" is from Luke 14:14.
16. For "Joshua's Vision" see Joshua 5:13-15.
17. *Revenants:* "returners," as from exile or death.
18. "Lively hope" is from I Peter 1:3.
19. "The wrestling angel grasped Jacob" describes Genesis 32:24.
20. Jacob's "mysterious sleep" is described in Genesis 28:11-15.
21. The "bells and pomegranates" are from Exodus 39:24-26; there is presumably no reference to Browning here, though he had used the phrase as the title of a series of verse-pamphlets.
22. "Burden" means a bass under-part here.
23. For "Moses' tabernacle" see Exodus 25-27.
24. For "the House of Bethany" see Matthew 26:6-13.

from *The Renaissance:*
Studies in Art and Poetry

Preface

Many attempts have been made by writers on art and poetry to define beauty in the abstract, to express it in the most general terms, to find a universal formula for it.[1] The value of these attempts has most often been in the suggestive and penetrating things said by the way. Such discussions help us very little to enjoy what has been well done in art or poetry, to discriminate between what is more and what is less excellent in them, or to use words like beauty, excellence, art, poetry, with a more precise meaning than they would otherwise have. Beauty, like all other qualities presented to human experience, is relative; and the definition of it becomes unmeaning and useless in proportion to its abstractness. To define beauty, not in the most abstract, but in the most concrete terms possible, to find, not a universal formula for it, but the formula which expresses most adequately this or that special manifestation of it, is the aim of the true student of aesthetics.

"To see the object as in itself it really is,"[2] has been justly said to be the aim of all true criticism whatever; and in aesthetic criticism the first step towards seeing one's object as it really is, is to know one's own impression as it really is, to discriminate it, to realise it distinctly. The objects with which aesthetic criticism deals—music, poetry, artistic and accomplished forms of human life—are indeed receptacles of so many powers or forces; they possess, like the products of nature, so many virtues or qualities. What is this song or picture, this engaging personality presented in life or in a book, to *me*?[3] What effect does it really produce on me? Does it give me pleasure? and if so, what sort or degree of pleasure? How is my nature modified by its presence, and under its influence? The answers to these questions are the original facts with which the aesthetic critic has to do; and, as in the study of light, of morals, of number, one must realise such primary data for oneself, or not at all. And he who experiences these impressions strongly, and drives directly at the discrimination and analysis of them, has no need to trouble himself with the abstract question what beauty is in itself, or what its exact relation to truth or experience—metaphysical questions, as unprofitable as metaphysical questions elsewhere. He may pass them all by as being, answerable or not, of no interest to him.

The aesthetic critic, then, regards all the objects with which he has to do, all works of art, and the fairer forms of nature and human life, as powers or forces producing pleasurable sensations, each of a more or less peculiar and unique kind. This influence he feels, and wishes to explain, analysing it, and reducing it to its elements. To him, the picture, the landscape, the engaging personality in life or in a book, *La Gioconda*, the hills of Carrara, Pico of Mirandola,[4] are valuable for their virtues,[5] as we say, in speaking of a herb, a wine, a gem; for the property each has of affecting one with a special, a unique, impression of pleasure. Our education becomes complete in proportion as our susceptibility to these impressions increases in depth and variety. And the function of the aesthetic critic is to distinguish, analyse, and separate from its adjuncts, the virtue by which a picture, a landscape, a fair personality in life or in a book, produces this special impression of beauty or pleasure, to indicate what the source of that impression is, and under what conditions it is experienced. His end is reached when he has disengaged that virtue, and noted it, as a chemist notes some natural element, for himself and others; and the rule for those who would reach this end is stated with great exactness in the words of a recent critic of Sainte-Beuve:—*De se borner à connaître de près les belles choses, et à s'en nourrir en exquis amateurs, en humanistes accomplis.*[6]

What is important, then, is not that the critic should possess a correct abstract definition of beauty for the intellect, but a certain kind of temperament, the power of being deeply moved by the presence of beautiful objects. He will remember always that beauty exists in many forms. To him all periods, types, schools of taste, are in themselves equal. In all ages there have been some excellent workmen, and some excellent work done. The question he asks is always:—In whom did the stir, the genius, the sentiment of the period find itself? where was the receptacle of its refinement, its elevation, its taste? "The ages are all equal," says William Blake, "but genius is always above its age."[7]

Often it will require great nicety to disengage this virtue from the commoner elements with which it may be found in combination. Few artists, not Goethe or Byron even,[8] work quite cleanly, casting off all *débris*, and leaving us only what the heat of their imagination has wholly fused and transformed. Take, for instance, the writings of Wordsworth. The heat of his genius, entering into the substance of his work, has crystallised a part, but only a part, of it; and in that great mass of verse there is much which might well be forgotten. But scattered up and down it, sometimes fusing and transforming entire compositions, like the Stanzas on *Resolution and Independence*, and the Ode on the *Recollections of Childhood*,[9] sometimes, as if at random, depositing a fine crystal here or there, in a matter it does not wholly search through and transform, we trace the action of his unique, incommunicable faculty, that strange, mystical sense of a life in natural things, and of man's life as a part of nature, drawing strength and colour and character from local influences, from the hills and streams, and from natural sights and sounds. Well! that is the *virtue*, the active principle in Wordsworth's poetry; and then the function of the critic of Wordsworth is to follow up that active principle, to disengage it, to mark the degree in which it penetrates his verse.[10]

The subjects of the following studies are taken from the history of the *Renaissance*,[11] and touch what I think the chief points in that complex, many-sided movement. I have explained in the first of them what I understand by the word, giving it a much wider scope than was intended by those who originally used it to denote only that revival of classical antiquity in the fifteenth century which was but one of many results of a general excitement and enlightening of the human mind, of which the great aim and achievements of what, as Christian art, is often falsely opposed to the Renaissance, were another result. This outbreak of the human spirit may be traced far into the middle age itself, with its qualities already clearly pronounced, the care for physical beauty, the worship of the body, the breaking down of those limits which the religious system of the middle age imposed on the heart and the imagination. I have taken as an example of this movement, this earlier Renaissance within the middle age itself, and as an expression of its qualities, two little compositions in early French; not because they constitute the best possible expression of them, but because they help the unity of my series, inasmuch as the Renaissance ends also in France, in French poetry, in a phase of which the writings of Joachim du Bellay[12] are in many ways the most perfect illustration; the Renaissance thus putting forth in France an aftermath, a wonderful later growth, the products of which have to the full that subtle and delicate sweetness which belongs to a refined and comely decadence; just as its earliest phases have the freshness which belongs to all periods of growth in art, the charm of *ascêsis*,[13] of the austere and serious girding of the loins in youth.

But it is in Italy, in the fifteenth century, that the interest of the Renaissance mainly lies,—in that solemn fifteenth century which can hardly be studied too much, not merely for its positive results in the things of the intellect and the imagination, its concrete works of art, its special and prominent personalities, with their profound aesthetic charm, but for its general spirit and character, for the ethical qualities of which it is a consummate type.

The various forms of intellectual activity which together make up the culture of an age, move for the most part from different starting-points, and by unconnected roads. As products of the same generation they partake indeed of a common character, and unconsciously illustrate each other; but of the producers themselves, each group is solitary, gaining what advantage or disadvantage there may be in intellectual isolation. Art and poetry, philosophy and the religious life, and that other life of refined pleasure and action in. the open places of the world, are each of them confined to its own circle of ideas, and those who prosecute either of them are generally little curious of the thoughts of others. There come, however, from time to time, eras of more favorable conditions, in which the thoughts of men draw nearer together than is their wont, and the many interests of the intellectual world combine in one complete type of general culture. The fifteenth century in Italy is one of these happier eras; and what is sometimes said of the age of Pericles is true of that of Lorenzo:[14]—it is an age productive in personalities, many-sided, centralised, complete. Here, artists and philosophers and those whom the action of the world has elevated and made keen, do not live in isolation, but breathe a common air, and catch light and heat from each other's thoughts. There is a spirit of general elevation and enlightenment in which all alike communicate. It is the unity of this spirit which gives unity to all the various products of the Renaissance; and it is to this intimate alliance with mind, this participation in the best thoughts which that age produced, that the art of Italy in the fifteenth century owes much of its grave dignity and influence.

I have added an essay on Winckelmann, as not incongruous with the studies which precede it, because Winckelmann, coming in the eighteenth century, really belongs in spirit to an earlier age. By his enthusiasm for things of the intellect and the imagination for their own sake, by his Hellenism, his life-long struggle to attain to the Greek spirit, he is in sympathy with the humanists of an earlier century. He is the last fruit of the Renaissance, and explains in a striking way its motive and tendencies.[15]

1873

NOTES

1. "A universal formula" refers to German philosophical aesthetics, which Pater dismisses as not his concern; rejecting discussions of "beauty in the abstract," Pater seeks to return to the Greek root of the word "aesthetic," which means "perception."
2. Pater deliberately alludes to the opening of Matthew Arnold's "The Function of Criticism at the Present Time."
3. Another allusion to Arnold, here to the essay "Heinrich Heine," and to a passage where Goethe is praised for his profound naturalism.
4. *La Gioconda,* the "Mona Lisa," is the portrait by Leonardo da Vinci (at the Louvre) that Pater's most famous passage impressionalistically "describes." Carrara is an Italian region known for its marble. Giovanni Pico, Count of Mirandola (1463–1494), was a Neoplatonist philosopher to whom Pater devotes one of the essays of *The Renaissance.*
5. "Virtues" here means "power."
6. "To limit themselves to knowing at first hand beautiful things, and to develop themselves as sensitive amateurs by these, as accomplished humanists."

7. From Blake's "Annotations" to *The Works of Sir Joshua Reynolds.* Blake's actual wording: "Ages are All Equal, But Genius is Always Above The Age." See *The Poetry and Prose of William Blake,* edited by David V. Erdman (New York, 1965, 1970), p. 638.

8. The "Byron even," in this context, is strange for Pater, and a difficult estimate to justify critically.

9. The correct title of Wordsworth's poem is: "Ode: Intimations of Immortality from Recollections of Early Childhood."

10. Pater follows Arnold here in the view that Wordsworth requires rigorous selectivity on the critic's part.

11. *Renaissance* (French for "rebirth") is defined by Pater as commencing in France toward the close of the twelfth century. The more common nineteenth-century English view located the Renaissance in Italy, between the fourteenth and sixteenth centuries. Essentially, Pater turns to the Renaissance as a counterpoise to Ruskin's exaltation of the Middle Ages, particularly in *The Stones of Venice.*

12. Joachim du Bellay (1522–1560), French poet and humanist, the subject of one of the essays in Pater's *The Renaissance.*

13. "The charm of *ascêsis*" is one of Pater's crucial ideas, partly outlined in my "Introduction"; in his essay "Style," Pater defines *ascêsis* as "self-restraint, a skilful economy of means."

14. Pericles, dominant in Athens in the fifth century B.C., led the city to its greatest achievement in the arts; Lorenzo de Medici (1449–1492) was the Pericles of Florence as its prince, and another major patron of the arts.

15. Johann Joachim Winckelmann (1717–1768), German classical scholar, and one of Pater's heroic precursors, to whom one of the essays in *The Renaissance* is devoted.

Sandro Botticelli

In Leonardo's treatise on painting[1] only one contemporary is mentioned by name—Sandro Botticelli. This preëminence may be due to chance only, but to some will rather appear a result of deliberate judgment; for people have begun to find out the charm of Botticelli's work, and his name, little known in the last century, is quietly becoming important.[2] In the middle of the fifteenth century[3] he had already anticipated much of that meditative subtlety, which is sometimes supposed peculiar to the great imaginative workmen of its close.[4] Leaving the simple religion which had occupied the followers of Giotto[5] for a century, and the simple naturalism which had grown out of it, a thing of birds and flowers only, he sought inspiration in what to him were works of the modern world, the writings of Dante and Boccaccio,[6] and in new readings of his own classical stories[7]: or, if he painted religious incidents, painted them with an under-current of original sentiment, which touches you as the real matter of the picture through the veil of its ostensible subject. What is the peculiar sensation, what is the peculiar quality of pleasure, which his work has the property of exciting in us, and which we cannot get elsewhere? For this, especially when he has to speak for a comparatively unknown artist, is always the chief question which a critic has to answer.

In an age when the lives of artists were full of adventure, his life is almost colourless. Criticism indeed has cleared away much of the gossip which Vasari[8] accumulated, has touched the legend of Lippo and Lucrezia, and rehabilitated the character of Andrea del Castagno; but in Botticelli's case there is no legend to dissipate. He did not even go by his true name:

Sandro is a nickname,[9] and his true name is Filipepi, Botticelli being only the name of the goldsmith who first taught him art. Only two things happened to him, two things which he shared with other artists:—he was invited to Rome to paint in the Sistine Chapel, and he fell in later life under the influence of Savonarola,[10] passing apparently almost out of men's sight in a sort of religious melancholy, which lasted till his death in 1515, according to the received date. Vasari says that he plunged into the study of Dante, and even wrote a comment on the *Divine Comedy*. But it seems strange that he should have lived on inactive so long; and one almost wishes that some document might come to light, which, fixing the date of his death earlier, might relieve one, in thinking of him, of his dejected old age.

He is before all things a poetical painter, blending the charm of story and sentiment, the medium of the art of poetry, with the charm of line and colour, the medium of abstract painting. So he becomes the illustrator of Dante. In a few rare examples of the edition of 1481, the blank spaces, left at the beginning of every canto for the hand of the illuminator, have been filled, as far as the nineteenth canto of the *Inferno*, with impressions of engraved plates, seemingly by way of experiment, for in the copy in the Bodleian Library, one of the three impressions it contains has been printed upside down, and much awry, in the midst of the luxurious printed page. Giotto, and the followers of Giotto, with their almost childish religious aim, had not learned to put that weight of meaning into outward things, light, colour, everyday gesture, which the poetry of the *Divine Comedy* involves, and before the fifteenth century Dante could hardly have found an illustrator. Botticelli's illustrations are crowded with incident, blending with a naïve carelessness of pictorial propriety, three phases of the same scene into one plate. The grotesques, so often a stumbling-block to painters who forget that the words of a poet, which only feebly present an image to the mind, must be lowered in key when translated into form, make one regret that he has not rather chosen for illustration the more subdued imagery of the *Purgatorio*.[11] Yet in the scene of those who "go down quick into hell," there is an invention about the fire taking hold on the upturned soles of the feet, which proves that the design is no mere translation of Dante's words, but a true painter's vision; while the scene of the Centaurs wins one at once, for, forgetful of the actual circumstances of their appearance, Botticelli has gone off with delight on the thought of the Centaurs themselves, bright, small creatures of the woodland, with arch baby faces and mignon forms, drawing tiny bows.

Botticelli lived in a generation of naturalists, and he might have been a mere naturalist among them. There are traces enough in his work of that alert sense of outward things, which, in the pictures of that period, fills the lawns with delicate living creatures, and the hillsides with pools of water, and the pools of water with flowering reeds. But this was not enough for him; he is a visionary painter, and in his visionariness he resembles Dante. Giotto, the tried companion of Dante, Masaccio, Ghirlandajo even, do but transcribe, with more or less refining, the outward image; they are dramatic, not visionary painters;[12] they are almost impassive spectators of the action before them. But the genius of which Botticelli is the type usurps the data before it as the exponent of ideas, moods, visions of its own; in this interest it plays fast and loose with those data, rejecting some and isolating others, and always combining them anew. To him, as to Dante, the scene, the colour, the outward image or gesture, comes with all its incisive and importunate reality; but awakes in him, moreover, by some subtle law of his own structure, a mood which it awakes in no one else, of which it is the double or repetition, and which it clothes, that all may share it, with sensuous circumstance.

But he is far enough from accepting the conventional orthodoxy of Dante which, referring all human action to the simple formula of purgatory, heaven and hell, leaves an insoluble element of prose in the depths of Dante's poetry. One picture of his, with the portrait of the donor, Matteo Palmieri, below, had the credit or discredit of attracting some shadow of ecclesiastical censure. This Matteo Palmieri—two dim figures move under that name in contemporary history—was the reputed author of a poem, still unedited, *La Città Divina*, which represented the human race as an incarnation of those angels who, in the revolt of Lucifer, were neither for Jehovah nor for His enemies, a fantasy of that earlier Alexandrian philosophy about which the Florentine intellect in that century was so curious. Botticelli's picture may have been only one of those familiar compositions in which religious reverie has recorded its impressions of the various forms of beatified existence—*Glorias*, as they were called, like that in which

Giotto painted the portrait of Dante; but somehow it was suspected of embodying in a picture the wayward dream of Palmieri, and the chapel where it hung was closed. Artists so entire as Botticelli are usually careless about philosophical theories, even when the philosopher is a Florentine of the fifteenth century, and his work a poem in *terza rima*. But Botticelli, who wrote a commentary on Dante, and became the disciple of Savonarola, may well have let such theories come and go across him. True or false, the story interprets much of the peculiar sentiment with which he infuses his profane and sacred persons, comely, and in a certain sense like angels, but with a sense of displacement or loss about them—the wistfulness of exiles,[13] conscious of a passion and energy greater than any known issue of them explains, which runs through all his varied work with a sentiment of ineffable melancholy.

So just what Dante scorns as unworthy alike of heaven and hell, Botticelli accepts, that middle world in which men take no side in great conflicts, and decide no great causes, and make great refusals.[14] He thus sets for himself the limits within which art, undisturbed by any moral ambition, does its most sincere and surest work. His interest is neither in the untempered goodness of Angelico's saints, nor the un-tempered evil of Orcagna's *Inferno*; but with men and women, in their mixed and uncertain condition, always attractive, clothed sometimes by passion with a character of loveliness and energy, but saddened perpetually by the shadow upon them of the great things from which they shrink. His morality is all sympathy; and it is this sympathy, conveying into his work somewhat more than is usual of the true complexion of humanity, which makes him, visionary as he is, so forcible a realist.

It is this which gives to his Madonnas their unique expression and charm. He has worked out in them a distinct and peculiar type, definite enough in his own mind, for he has painted it over and over again, sometimes one might think almost mechanically, as a pastime during that dark period when his thoughts were so heavy upon him. Hardly any collection of note is without one of these circular pictures, into which the attendant angels depress their heads so naïvely. Perhaps you have sometimes wondered why those peevish-looking Madonnas, conformed to no acknowledged or obvious type of beauty, attract you more and more, and often come back to you when the Sistine Madonna and the Virgins of Fra Angelico are forgotten. At first, contrasting them with those, you may have thought that there was something in them mean or abject even, for the abstract lines of the face have little nobleness, and the colour is wan. For with Botticelli she too, though she holds in her hands the "Desire of all nations," is one of those who are neither for Jehovah nor for His enemies; and her choice is on her face. The white light on it is cast up hard and cheerless from below, as when snow lies upon the ground, and the children look up with surprise at the strange whiteness of the ceiling. Her trouble is in the very caress of the mysterious child, whose gaze is always far from her, and who has already that sweet look of devotion which men have never been able altogether to love, and which still makes the born saint an object almost of suspicion to his earthly brethren. Once, indeed,[15] he guides her hand to transcribe in a book the words of her exaltation, the *Ave*, and the *Magnificat*, and the *Gaude Maria*, and the young angels, glad to rouse her for a moment from her dejection, are eager to hold the inkhorn and to support the book; but the pen almost drops from her hand, and the high cold words have no meaning for her, and her true children are those others, among whom, in her rude home, the intolerable honour came to her, with that look of wistful inquiry on their irregular faces which you see in startled animals—gipsy children, such as those who, in Apennine villages, still hold out their long brown arms to beg of you, but on Sundays become *enfants du chœur*, with their thick black hair nicely combed, and fair white linen on their sunburnt throats.

What is strangest is that he carries this sentiment into classical subjects, its most complete expression being a picture in the *Uffizii*, of Venus rising from the sea, in which the grotesque emblems of the middle age, and a landscape full of its peculiar feeling, and even its strange draperies, powdered all over in the Gothic manner with a quaint conceit of daisies, frame a figure that reminds you of the faultless nude studies of Ingres.[16] At first, perhaps, you are attracted only by a quaintness of design, which seems to recall all at once whatever you have read of Florence in the fifteenth century; afterwards you may think that this quaintness must be incongruous with the subject, and that the colour is cadaverous or at least cold. And yet, the more you come to understand what imaginative colouring really is, that all colour is no mere delightful quality of natural things, but a spirit upon them by which they become expressive to the spirit, the better you will like this peculiar quality of colour; and you will find that quaint design of Botticelli's a more direct inlet into the Greek temper than the works of the Greeks themselves even of the finest period. Of the Greeks as they really were, of their difference from ourselves, of the aspects of their outward life, we know far more than Botticelli, or his most learned contemporaries; but for us long familiarity has taken off the edge of the lesson, and we are hardly conscious of what we owe to the Hellenic spirit. But in pictures like this of Botticelli's you have a record of the first impression make by it on minds turned back towards it, in almost painful aspiration, from a world in which it had been ignored so long; and in the passion, the energy, the industry of realisation, with which Botticelli carries out his intention, is the exact measure of the legitimate influence over the human mind of the imaginative system of which this is the central myth. The light is indeed cold—mere sunless dawn; but a later painter would have cloyed you with sunshine; and you can see the better for that quietness in the morning air each long promontory, as it slopes down to the water's edge. Men go forth to their labours until the evening; but she is awake before them, and you might think that the sorrow in her face was at the thought of the whole long day of love yet to come. An emblematical figure of the wind blows hard across the grey water, moving forward the dainty-lipped shell on which she sails, the sea "showing his teeth" as it moves in thin lines of foam, and sucking in, one by one, the falling roses, each severe in outline, plucked off short at the stalk, but embrowned a little, as Botticelli's flowers always are. Botticelli meant all that imagery to be altogether pleasurable; and it was partly an incompleteness of resources, inseparable from the art of that time, that subdued and chilled it; but his predilection for minor tones counts also; and what is unmistakable is the sadness with which he has conceived the goddess of pleasure, as the depositary of a great power over the lives of men.

I have said that the peculiar character of Botticelli is the result of a blending in him of a sympathy for humanity in its uncertain condition, its attractiveness, its investiture at rarer moments in a character of loveliness and energy, with his consciousness of the shadow upon it of the great things from which it shrinks, and that this conveys into his work somewhat more than painting usually attains of the true complexion of humanity. He paints the story of the goddess of pleasure in other episodes besides that of her birth from the sea, but never without some shadow of death in the grey flesh and wan flowers.[17] He paints Madonnas, but they shrink from the pressure of the divine child, and plead in unmistakable undertones for a warmer, lower humanity. The same figure—tradition connects it with Simonetta, the mistress of Giuliano de' Medici—appears again as Judith, returning home across the hill country, when the great deed is over, and the moment of revulsion come, when the olive branch in her hand is becoming a burthen; as *Justice*, sitting on a throne, but with a fixed look of self-hatred which makes the sword in her hand seem that of a suicide; and again as *Veritas*, in the allegorical picture of *Calumnia*, where one may note in passing the suggestiveness of an accident which identifies the image of Truth with the person of Venus. We might trace the same sentiment through his engravings; but his share in them is doubtful, and the object of this brief study has been attained, if I have defined aright the temper in which he worked.

But, after all, it may be asked, is a painter like Botticelli—a secondary painter, a proper subject for general criticism? There are a few great painters, like Michelangelo or Leonardo, whose work has become a force in general culture, partly for this very reason that they have absorbed into themselves all such workmen as Sandro Botticelli; and, over and above mere technical or antiquarian criticism, general criticism may be very well employed in that sort of interpretation which adjusts the position of these men to general culture, whereas smaller men can be the proper subjects only of technical or antiquarian treatment. But, besides those great men, there is a certain number of artists who have a distinct faculty of their own by which they convey to us a peculiar quality of pleasure which we cannot get elsewhere; and these, too, have their place in general culture, and must be interpreted to it by those who have felt their charm strongly, and are often the objects of a special diligence and a consideration wholly affectionate, just because there is not about them the stress of a great name and authority. Of this select number Botticelli is one; he has the freshness, the uncertain and diffident promise which belongs to the earlier Renaissance itself, and makes it perhaps the most interesting period in the history of the mind: in studying his work one begins to understand to how great a place in human culture the art of Italy had been called.

1870

NOTES

1. See Pater's essay on Leonardo, where the reference is to a French compiler of this treatise, Raffaelle du Fresne.
2. The interest in Botticelli, in England, was largely due to the Pre-Raphaelite Movement, since Ruskin ignored Botticelli until after the early 1870's. Pater is asserting a priority here against Ruskin's authority.
3. Botticelli's dates are 1444?–1510, but his major work was done early.
4. These "great imaginative workmen" must be Leonardo, Michelangelo, and Raphael.
5. Giotto (1276–1337) was contemporary with Dante.
6. Dante (1265–1321) and Boccaccio (1313–1375) are seen here as Botticelli's major precursors.
7. Perhaps a reference to Botticelli's own myth-makings in paintings like the *Primavera* or the *Mars and Venus*.
8. Vasari wrote the *Lives of the Painters* (1550).
9. The habit of nicknames for the Renaissance masters fascinated Browning also, as in his name for Massacio, "Hulking Tom," in his great poem, "Fra Lippo Lippi."
10. Savonarola's brief religious movement came in 1492.
11. A mistake on Pater's part, as Botticelli did illustrate the whole of Dante's poem. But the "mistake" is revelatory and brings Botticelli closer to Pater.
12. The difficult distinction between "dramatic" and "visionary" here is central to Pater, and to Yeats after him. Behind the distinction is a Romantic aesthetic preference that can be traced from Blake and Coleridge down through the nineteenth century's continuous success at visionary art, and almost as continuous failure at drama.
13. Pater's Botticelli is essentially Pater; "the wistfulness of exiles" describes all of Pater's imaginary portraits, and Pater himself as well.
14. This is again as much Pater as Botticelli, for "the middle world" of "great refusals" is the realm of Pater's *askesis*, his version of a purgatorial self-curtailment.
15. This is the picture of the Madonna in the Uffizi.
16. Pater must have the great *La Source* of Ingres, at the Louvre, in mind.
17. Pater is thinking of the *Mars and Venus* (National Gallery, London).

Leonardo da Vinci

Homo Minister et Interpres Naturae[1]

In Vasari's life of Leonardo da Vinci as we now read it
there are some variations from the first edition.[2] There,
the painter who has fixed the outward type of Christ for succeeding centuries was a bold speculator, holding lightly by
other men's beliefs, setting philosophy above Christianity.
Words of his, trenchant enough to justify this impression, are
not recorded, and would have been out of keeping with a
genius of which one characteristic is the tendency to lose itself
in a refined and graceful mystery. The suspicion was but the
time-honoured mode in which the world stamps its appreciation of one who has thoughts for himself alone, his high
indifference, his intolerance of the common forms of
things; and in the second edition the image was changed into
something fainter and more conventional. But it is still by a
certain mystery in his work, and something enigmatical
beyond the usual measure of great men, that he fascinates,
or perhaps half repels. His life is one of sudden revolts, with
intervals in which he works not at all, or apart from the
main scope of his work. By a strange fortune the works on
which his more popular fame rested disappeared early from
the world, as the *Battle of the Standard*; or are mixed
obscurely with the work of meaner hands, as the *Last
Supper*. His type of beauty is so exotic that it fascinates a
larger number than it delights, and seems more than that of
any other artist to reflect ideas and views and some scheme
of the world within; so that he seemed to his contemporaries
to be the possessor of some unsanctified and secret wisdom;
as to Michelet[3] and others to have anticipated modern ideas.
He trifles with his genius, and crowds all his chief work into

a few tormented years of later life; yet he is so possessed by his genius that he passes unmoved through the most tragic events, overwhelming his country and friends, like one who comes across them by chance on some secret errand.

His *legend*,[4] as the French say, with the anecdotes which every one knows, is one of the most brilliant in Vasari. Later writers merely copied it, until, in 1804, Carlo Amoretti[5] applied to it a criticism which left hardly a date fixed, and not one of those anecdotes untouched. The various questions thus raised have since that time become, one after another, subjects of special study, and mere antiquarianism has in this direction little more to do. For others remain the editing of the thirteen books of his manuscripts, and the separation by technical criticism of what in his reputed works is really his, from what is only half his, or the work of his pupils. But a lover of strange souls may still analyse for himself the impression made on him by those works, and try to reach through it a definition of the chief elements of Leonardo's genius. The *legend*, corrected and enlarged by its critics, may now and then intervene to support the results of this analysis.

His life has three divisions—thirty years at Florence, nearly twenty years at Milan, then nineteen years of wandering, till he sinks to rest under the protection of Francis the First at the *Château de Clou*.[6] The dishonour of illegitimacy hangs over his birth. Piero Antonio, his father, was of a noble Florentine house, of Vinci in the *Val d'Arno*,[7] and Leonardo, brought up delicately among the true children of that house, was the love-child of his youth, with the keen, puissant nature such children often have. We see him in his youth fascinating all men by his beauty, improvising music and songs, buying the caged birds and setting them free, as he walked the streets of Florence, fond of odd bright dresses and spirited horses.

From his earliest years he designed many objects, and constructed models in relief, of which Vasari mentions some of women smiling. His father, pondering over this promise in the child, took him to the workshop of Andrea del Verrocchio, then the most famous artist in Florence. Beautiful objects lay about there—reliquaries, pyxes,[8] silver images for the pope's chapel at Rome, strange fancy-work of the middle age, keeping odd company with fragments of antiquity, then but lately discovered. Another student Leonardo may have seen there— a boy into whose soul the level light and aërial illusions of Italian sunsets had passed, in after days famous as Perugino.[9]

Verrocchio was an artist of the earlier Florentine type, carver, painter, and worker in metals, in one; designer, not of pictures only, but of all things for sacred or household use, drinking-vessels, ambries,[10] instruments of music, making them all fair to look upon, filling the common ways of life with the reflexion of some far-off brightness; and years of patience had refined his hand till his work was now sought after from distant places.

It happened that Verrocchio was employed by the brethren of Vallombrosa[11] to paint the Baptism of Christ, and Leonardo was allowed to finish an angel in the left-hand corner. It was one of those moments in which the progress of a great thing—here, that of the art of Italy—presses hard and sharp on the happiness of an individual, through whose discouragement and decrease, humanity, in more fortunate persons, comes a step nearer to its final success.

For beneath the cheerful exterior of the mere well-paid craftsman, chasing brooches for the copes of *Santa Maria Novella*,[12] or twisting metal screens for the tombs of the Medici,[13] lay the ambitious desire of expanding the destiny of Italian art by a larger knowledge and insight into things, a purpose in art not unlike Leonardo's still unconscious purpose; and often, in the modelling of drapery, or of a lifted arm, or of hair cast back from the face there came to him something of the freer manner and richer humanity of a later age. But in this *Baptism* the pupil had surpassed the master; and Verrocchio turned away as one stunned, and as if his sweet earlier work must thereafter be distasteful to him, from the bright animated angel of Leonardo's hand.

The angel may still be seen in Florence, a space of sunlight in the cold, laboured old picture; but the legend is true only in sentiment, for painting had always been the art by which Verrocchio set least store. And as in a sense he anticipates Leonardo, so to the last Leonardo recalls the studio of Verrocchio, in the love of beautiful toys, such as the vessel of water for a mirror, and lovely needlework about the implicated hands in the *Modesty and Vanity*, and of reliefs, like those cameos which in the *Virgin of the Balances* hang all round the girdle of Saint Michael, and of bright variegated stones, such as the agates in the *Saint Anne*, and in a hieratic preciseness and grace, as of a sanctuary swept and garnished. Amid all the cunning and intricacy of his Lombard[14] manner this never left him. Much of it there must have been in that lost picture of *Paradise*, which he prepared as a cartoon[15] for tapestry, to be woven in the looms of Flanders. It was the perfection of the older Florentine style of miniature-painting, with patient putting of each leaf upon the trees and each flower in the grass, where the first man and woman were standing.

And because it was the perfection of that style, it awoke in Leonardo some seed of discontent which lay in the secret places of his nature. For the way to perfection is through a series of disgusts; and this picture—all that he had done so far in his life at Florence—was after all in the old slight manner. His art, if it was to be something in the world, must be weighted with more of the meaning of nature and purpose of humanity. Nature was "the true mistress of higher intelligences." So he plunged into the study of nature. And in doing this he followed the manner of the older students; he brooded over the hidden virtues of plants and crystals, the lines traced by the stars as they moved in the sky, over the correspondences which exist between the different orders of living things, through which, to eyes opened, they interpret each other; and for years he seemed to those about him as one listening to a voice, silent for other men.

He learned here the art of going deep, of tracking the sources of expression to their subtlest retreats, the power of an intimate presence in the things he handled. He did not at once or entirely desert his art; only he was no longer the cheerful, objective painter, through whose soul, as through clear glass, the bright figures of Florentine life, only made a little mellower and more pensive by the transit, passed on to the white wall. He wasted many days in curious tricks of design, seeming to lose himself in the spinning of intricate devices of lines and colours. He was smitten with a love of the impossible—the perforation of mountains, changing the course of rivers, raising great buildings, such as the church of *San Giovanni*, in the air; all those feats for the performance of which natural magic professed to have the key. Later writers, indeed, see in these efforts an anticipation of modern mechanics; in him they were rather dreams, thrown off by the overwrought and labouring brain. Two ideas were especially fixed in him, as reflexes of things that had touched his brain in childhood beyond the measure of other impressions —the smiling of women and the motion of great waters.

And in such studies some interfusion of the extremes of

beauty and terror shaped itself, as an image that might be seen and touched, in the mind of this gracious youth, so fixed that for the rest of his life it never left him; and as catching glimpses of it in the strange eyes or hair of chance people, he would follow such about the streets of Florence till the sun went down, of whom many sketches of his remain. Some of these are full of a curious beauty, that remote beauty apprehended only by those who have sought it carefully; who, starting with acknowledged types of beauty, have refined as far upon these, as these refine upon the world of common forms. But mingled inextricably with this there is an element of mockery also; so that, whether in sorrow or scorn, he caricatures Dante even. Legions of grotesques sweep under his hand; for has not nature too her grotesques—the rent rock, the distorting light of evening on lonely roads, the unveiled structure of man in the embryo, or the skeleton?

All these swarming fancies unite in the *Medusa* of the *Uffizi*.[16] Vasari's story of an earlier Medusa, painted on a wooden shield, is perhaps an invention; and yet, properly told, has more of the air of truth about it than anything else in the whole legend. For its real subject is not the serious work of a man, but the experiment of a child. The lizards and glowworms and other strange small creatures which haunt an Italian vineyard bring before one the whole picture of a child's life in a Tuscan dwelling—half castle, half farm— and are as true to nature as the pretended astonishment of the father for whom the boy has prepared a surprise.[17] It was not in play that he painted that other Medusa, the one great picture which he left behind him in Florence. The subject has been treated in various ways; Leonardo alone cuts to its centre; he alone realises it as the head of a corpse, exercising its powers through all the circumstances of death. What may be called the fascination of corruption penetrates in every touch its exquisitely finished beauty. About the dainty lines of the cheek the bat flits unheeded. The delicate snakes seem literally strangling each other in terrified struggle to escape from the Medusa brain. The hue which violent death always brings with it is in the features: features singularly massive and grand, as we catch them inverted, in a dexterous foreshortening, sloping upwards, almost sliding down upon us, crown foremost, like a great calm stone against which the wave of serpents breaks. But it is a subject that may well be left to the beautiful verses of Shelley.[18]

The science of that age was all divination, clairvoyance, unsubjected to our exact modern formulas, seeking in an instant of vision to concentrate a thousand experiences. Later writers, thinking only of the well-ordered treatise on painting which a Frenchman, Raffaelle du Fresne,[19] a hundred years afterwards, compiled from Leonardo's bewildered manuscripts, written strangely, as his manner was, from right to left, have imagined a rigid order in his inquiries. But this rigid order was little in accordance with the restlessness of his character; and if we think of him as the mere reasoner who subjects design to anatomy, and composition to mathematical rules, we shall hardly have of him that impression which those about him received from him. Poring over his crucibles, making experiments with colour, trying, by a strange variation of the alchemist's dream, to discover the secret, not of an elixir to make man's natural life immortal, but rather of giving immortality to the subtlest and most delicate effects of painting, he seemed to them rather the sorcerer or the magician, possessed of curious secrets and a hidden knowledge, living in a world of which he alone possessed the key. What his philosophy seems to have been most like is that of Paracelsus or Cardan;[20] and much of the spirit of the older alchemy still hangs about it, with its confidence in short cuts and odd byways to knowledge. To him philosophy was to be something giving strange swiftness and double sight, divining the sources of springs beneath the earth or of expression beneath the human countenance, clairvoyant of occult gifts in common or uncommon things, in the reed at the brook-side, or the star which draws near to us but once in a century. How, in this way, the clear purpose was overclouded, the fine chaser's hand perplexed, we but dimly see; the mystery which at no point quite lifts from Leonardo's life is deepest here. But it is certain that at one period of his life he had almost ceased to be an artist.

The year 1483—the year of the birth of Raffaelle and the thirty-first of Leonardo's life—is fixed as the date of his visit to Milan by the letter in which he recommends himself to Ludovico Sforza,[21] and offers to tell him, for a price, strange secrets in the art of war. It was that Sforza who murdered his young nephew by slow poison, yet was so susceptible of religious impressions that he blended mere earthly passions with a sort of religious sentimentalism, and who took for his device the mulberry-tree—symbol, in its long delay and sudden yielding of flowers and fruit together, of a wisdom which economises all forces for an opportunity of sudden and sure effect. The fame of Leonardo had gone before him, and he was to model a colossal statue of Francesco, the first Duke of Milan. As for Leonardo himself, he came not as an artist at all, or careful of the fame of one; but as a player on the harp, a strange harp of silver of his own construction, shaped in some curious likeness to a horse's skull. The capricious spirit of Ludovico was susceptible also of the charm of music, and Leonardo's nature had a kind of spell in it. Fascination is always the word descriptive of him. No portrait of his youth remains; but all tends to make us believe that up to this time some charm of voice and aspect, strong enough to balance the disadvantage of his birth, had played about him. His physical strength was great; it was said that he could bend a horse-shoe like a coil of lead.

The *Duomo*,[22] the work of artists from beyond the Alps, so fantastic to the eye of a Florentine used to the mellow, unbroken surfaces of Giotto and Arnolfo,[23] was then in all its freshness; and below, in the streets of Milan, moved a people as fantastic, changeful, and dreamlike. To Leonardo least of all men could there be anything poisonous in the exotic flowers of sentiment which grew there. It was a life of brilliant sins and exquisite amusements: Leonardo became a celebrated designer of pageants: and it suited the quality of his genius, composed in almost equal parts of curiosity and the desire of beauty, to take things as they came.

Curiosity and the desire of beauty—these are the two elementary forces in Leonardo's genius; curiosity often in conflict with the desire of beauty, but generating, in union with it, a type of subtle and curious grace.

The movement of the fifteenth century was twofold; partly the Renaissance, partly also the coming of what is called the "modern spirit," with its realism, its appeal to experience: it comprehended a return to antiquity, and a return to nature. Raffaelle represents the return to antiquity, and Leonardo the return to nature. In this return to nature, he was seeking to satisfy a boundless curiosity by her perpetual surprises, a microscopic sense of finish by her *finesse*, or delicacy of operation, that *subtilitas naturae* which Bacon notices.[24] So we find him often in intimate relations with men of science,— with Fra Luca Paccioli the mathematician, and the anatomist Marc Antonio della Torre. His observations and experiments fill thirteen volumes of manuscript; and those who can judge describe him as anticipating long before, by rapid intuition, the later ideas of science. He explained the obscure light of the unilluminated part of the moon, knew that the sea had once covered the mountains which contain shells, and the gathering of the equatorial waters above the polar.

He who thus penetrated into the most secret parts of nature preferred always the more to the less remote, what, seeming exceptional, was an instance of law more refined, the construction about things of a peculiar atmosphere and mixed lights. He paints flowers with such curious felicity that different writers have attributed to him a fondness for particular flowers, as Clement the cyclamen, and Rio the jasmin;[25] while, at Venice, there is a stray leaf from his portfolio dotted all over with studies of violets and the wild rose. In him first appears the taste for what is *bizarre* or *recherché*[26] in landscape; hollow places full of the green shadow of bituminous rocks, ridged reefs of trap-rock which cut the water into quaint sheets of light—their exact antitype is in our own western seas;[27] all the solemn effects of moving water; you may follow it springing from its distant source among the rocks on the heath of the *Madonna of the Balances*, passing, as a little fall, into the treacherous calm of the *Madonna of the Lake*, next, as a goodly river, below the cliffs of the *Madonna of the Rocks*, washing the white walls of its distant villages, stealing out in a network of divided streams in *La Gioconda* to the seashore of the *Saint Anne*—that delicate place, where the wind passes like the hand of some fine etcher over the surface, and the untorn shells are lying thick upon the sand, and the tops of the rocks, to which the waves never rise, are green with grass, grown fine as hair. It is the landscape, not of dreams or of fancy, but of places far withdrawn, and hours selected from a thousand with a miracle of *finesse*. Through Leonardo's strange veil of sight things reach him so; in no ordinary night or day, but as in faint light of eclipse, or in some brief interval of falling rain at daybreak, or through deep water.

And not into nature only; but he plunged also into human personality, and became above all a painter of portraits; faces of a modelling more skilful than has been seen before or since, embodied with a reality which almost amounts to illusion, on dark air. To take a character as it was, and delicately sound its stops,[28] suited one so curious in observation, curious in invention. So he painted the portraits of Ludovico's mistresses, Lucretia Crivelli and Cecilia Galerani the poetess, of Ludovico himself, and the Duchess Beatrice. The portrait of Cecilia Galerani is lost, but that of Lucretia Crivelli has been identified with *La Belle Feronière* of the Louvre, and Ludovico's pale, anxious face still remains in the Ambrosian library.[29] Opposite is the portrait of Beatrice d'Este[30] in whom Leonardo seems to have caught some presentiment of early death, painting her precise and grave, full of the refinement of the dead, in sad earth-coloured raiment, set with pale stones.

Sometimes this curiosity came in conflict with the desire of beauty; it tended to make him go too far below that outside of things in which art begins and ends. This struggle between the reason and its ideas, and the senses, the desire of beauty, is the key to Leonardo's life at Milan—his restlessness, his endless re-touchings, his odd experiments with colour. How much must he leave unfinished, how much recommence! His problem was the transmutation of ideas into images. What he had attained so far had been the mastery of that earlier Florentine style, with its naïve and limited sensuousness. Now he was to entertain in this narrow medium those divinations of a humanity too wide for it, that larger vision of the opening world, which is only not too much for the great, irregular art of Shakspere; and everywhere the effort is visible in the work of his hands. This agitation, this perpetual delay, give him an air of weariness and *ennui*. To others he seems to be aiming at an impossible effect, to do something that art, that painting, can never do. Often the expression of physical beauty at this or that point seems strained and marred in the effort, as in those heavy German foreheads—too German and heavy for perfect beauty.

For there was a touch of Germany in that genius which, as Goethe said, had "thought itself weary"—*müde sich gedacht*. What an anticipation of modern Germany, for instance, in that debate on the question whether sculpture or painting is the nobler art.* But there is this difference between him and the German, that, with all that curious science, the German would have thought nothing more

---

* How princely, how characteristic of Leonardo, the answer, *Quanto più, un' arte porta seco fatica di corpo, tanto più è vile!* ("The more evidence of physical strain an art reveals in its product, the lower it is"!) —Pater's own note.

was needed; and the name of Goethe himself reminds one how great for the artist may be the danger of over-much science; how Goethe, who, in the *Elective Affinities* and the first part of *Faust*, does transmute ideas into images, who wrought many such transmutations, did not invariably find the spell-word, and in the second part of *Faust* presents us with a mass of science which has almost no artistic character at all. But Leonardo will never work till the happy moment comes—that moment of *bien-être*,[81] which to imaginative men is a moment of invention. On this moment he waits; other moments are but a preparation, or after-taste of it. Few men distinguish between them as jealously as he did. Hence, so many flaws even in the choicest work. But for Leonardo the distinction is absolute, and, in the moment of *bien-être*, the alchemy complete: the idea is stricken into colour and imagery: a cloudy mysticism is refined to a subdued and graceful mystery, and painting pleases the eye while it satisfies the soul.

This curious beauty is seen above all in his drawings, and in these chiefly in the abstract grace of the bounding lines. Let us take some of these drawings, and pause over them awhile; and, first, one of those at Florence—the heads of a woman and a little child, set side by side, but each in its own separate frame. First of all, there is much pathos in the reappearance in the fuller curves of the face of the child, of the sharper, more chastened lines of the worn and older face, which leaves no doubt that the heads are those of a little child and its mother. A feeling for maternity is indeed always characteristic of Leonardo; and this feeling is further indicated here by the half-humorous pathos of the diminutive, rounded shoulders of the child. You may note a like pathetic power in drawings of a young man seated in a stooping posture, his face in his hands, as in sorrow; of a slave sitting in an uneasy inclined posture, in some brief interval of rest; of a small Madonna and Child, peeping sideways in half-reassured terror, as a mighty griffin with batlike wings, one of Leonardo's finest *inventions*, descends suddenly from the air to snatch up a lion wandering near them. But note in these, as that which especially belongs to art, the contour of the young man's hair, the poise of the slave's arm above his head, and the curves of the head of the child, following the little skull within, thin and fine as some sea-shell worn by the wind.

Take again another head, still more full of sentiment, but

of a different kind, a little drawing in red chalk which every one remembers who has examined at all carefully the drawings by old masters at the Louvre. It is a face of doubtful sex, set in the shadow of its own hair, the cheek-line in high light against it, with something voluptuous and full in the eyelids and the lips. Another drawing might pass for the same face in childhood, with parched and feverish lips, but with much sweetness in the loose, short-waisted childish dress, with necklace and *bulla*,[32] and in the daintily bound hair. We might take the thread of suggestion which these two drawings offer, when thus set side by side, and, following it through the drawings at Florence, Venice, and Milan, construct a sort of series, illustrating better than anything else Leonardo's type of womanly beauty. Daughters of Herodias,[33] with their fantastic head-dresses knotted and folded so strangely to leave the dainty oval of the face disengaged, they are not of the Christian family, or of Raffaelle's. They are the clairvoyants, through whom, as through delicate instruments, one becomes aware of the subtler forces of nature, and the modes of their action, all that is magnetic in it, all those finer conditions wherein material things rise to that subtlety of operation which constitutes them spiritual, where only the finer nerve and the keener touch can follow: it is as if in certain revealing instances we actually saw them at their work on human flesh. Nervous, electric, faint always with some inexplicable faintness, they seem to be subject to exceptional conditions, to feel powers at work in the common air unfelt by others, to become as it were, receptacles of them, and pass them on to us in a chain of secret influences.

But among the more youthful heads there is one at Florence which Love chooses for its own—the head of a young man, which may well be the likeness of Andrea Salaino, beloved of Leonardo for his curled and waving hair—*belli capelli ricci e inanellati*[34]—and afterwards his favourite pupil and servant. Of all the interests in living men and women which may have filled his life at Milan, this attachment alone is recorded; and in return Salaino identified himself so entirely with Leonardo, that the picture of *Saint Anne*, in the Louvre, has been attributed to him. It illustrates Leonardo's usual choice of pupils, men of some natural charm of person or intercourse like Salaino, or men of birth and princely habits of life like Francesco Melzi[35]—men with just enough genius to be capable of initiation into his secret, for the sake of which they were ready to efface their own individuality. Among them, retiring often to the villa of the Melzi at *Canonica al Vaprio*, he worked at his fugitive manuscripts and sketches, working for the present hour, and for a few only, perhaps chiefly for himself. Other artists have been as careless of present or future applause, in self-forgetfulness, or because they set moral or political ends above the ends of art; but in him this solitary culture of beauty seems to have hung upon a kind of self-love, and a carelessness in the work of art of all but art itself. Out of the secret places of a unique temperament he brought strange blossoms and fruits hitherto unknown; and for him, the novel impression conveyed, the exquisite effect woven, counted as an end in itself—a perfect end.

And these pupils of his acquired his manner so thoroughly, that though the number of Leonardo's authentic works is very small indeed, there is a multitude of other men's pictures through which we undoubtedly see him, and come very near to his genius. Sometimes, as in the little picture of the *Madonna of the Balances*, in which, from the bosom of His mother, Christ weighs the pebbles of the brook against the sins of men, we have a hand, rough enough by contrast, working upon some fine hint or sketch of his. Sometimes, as in the subjects of the *Daughter of Herodias* and the *Head of John the Baptist*, the lost originals have been re-echoed and varied upon again and again by Luini[36] and others. At other times the original remains, but has been a mere theme or motive, a type of which the accessories might be modified or changed; and these variations have but brought out the more the purpose, or expression of the original. It is so with the so-called *Saint John the Baptist* of the Louvre—one of the few naked figures Leonardo painted—whose delicate brown flesh and woman's hair no one would go out into the wilderness to seek, and whose treacherous smile would have us understand something far beyond the outward gesture or circumstance. But the long, reed-like cross in the hand, which suggests Saint John the Baptist, becomes faint in a copy at the Ambrosian library, and disappears altogether in another, in the *Palazzo Rosso* at Genoa. Returning from the last to the original, we are no longer surprised by Saint John's strange likeness to the *Bacchus* which hangs near it, which set Théophile Gautier thinking of Heine's notion of decayed gods, who, to maintain themselves, after the fall of paganism, took employment in the new religion.[87] We recognise one of those symbolical inventions in which the ostensible subject is used, not as matter for definite pictorial realisation, but as the starting-point of a train of sentiment, as subtle and vague as a piece of music. No one ever ruled over his subject more entirely than Leonardo, or bent it more dexterously to purely artistic ends. And so it comes to pass that though he handles sacred subjects continually, he is the most profane of painters; the given person or subject, Saint John in the Desert, or the Virgin on the knees of Saint Anne, is often merely the pretext for a kind of work which carries one quite out of the range of its conventional associations.

About the *Last Supper*, its decay and restorations, a whole literature has risen up, Goethe's pensive sketch of its sad fortunes being far the best.[38] The death in childbirth of the Duchess Beatrice was followed in Ludovico by one of those paroxysms of religious feeling which in him were constitutional. The low, gloomy Dominican church of *Saint Mary of the Graces* had been the favourite shrine of Beatrice. She had spent her last days there, full of sinister presentiments; at last it had been almost necessary to remove her from it by force; and now it was here that mass was said a hundred times a day for her repose. On the damp wall of the refectory, oozing with mineral salts, Leonardo painted the *Last Supper*. A hundred anecdotes were told about it, his retouchings and delays. They show him refusing to work except at the moment of invention, scornful of whoever thought that art was a work of mere industry and rule, often coming the whole length of Milan to give a single touch. He painted it, not in fresco,[39] where all must be *impromptu*, but in oils, the new method which he had been one of the first to welcome, because it allowed of so many after-thoughts, so refined a working out of perfection. It turned out that on a plastered wall no process could have been less durable. Within fifty years it had fallen into decay. And now we have to turn back to Leonardo's own studies, above all to one drawing of the central head at the *Brera*,[40] which, in a union of tenderness and severity in the face-lines, reminds one of the monumental work of Mino da Fiesole,[41] to trace it as it was.

It was another effort to lift a given subject out of the range of its conventional associations. Strange, after all the misrepresentations of the middle age, was the effort to see it, not as the pale Host of the altar,[42] but as one taking leave

of his friends. Five years afterwards the young Raffaelle, at
Florence, painted it with sweet and solemn effect in the refectory of Saint Onofrio; but still with all the mystical unreality
of the school of Perugino. Vasari pretends that the central
head was never finished; but finished or unfinished, or owing
part of its effect to a mellowing decay, this central head does
but consummate the sentiment of the whole company—
ghosts through which you see the wall, faint as the shadows
of the leaves upon the wall on autumn afternoons: this figure
is but the faintest, most spectral of them all. It is the image
of what the history it symbolises has more and more become
for the world, paler and paler as it recedes into the distance.
Criticism came with its appeal from mystical unrealities to
originals, and restored no lifelike reality but these transparent
shadows, spirits which have not flesh and bones.

The *Last Supper* was finished in 1497; in 1498 the French
entered Milan, and whether or not the Gascon bowmen used
it as a mark for their arrows, the model of Francesco Sforza
certainly did not survive. What, in that age, such work was
capable of being—of what nobility, amid what racy truthful-
ness to fact—we may judge from the bronze statue of Bartolomeo Colleoni[43] on horseback, modelled by Leonardo's
master, Verrocchio (he died of grief, it was said, because, the
mould accidentally failing, he was unable himself to complete
it), still standing in the *piazza*[44] of Saint John and Saint Paul
at Venice. Some traces of the thing may remain in certain of
Leonardo's drawings, and also, perhaps, by a singular circumstance, in a far-off town of France. For Ludovico became
a prisoner, and ended his days at Loches in Touraine;[45]—
allowed at last, it is said, to breathe fresher air for awhile in
one of the rooms of a high tower there, after many years of
captivity in the dungeons below, where all seems sick with
barbarous feudal memories, and where his prison is still
shown, its walls covered with strange painted arabesques,
ascribed by tradition to his hand, amused a little, in this way,
through the tedious years:—vast helmets and faces and
pieces of armour, among which, in great letters, the motto
Infelix Sum[46] is woven in and out, and in which, perhaps,
it is not too fanciful to see the fruit of a wistful after-dream-
ing over all those experiments with Leonardo on the armed
figure of the great duke, that had occupied the two so often
during the days of his good fortune at Milan.

The remaining years of Leonardo's life are more or less

years of wandering. From his brilliant life at court he had
saved nothing, and he returned to Florence a poor man. Perhaps necessity kept his spirit excited: the next four years are
one prolonged rapture or ecstasy of invention. He painted the
pictures of the Louvre, his most authentic works, which came
there straight from the cabinet of Francis the First, at Fontain-
bleau. One picture of his, the *Saint Anne*—not the *Saint Anne*
of the Louvre, but a mere cartoon, now in London—revived
for a moment a sort of appreciation more common in an
earlier time, when good pictures had still seemed miraculous;
and for two days a crowd of people of all qualities passed in
naïve excitement through the chamber where it hung, and
gave Leonardo a taste of Cimabue's triumph.[47] But his
work was less with the saints than with the living women of
Florence; for he lived still in the polished society that he loved,
and in the houses of Florence, left perhaps a little subject to
light thoughts by the death of Savonarola[48]—the latest gossip
(1869) is of an undraped Monna Lisa,[49] found in some out-
of-the-way corner of the late *Orleans* collection—he saw
Ginevra di Benci, and Lisa, the young third wife of Francesco
del Giocondo. As we have seen him using incidents of sacred
story, not for their own sake, or as mere subjects for pictorial
realisation, but as a symbolical language for fancies all his
own, so now he found a vent for his thoughts in taking one of
these languid women, and raising her, as Leda or Pomona,[50]
Modesty or Vanity, to the seventh heaven of symbolical
expression.

La Gioconda is, in the truest sense, Leonardo's masterpiece,
the revealing instance of his mode of thought and work. In
suggestiveness, only the *Melancholia* of Dürer[51] is comparable
to it; and no crude symbolism disturbs the effect of its subdued and graceful mystery. We all know the face and hands
of the figure, set in its marble chair, in that cirque of fantastic
rocks, as in some faint light under sea. Perhaps of all ancient
pictures time has chilled it least.* As often happens with
works in which invention seems to reach its limit, there is an
element in it given to, not invented by, the master. In that
inestimable folio of drawings, once in the possession of Vasari,
were certain designs by Verrocchio, faces of such impressive
beauty that Leonardo in his boyhood copied them many times.

___

* Yet for Vasari there was some further magic of crimson in the lips
and cheeks, lost for us. (Pater's own note.)

It is hard not to connect with these designs of the elder, by-past master, as with its germinal principle, the unfathomable smile, always with a touch of something sinister in it, which plays over all Leonardo's work. Besides, the picture is a portrait. From childhood we see this image defining itself on the fabric of his dreams; and but for express historical testimony, we might fancy that this was but his ideal lady, embodied and beheld at last. What was the relationship of a living Florentine to this creature of his thought? By means of what strange affinities had the person and the dream grown up thus apart, and yet so closely together? Present from the first incorporeally in Leonardo's thought, dimly traced in the designs of Verrocchio, she is found present at last in *Il Giocondo's* house. That there is much of mere portraiture in the picture is attested by the legend that by artificial means, the presence of mimes[52] and flute-players, that subtle expression was protracted on the face. Again, was it in four years and by renewed labour never really completed, or in four months and as by stroke of magic, that the image was projected?

The presence that thus rose so strangely beside the waters, is expressive of what in the ways of a thousand years men had come to desire. Hers is the head upon which all "the ends of the world are come,"[53] and the eyelids are a little weary. It is a beauty wrought out from within upon the flesh, the deposit, little cell by cell, of strange thoughts and fantastic reveries and exquisite passions. Set it for a moment beside one of those white Greek goddesses or beautiful women of antiquity, and how would they be troubled by this beauty, into which the soul with all its maladies has passed! All the thoughts and experience of the world have etched and moulded there, in that which they have of power to refine and make expressive the outward form, the animalism of Greece, the lust of Rome, the reverie of the middle age with its spiritual ambition and imaginative loves, the return of the Pagan world, the sins of the Borgias.[54] She is older than the rocks among which she sits; like the vampire, she has been dead many times, and learned the secrets of the grave; and has been a diver in deep seas, and keeps their fallen day about her; and trafficked for strange webs with Eastern merchants: and, as Leda, was the mother of Helen of Troy, and, as Saint Anne, the mother of Mary; and all this has been to her but as the sound of lyres and flutes, and lives only in the delicacy with which it has moulded the changing lineaments, and tinged the eyelids and the hands.[55] The fancy of a perpetual life, sweeping together ten thousand experiences, is an old one; and modern thought has conceived the idea of humanity as wrought upon by, and summing up in itself, all modes of thought and life. Certainly Lady Lisa might stand as the embodiment of the old fancy, the symbol of the modern idea.

During these years at Florence Leonardo's history is the history of his art; he himself is lost in the bright cloud of it. The outward history begins again in 1502, with a wild journey through central Italy, which he makes as the chief engineer of Cæsar Borgia. The biographer, putting together the stray jottings of his manuscripts, may follow him through every day of it, up the strange tower of Siena, which looks towards Rome, elastic like a bent bow, down to the seashore at Piombino, each place appearing as fitfully as in a fever dream.

One other great work was left for him to do, a work all trace of which soon vanished, *The Battle of the Standard*, in which he had Michelangelo for his rival. The citizens of Florence, desiring to decorate the walls of the great council-chamber, had offered the work for competition, and any subject might be chosen from the Florentine wars of the fifteenth century. Michelangelo chose for his cartoon an incident of the war with Pisa, in which the Florentine soldiers, bathing in the Arno, are surprised by the sound of trumpets, and run to arms.[56] His design has reached us only in an old engraving, which perhaps helps us less than what we remember of the background of his *Holy Family* in the *Uffizii* to imagine in what superhuman form, such as might have beguiled the heart of an earlier world, those figures may have risen from the water. Leonardo chose an incident from the battle of Anghiari, in which two parties of soldiers fight for a standard. Like Michelangelo's, his cartoon is lost, and has come to us only in sketches, and in a fragment of Rubens.[57] Through the accounts given we may discern some lust of terrible things in it, so that even the horses tore each other with their teeth; and yet one fragment of it, in a drawing of his at Florence, is far different—a waving field of lovely armour, the chased edgings running like lines of sunlight from side to side. Michelangelo was twenty-seven years old; Leonardo more than fifty; and Raffaelle, then nineteen years old, visiting Florence for the first time, came and watched them as they worked.

We catch a glimpse of him again, at Rome in 1514, surrounded by his mirrors and vials and furnaces, making strange toys that seemed alive of wax and quicksilver. The hesitation which had haunted him all through life, and made him like one under a spell, was upon him now with double force. No one had ever carried political indifferentism farther; it had always been his philosophy to "fly before the storm;" he is for the Sforzas, or against them, as the tide of their fortune turns. Yet now in the political society of Rome, he came to be suspected of concealed French sympathies. It paralysed him to find himself among enemies; and he turned wholly to France, which had long courted him.

France was about to become an Italy more Italian than Italy itself. Francis the First, like Louis the Twelfth[58] before him, was attracted by the *finesse* of Leonardo's work; *La Gioconda* was already in his cabinet, and he offered Leonardo the little *Château de Clou*, with its vineyards and meadows, in the pleasant valley of the Masse, just outside the walls of the town of Amboise, where, especially in the hunting season, the court then frequently resided. *A Monsieur Lyonard, peinteur du Roy pour Amboyse*[59]—so the letter of Francis the First is headed. It opens a prospect, one of the most interesting in the history of art, where, under a strange mixture of lights, Italian art dies away as a French exotic.

Two questions remain, after much busy antiquarianism, concerning Leonardo's death—the question of the precise form of his religion, and the question whether Francis the First was present at the time. They are of about equally little importance in the estimate of Leonardo's genius. The directions in his will about the thirty masses and the great candles for the church of Saint Florentin are things of course, their real purpose being immediate and practical; and on no theory of religion could these hurried offices be of much consequence. We forget them in speculating how one who had been always so desirous of beauty, but desired it always in such definite and precise forms, as hands or flowers or hair, looked forward now into the vague land, and experienced the last curiosity.[60]

1869

NOTES

1. *Homo Minister et Interpres Naturæ:* "A man, servant and interpreter of Nature"; for this phrase see Francis Bacon's *Novum Organum*, First Book of Aphorisms, No. I.
2. Vasari's *Lives* (1550) included a Life of Leonardo (1452–1519).
3. Jules Michelet (1798–1874), great Viconian historian of France, who wrote on Leonardo in *La Renaissance* (1855).
4. *Legend:* crucial aspects of his life.
5. Carlo Amoretti's important study of Leonardo was published in Milan in 1804.
6. Francis I (1494–1547) assigned this castle to Leonardo; Pater returns to this point in this essay's penultimate paragraph.
7. *Val d'Arno:* "The Valley of the Arno," where Florence is located.
8. Pyxes: boxes for consecrated bread of the Mass; Verrocchio (1435–1488).
9. Perugino: actual name was Pietro Vannucci (1446–1523).
10. *Ambries:* chests.
11. "The brethren of Vallombrosa" were a monkish order, founded in the eleventh century, near Florence.
12. "Chasing brooches for the capes of *Santa Maria Novella*": engraving decorative clasps for the cloaks to be used in the New Church of St. Mary.
13. "The Medici": Florentine political and commercial family, powerful throughout the fourteenth to sixteenth century.
14. "Lombard": North Italian.
15. *Cartoon:* design.
16. The Uffizi gallery in Florence, where Pater saw this painting of the Medusa, a Gorgon-woman with snaky locks, whose glance turned men to stone.
17. "Prepared a surprise": a story in Vasari that the young Leonardo frightened his father by painting a monster on a wooden shield, the vision of the monster being compounded from various small, strange animals that the boy had collected; the story has very dark psychic overtones.
18. See Shelley's disturbing poem of 1819, "On the Medusa of Leonardo da Vinci," which influenced Pater's description of *La Gioconda*.
19. Raphael Trichet Du Fresne (1611–1661).
20. Paracelsus: Theophrastus Bombastus von Hohenheim, 1493?–1541), from whose name we take the fine word "bombast," a German alchemical speculator who held a doctrine of correspondence.

21. Ludovico Sforza (1451–1508), high nobleman of Milan, a patron of Leonardo.
22. *Duomo:* Dome or Cathedral of Milan.
23. Giotto (1276–1337), major painter and architect; Arnolfo di Cambio (1250–1302), also an architect, and a sculptor.
24. *Subtilas naturæ:* "subtlety of nature," Francis Bacon, *Novum Organum,* First Book of Aphorisms, X.
25. Charles Clement wrote a book on Leonardo and his contemporaries (Paris, 1861); Alexis François Rio wrote a book on Leonardo and his school (Paris, 1855).
26. *Recherché:* "rare, quested-after strangeness."
27. English seas, therefore west from an Italian perspective.
28. Stops: holes of a flute.
29. "Ambrosian library": in Milan; it is also an art gallery.
30. Beatrice d'Este (1475-1497), was Duchess of Milan, known for her beauty.
31. *Bien-être:* "well-being."
32. *Bulla:* throat pendant, or other ornament.
33. "Daughters of Herodias": Herodias was the mother of Salome, and wife of the Herod who executed John the Baptist.
34. *Belli capelli ricci e inanellati:* "beautiful hair, curled and plentiful."
35. Francesco Melzi (1492–1568), pupil of Leonardo.
36. Bernardino Luini (1475–1533), noted painter.
37. Heine's vision of the displacement of the pagan gods haunted Pater, and can be met many times in his work.
38. Goethe wrote an essay on Leonardo's *Last Supper;* see his *Werke,* XVIII, 362.
39. *Fresco* (literally "fresh") is done by painting upon still-moist plaster.
40. *Brera:* Milanese art gallery.
41. Mino da Fiesole (1400–1486), major Florentine sculptor.
42. Here Christ is both Host at the Last Supper, and the "Host" of consecrated wafer in the Mass.
43. Bartolomeo Colleoni (1400–1475), illustrious mercenary captain.
44. *Piazza:* "square."
45. Touraine: western province of France.
46. *Infelix Sum:* "I am unhappy."
47. Giovanni Cimabue (1240–1302), Florentine painter.
48. Girolamo Savonarola (1452–1498), Florentine religious revolutionary.
49. "An undraped Monna Lisa": presumably a naked version of *La Gioconda.*
50. Leda, raped by Zeus in his swan-form, bore him Castor, Pollux, Helen of Troy, and Clytemnestra. Pomona was the archaic Italian goddess and protectress of the fruit harvest.

51. Albrecht Dürer (1471–1528), major German painter-engraver.
52. Mimes: "clowns or mimics."
53. "The ends of the world are come," from I Corinthians 10:11.
54. "The sins of the Borgias" presumably refer to the vehement activities of Cesare Borgia (1476–1507), a rather military cardinal, and of his sister Lucretia (1480–1519), who was Duchess of Ferrara, and did not altogether deserve her extraordinary reputation.
55. This extraordinary sentence, Pater's most notorious, is partially analyzed in my "Introduction."
56. See the fine poem founded on this cartoon, F. T. Prince's "Soldiers Bathing."
57. Peter Paul Rubens (1577–1640), greatest of Flemish painters.
58. Louis the Twelfth (1462–1515), King of France.
59. *A Monsieur Lyonard, peinteur du Roy pour Amboyse:* "To Mr. Leonardo, King's painter at Amboise."
60. This last sentence of Pater's "Leonardo" should be read against the "Conclusion" to *The Renaissance.*

The School of Giorgione (excerpt)

It is the mistake of much popular criticism to regard poetry, music, and painting—all the various products of art—as but translations into different languages of one and the same fixed quantity of imaginative thought, supplemented by certain technical qualities of colour, in painting—of sound, in music—of rhythmical words, in poetry. In this way, the sensuous element in art, and with it almost everything in art that is essentially artistic, is made a matter of indifference; and a clear apprehension of the opposite principle—that the sensuous material of each art brings with it a special phase or quality of beauty, untranslatable into the forms of any other, an order of impressions distinct in kind—is the beginning of all true æsthetic criticism. For, as art addresses not pure sense, still less the pure intellect, but the "imaginative reason"[1] through the senses, there are differences of kind in æsthetic beauty, corresponding to the differences in kind of the gifts of sense themselves. Each art, therefore, having its own peculiar and incommunicable sensuous charm, has its own special mode of reaching the imagination, its own special responsibilities to its material. One of the functions of æsthetic criticism is to define these limitations; to estimate the degree in which a given work of art fulfils its responsibilities to its special material; to note in a picture that true pictorial charm, which is neither a mere poetical thought nor sentiment, on the one hand, nor a mere result of communicable technical skill in colour or design, on the other; to define in a poem that true poetical quality, which is neither descriptive nor meditative merely, but comes of an inventive handling of rhythmical language—the element of song in the singing; to note in music the musical charm—that essential music, which presents no words, no matter of sentiment or thought, separable from the special form in which it is conveyed to us.

To such a philosophy of the variations of the beautiful, Lessing's analysis of the spheres of sculpture and poetry, in the *Laocoon*,[2] was a very important contribution. But a true appreciation of these things is possible only in the light of a whole system of such art-casuistries. And it is in the criticism of painting that this truth most needs enforcing, for it is in popular judgments on pictures that false generalisation of all art into forms of poetry is most prevalent. To suppose that all is mere technical acquirement in delineation or touch, working through and addressing itself to the intelligence, on the one side, or a merely poetical, or what may be called literary interest, addressed also to the pure intelligence, on the other; —this is the way of most spectators, and of many critics, who have never caught sight, all the time, of that true pictorial quality which lies between (unique pledge of the possession of the pictorial gift) the inventive or creative handling of pure line and colour, which, as almost always in Dutch painting, as often also in the works of Titian or Veronese, is quite independent of anything definitely poetical in the subject it accompanies. It is the *drawing*—the design projected from that peculiar pictorial temperament or constitution, in which, while it may possibly be ignorant of true anatomical proportions, all things whatever, all poetry, every idea however abstract or obscure, floats up as a visible scene or image: it is the *colouring*—that weaving as of just perceptible gold threads of light through the dress, the flesh, the atmosphere, in Titian's *Lace-girl*—the staining of the whole fabric of the thing with a new, delightful physical quality. This *drawing*, then—the arabesque traced in the air by Tintoret's flying figures, by Titian's forest branches; this colouring—the magic conditions of light and hue in the atmosphere of Titian's *Lace-girl*, or Rubens's *Descent from the Cross:*—these essential pictorial qualities must first of all delight the sense, delight it as directly and sensuously as a fragment of Venetian glass; and through this delight only be the medium of whatever poetry or science may lie beyond them, in the intention of the composer. In its primary aspect, a great picture has no more definite message for us than an accidental play of sunlight and shadow for a moment, on the wall or floor: is itself, in truth, a space of such fallen light, caught as the colours are caught in an Eastern carpet, but refined upon, and dealt with more subtly and exquisitely than by nature itself. And this primary and essential condition fulfilled, we may trace the coming of poetry into painting, by fine gradations upwards; from Japanese fan-painting, for instance, where we get, first, only abstract colour; then, just a little interfused sense of the poetry of flowers; then, sometimes, perfect flower-painting; and so, onwards, until in Titian we have, as his poetry in the *Ariadne*, so actually a touch of true childlike humour in the diminutive, quaint figure with its silk gown, which ascends the temple stairs, in his picture of the *Presentation of the Virgin*, at Venice.

But although each art has thus its own specific order of impressions, and an untranslatable charm, while a just apprehension of the ultimate differences of the arts is the beginning of æsthetic criticism, yet it is noticeable that, in its special mode of handling its given material, each art may be observed to pass into the condition of some other art, by what German critics term an *Anders-streben*[3]—a partial alienation from its own limitations, by which the arts are able, not indeed to supply the place of each other, but reciprocally to lend each other new forces.

Thus some of the most delightful music seems to be always approaching to figure, to pictorial definition. Architecture, again, though it has its own laws—laws esoteric enough, as the true architect knows only too well—yet sometimes aims at fulfilling the conditions of a picture, as in the *Arena* chapel; or of sculpture, as in the flawless unity of Giotto's tower at Florence; and often finds a true poetry, as in those strangely twisted staircase of the *châteaux* of the country of the Loire, as if it were intended that among their odd turnings the actors in a wild life might pass each other unseen: there being a poetry also of memory and of the mere effect of time, by which it often profits greatly. Thus, again, sculpture aspires out of the hard limitation of pure form towards colour, or its equivalent; poetry also, in many ways, finding guidance from the other arts, the analogy between a Greek tragedy and a work of Greek sculpture, between a sonnet and a relief, of French poetry generally with the art of engraving, being more than mere figures of speech; and all the arts in common aspiring towards the principle of music; music being the typical, or ideally consummate art, the object of the great *Anders-*

streben of all art, of all that is artistic, or partakes of artistic qualities.

All art constantly aspires towards the condition of music.[4] For while in all other works of art it is possible to distinguish the matter from the form, and the understanding can always make this distinction, yet it is the constant effort of art to obliterate it. That the mere matter of a poem, for instance— its subject, its given incidents or situation; that the mere matter of a picture—the actual circumstances of an event, the actual topography of a landscape—should be nothing without the form, the spirit, of the handling; that this form, this mode of handling, should become an end in itself, should penetrate every part of the matter:—this is what all art constantly strives after, and achieves in different degrees.

This abstract language becomes clear enough, if we think of actual examples. In an actual landscape we see a long white road, lost suddenly on the hill-verge. That is the matter of one of the etchings of M. Legros: only, in this etching, it is informed by an indwelling solemnity of expression, seen upon it or half-seen, within the limits of an exceptional moment, or caught from his own mood perhaps, but which he maintains as the very essence of the thing, throughout his work. Sometimes a momentary tint of stormy light may invest a homely or too familiar scene with a character which might well have been drawn from the deep places of the imagination. Then we might say that this particular effect of light, this sudden inweaving of gold thread through the texture of the haystack, and the poplars, and the grass, gives the scene artistic qualities; that it is like a picture. And such tricks of circumstance are commonest in landscape which has little salient character of its own; because, in such scenery, all the material details are so easily absorbed by that informing expression of passing light, and elevated, throughout their whole extent, to a new and delightful effect by it. And hence the superiority, for most conditions of the picturesque, of a river-side in France to a Swiss valley, because, on the French river-side, mere topography, the simple material, counts for so little, and, all being so pure, untouched, and tranquil in itself, mere light and shade have such easy work in modulating it to one dominant tone. The Venetian landscape, on the other hand, has in its material conditions much which is hard, or harshly definite; but the masters of the Venetian school have shown themselves little burdened by them. Of its

Alpine background they retain certain abstracted elements only, of cool colour and tranquillising line; and they use its actual details, the brown windy turrets, the straw-coloured fields, the forest arabesques, but as the notes of a music which duly accompanies the presence of their men and women, presenting us with the spirit or essence only of a certain sort of landscape—a country of the pure reason or half-imaginative memory.

Poetry, again, works with words addressed in the first instance to the mere intelligence; and it deals, most often, with a definite subject or situation. Sometimes it may find a noble and quite legitimate function in the expression of moral or political aspiration, as often in the poetry of Victor Hugo. In such instances it is easy enough for the understanding to distinguish between the matter and the form, however much the matter, the subject, the element which is addressed to the mere intelligence, has been penetrated by the informing, artistic spirit. But the ideal types of poetry are those in which this distinction is reduced to its *minimum*; so that lyrical poetry, precisely because in it we are least able to detach the matter from the form, without a deduction of something from that matter itself, is, at least artistically, the highest and most complete form of poetry. And the very perfection of such poetry often seems to depend, in part, on a certain suppression or vagueness of mere subject, so that the meaning reaches us through ways not distinctly traceable by the understanding, as in some of the most imaginative compositions of William Blake, and often in Shakspere's songs, as preëminently in that song of Mariana's page in *Measure for Measure*,[5] in which the kindling force and poetry of the whole play seems to pass for a moment into an actual strain of music.

And this principle holds good of all things that partake in any degree of artistic qualities, of the furniture of our houses, and of dress, for instance, of life itself, of gesture and speech, and the details of daily intercourse; these also, or the wise, being susceptible of a suavity and charm, caught from the way in which they are done, which gives them a worth in themselves; wherein, indeed, lies what is valuable and justly attractive, in what is called the fashion of a time, which elevates the trivialities of speech, and manner, and dress, into "ends in themselves," and gives them a mysterious grace and attractiveness in the doing of them.

Art, then, is thus always striving to be independent of the

mere intelligence, to become a matter of pure perception, to get rid of its responsibilities to its subject or material; the ideal examples of poetry and painting being those in which the constituent elements of the composition are so welded together, that the material or subject no longer strikes the intellect only; nor the form, the eye or the ear only; but form and matter, in their union or identity, present one single effect to the "imaginative reason," that complex faculty for which every thought and feeling is twin-born with its sensible analogue or symbol.

It is the art of music which most completely realises this artistic ideal, this perfect identification of form and matter. In its ideal, consummate moments, the end is not distinct from the means, the form from the matter, the subject from the expression; they inhere in and completely saturate each other; and to it, therefore, to the condition of its perfect moments, all the arts may be supposed constantly to tend and aspire. Music, then, and not poetry, as is so often supposed, is the true type or measure of perfected art. Therefore, although each art has its incommunicable element, its untranslatable order of impressions, its unique mode of reaching the "imaginative reason," yet the arts may be represented as continually struggling after the law or principle of music, to a condition which music alone completely realises; and one of the chief functions of æsthetic criticism, dealing with the products of art, new or old, is to estimate the degree in which each of those products approaches, in this sense, to musical law.

1877

NOTES

1. "imaginative reason": Pater cunningly quotes this phrase from a highly un-Paterian passage in Arnold's essay, "Pagan and Mediæval Religious Sentiment." Contrast the whole of Pater's opening paragraph to Arnold's passage: "The poetry of later paganism lived by the senses and understanding; the poetry of mediæval Christianity lived by the heart and imagination. But the main element of the modern spirit's life is neither the senses and understanding, nor the heart and imagination; it is the imaginative reason." Pater subverts this by suggesting that "art addresses . . . the 'imaginative reason' *through the*

senses" and further, that this address is most achieved as "that essential music" transcending all reason, however imaginative.

2. The *Laocoon* (more properly, *Laokoon*) is a crucial essay in criticism (1766) by Gotthold Ephraim Lessing, German dramatist and critic (1729–1781). Starting from the ancient Roman statuary of Laocoon and his son battling against sea serpents, Lessing attempted, by a contrast with Virgil, to distinguish between the plastic arts and poetry. Like his master, Ruskin, Pater works in the opposite direction.

3. *Anders-streben:* "striving after otherness" is one of Pater's crucial principles, closely related to his idea of *askesis.*

4. "The condition of music": This famous concept, ancestor of Yeats's "Condition of Fire" in the Paterian treatise, *Per Amica Silentia Lunae,* has little to do with music as such. It is Pater's synonym for what Coleridge called the Secondary Imagination or Yeats termed Phase 15 in *A Vision.*

5. *Measure for Measure:* Significantly, Pater's favorite among Shakespeare's plays, and the subject of one of the best essays in *Appreciations* (reprinted in this volume). The song referred to is "Take, O take those lips away," Act IV, Scene I, where a Boy sings to the forsaken Mariana at "the moated Grange." The scene inspired also Tennyson's superb lyric, "Mariana," which should be contrasted with this passage in "The School of Giorgione" and the parallel passage in Pater's essay on the play. Swinburne particularly commended Pater's insights here, which assimilate (somewhat) Shakespeare to the Aesthetic Sensibility.

Conclusion*

Λέγει που Ἡράκλειτος ὅτι πάντα χωρεῖ καὶ οὐδὲν μένει[1]

To regard all things and principles of things as inconstant modes or fashions has more and more become the tendency of modern thought.[2] Let us begin with that which is without

---

* This brief "Conclusion" was omitted in the second edition of this book, as I conceived it might possibly mislead some of those young men into whose hands it might fall. On the whole, I have thought it best to reprint it here, with some slight changes which bring it closer to my original meaning. I have dealt more fully in *Marius the Epicurean* with the thoughts suggested by it. (Pater's own note.)

—our physical life. Fix upon it in one of its more exquisite intervals, the moment, for instance, of delicious recoil from the flood of water in summer heat. What is the whole physical life in that moment but a combination of natural elements to which science gives their names? But these elements, phosphorus and lime and delicate fibres, are present not in the human body alone: we detect them in places most remote from it. Our physical life is a perpetual motion of them— the passage of the blood, the wasting and repairing of the lenses of the eye, the modification of the tissues of the brain by every ray of light and sound—processes which science reduces to simpler and more elementary forces. Like the elements of which we are composed, the action of these forces extends beyond us; it rusts iron and ripens corn. Far out on every side of us those elements are broadcast, driven by many forces; and birth and gesture[3] and death and the springing of violets from the grave[4] are but a few out of ten thousand resultant combinations. That clear, perpetual outline of face and limb is but an image of ours, under which we group them—a design in a web, the actual threads of which pass out beyond it. This at least of flame-like our life has, that it is but the concurrence, renewed from moment to moment, of forces parting sooner or later on their ways.

Or if we begin with the inward world of thought and feeling, the whirlpool is still more rapid, the flame more eager and devouring. There it is no longer the gradual darkening of the eye and fading of colour from the wall,—the movement of the shore-side, where the water flows down indeed, though in apparent rest,—but the race of the midstream, a drift of momentary acts of sight and passion and thought. At first sight experience seems to bury us under a flood of external objects, pressing upon us with a sharp and importunate reality, calling us out of ourselves in a thousand forms of action. But when reflexion begins to act upon those objects they are dissipated under its influence; the cohesive force seems suspended like a trick of magic; each object is loosed into a group of impressions—colour, odour, texture—in the mind of the observer.[5] And if we continue to dwell in thought on this world, not of objects in the solidity with which language invests them, but of impressions unstable, flickering, inconsistent, which burn and are extinguished with our consciousness of them, it contracts still further; the whole scope of observation is dwarfed to the narrow chamber of the individual mind. Experience, already reduced to a swarm of impressions, is ringed round for each one of us by that thick wall of personality through which no real voice has ever pierced on its way to us, or from us to that which we can only conjecture to be without.[6] Every one of those impressions is the impression of the individual in his isolation, each mind keeping as a solitary prisoner its own dream of a world.[7] Analysis goes a step farther still, and assures us that those impressions of the individual mind to which, for each one of us, experience dwindles down, are in perpetual flight; that each of them is limited by time, and that as time is infinitely divisible, each of them is infinitely divisible also; all that is actual in it being a single moment, gone while we try to apprehend it, of which it may ever be more truly said that it has ceased to be than that it is. To such a tremulous wisp constantly reforming itself on the stream, to a single sharp impression, with a sense in it, a relic more or less fleeting, of such moments gone by, what is real in our life fines itself down. It is with this movement, with the passage and dissolution of impressions, images, sensations, that analysis leaves off—that continual vanishing away, that strange, perpetual weaving and unweaving of ourselves.[8]

Philosophiren, says Novalis, *ist dephlegmatisiren vivificiren.*[9] The service of philosophy, of speculative culture, towards the human spirit is to rouse, to startle it[10] into sharp and eager observation. Every moment some form grows perfect in hand or face; some tone on the hills or the sea is choicer than the rest; some mood of passion or insight or intellectual excitement is irresistibly real and attractive for us,—for that moment only. Not the fruit of experience, but experience itself, is the end. A counted number of pulses only is given to us of a variegated, dramatic life. How may we see in them all that is to be seen in them by the finest senses? How shall we pass most swiftly from point to point, and be present always at the focus where the greatest number of vital forces unite in their purest energy?

To burn always with this hard, gemlike flame, to maintain this ecstasy, is success in life. In a sense it might even be said that our failure is to form habits: for, after all, habit is relative to a stereotyped world, and meantime it is only the roughness of the eye that makes any two persons, things, situations, seem alike. While all melts under our feet, we may well catch at any exquisite passion, or any contribution to knowledge that seems by a lifted horizon to set the spirit free for a moment, or any stirring of the senses, strange dyes, strange colours, and curious odours, or work of the artist's hands, or the face of one's friend. Not to discriminate every moment some passionate attitude in those about us, and in the brilliancy of their gifts some tragic dividing of forces on their ways, is, on this short day of frost and sun, to sleep before evening.[11] With this sense of the splendour of our experience and of its awful brevity, gathering all we are into one desperate effort to see and touch, we shall hardly have time to make theories about the things we see and touch. What we have to do is to be for ever curiously testing new opinions and courting new impressions, never acquiescing in a facile orthodoxy of Comte, or of Hegel,[12] or of our own. Philosophical theories or ideas,[13] as points of view, instruments of criticism, may help us to gather up what might otherwise pass unregarded by us. "Philosophy is the microscope of thought."[14] The theory or idea or system which requires of us the sacrifice of any part of this experience, in consideration of some interest into which we cannot enter, or some abstract theory we have not identified with ourselves, or what is only conventional, has no real claim upon us.

One of the most beautiful passages in the writings of Rousseau is that in the sixth book of the *Confessions*, where he describes the awakening in him of the literary sense. An undefinable taint of death had always clung about him, and now in early manhood he believed himself smitten by mortal disease. He asked himself how he might make as much as possible of the interval that remained; and he was not biassed by anything in his previous life when he decided that it must be by intellectual excitement, which he found just then in the clear, fresh writings of Voltaire.[15] Well! we are all *condamnés*, as Victor Hugo says: we are all under sentence of death but with a sort of indefinite reprieve—*les hommes sont tous condamnés à mort avec des sursis indéfinis:*[16] we have an interval, and then our place knows us no more. Some spend this interval in listlessness, some in high passions, the wisest, at least among "the children of this world,"[17] in art and song. For our one chance lies in expanding that interval, in getting as many pulsations as possible into the given time. Great passions[18] may give us this quickened sense of life, ecstasy and sorrow of love, the various forms of enthusiastic activity, disinterested or otherwise, which come naturally to many of us.[19] Only be sure it is passion—that it does yield you this fruit of a quickened, multiplied consciousness. Of this wisdom, the poetic passion, the desire of beauty, the love of art for art's sake,[20] has most; for art comes to you professing frankly to give nothing but the highest quality to your moments as they pass, and simply for those moments' sake.

1868

NOTES

1. Pater's translation of this epigraph: "Heracleitus says, 'All things give way; nothing remains',", from Plato's *Cratylus* 402A. Heraclitus (about 500 B.C.), Pre-Socratic seer of the flux, was an inevitable ancestor for Pater (and through Pater, for Yeats). Fire, the prime element for Heraclitus, becomes Pater's image of "this hard, gemlike flame."
2. "The tendency of modern thought": probably this was originally a Hegelian allusion, but by the third edition a Darwinian reference was quite likely.
3. "Gesture": used here in its ultimate etymological sense, as "activity" in general, from the Latin *gerere*, "conduct."
4. "The springing of violets from the grave": see Laertes, at the grave of Ophelia, *Hamlet*, Act V, Scene I, 246–247: "And from her fair and unpolluted flesh/May violets spring!"
5. "The mind of the observer": this powerful reduction insinuates that mere habit compels the momentary significances that we make out of the flux of sensations.
6. "We can only conjecture to be without": this ultimate skepticism is essentially that predicament of all Pater's *Imaginary Portraits*, and presumably of Pater himself.
7. "Its own dream of a world": the untenable position of solipsism, of the self certain only of itself, and finding unreal the outward world, and all other selves.
8. "Perpetual weaving and unweaving of ourselves": even the self is unstable and discontinuous; a product of the will and not part of given reality.
9. *"Philosophiren,* says Novalis, *ist dephlegmatisiren vivificiren"*: "To philosophize is to cast off inertia, to bring oneself to life." Novalis was the pen-name of Friedrich von Hardenberg (1772–1801), the most astonishing of German Romantic poets.
10. "To startle it": in the first edition, this read: "And of religion and culture as well to the human spirit is to startle it"; by changing this in the third edition, Pater sought to soften his antireligious stance.

11. "On this short day of frost and sun, to sleep before evening": Ian Fletcher observes the pungency of a typical Oxford winter day here.

12. "A facile orthodoxy of Comte, or of Hegel": Auguste Comte (1798–1857), French Positivist philosopher, and Georg Wilhelm Friedrich Hegel (1770–1831), German Idealist philosopher; Pater, who sympathized with both, is not attacking either but rather rejecting adherence to any metaphysic whatsoever.

13. "Philosophic theories or ideas": significantly altered from the first edition, which reads: "Theories, religious or philosophical ideas."

14. "Philosophy is the microscope of thought": from Victor Hugo's *Les Miserables* II.2., a most un-Paterian book astonishingly cited, for its greatness, at the end of the essay on "Style" in *Appreciations*.

15. "Which he found just then in the clear, fresh writings of Voltaire": Pater implies, rightly, that after this "just then" Rousseau turned against Voltaire.

16. "*—les hommes sont tous condamnés à mort avec des sursis indéfinis*": "Men are all condemned to death with indefinite reprieves."

17. "The children of this world": a qualification added in the third edition, the reference being to Luke 16:8, ". . . for the children of this world are in their generation wiser than the children of light."

18. "Great passions": "high passions" in the first edition.

19. "To many of us": in the first edition, this reads: "Political or religious enthusiasm . . . to many of us," but Pater again softened his anti-Christian overtness.

20. "Art for art's sake": the most misunderstood of Paterian expressions, probably because of Wilde's persuasive misinterpretation of it. Pater's Leonardo both naturalizes and humanizes his earlier aestheticism, and the closing sentences of "Style" suggest (though equivocally) a further modification of this apparently pure aestheticism. Still, Pater would have recoiled from Lawrence's variant, "Art for Life's sake," as a vulgarization. Pater probably intended an allusion here to Gautier.

from *Imaginary Portraits*

Sebastian van Storck*

It was a winter-scene, by Adrian van de Velde, or by Isaac van Ostade.[1] All the delicate poetry together with all the delicate comfort of the frosty season was in the leafless branches turned to silver, the furred dresses of the skaters, the warmth of the red-brick house-fronts under the gauze of white fog, the gleams of pale sunlight on the cuirasses of the mounted soldiers as they receded into the distance. Sebastian van Storck, confessedly the most graceful performer in all that skating multitude, moving in endless maze over the vast surface of the frozen water-meadow, liked best this season of the year for its expression of a perfect impassivity, or at least of a perfect repose. The earth was, or seemed to be, at rest, with a breathlessness of slumber which suited the young man's peculiar temper. The heavy summer, as it dried up the meadows now lying dead below the ice, set free a crowded and competing world of life, which, while it gleamed very pleasantly russet and yellow for the painter Albert Cuyp,[2] seemed wellnigh to suffocate Sebastian van Storck. Yet with all his appreciation of the national winter, Sebastian was not altogether a Hollander. His mother, of Spanish descent and Catholic, had given a richness of tone and form to the healthy freshness of the Dutch physiognomy, apt to preserve its youthfulness of aspect far beyond the period of life usual with other peoples. This mixed expression charmed the eye of Isaac van Ostade, who had painted his portrait from a sketch taken at one of those skating parties, with his plume of squirrel's tail and fur muff, in all the modest pleasantness of boy-

* Published in *Macmillan's Magazine*, March, 1886; reprinted as the third Portrait in *Imaginary Portraits*, 1887.

hood. When he returned home lately from his studies at a place far inland, at the proposal of his tutor, to recover, as the tutor suggested, a certain loss of robustness, something more than that cheerful indifference of early youth had passed away. The learned man, who held, as was alleged, the doctrines of a surprising new philosophy, reluctant to disturb too early the fine intelligence of the pupil entrusted to him, had found it, perhaps, a matter of honesty to send back to his parents one likely enough to catch from others any sort of theoretic light; for the letter he wrote dwelt much on the lad's intellectual fearlessness. "At present," he had written, "he is influenced more by curiosity than by a care for truth, according to the character of the young. Certainly, he differs strikingly from his equals in age, by his passion for a vigorous intellectual gymnastic, such as the supine character of their minds renders distasteful to most young men, but in which he shows a fearlessness that at times makes me fancy that his ultimate destination may be the military life; for indeed the rigidly logical tendency of his mind always leads him out upon the practical. Don't misunderstand me! At present, he is strenuous only intellectually; and has given no definite sign of preference, as regards a vocation in life. But he seems to me to be one practical in this sense, that his theorems will shape life for him, directly; that he will always seek, as a matter of course, the effective equivalent to—the line of being which shall be the proper continuation of—his line of thinking. This intellectual rectitude, or candour, which to my mind has a kind of beauty in it, has reacted upon myself, I confess, with a searching quality." That "searching quality," indeed, many others also, people far from being intellectual, had experienced—an agitation of mind in his neighborhood, oddly at variance with the composure of the young man's manner and surrounding, so jealously preserved.

In the crowd of spectators at the skating, whose eyes followed, so well-satisfied, the movements of Sebastian van Storck, were the mothers of marriageable daughters, who presently became the suitors of this rich and distinguished youth, introduced to them, as now grown to man's estate, by his delighted parents. Dutch aristocracy had put forth all its graces to become the winter morn: and it was characteristic of the period that the artist tribe was there, on a grand footing,—in waiting, for the lights and shadows they liked best. The artists were, in truth, an important body just then, as a natural consequence of the nation's hard-won prosperity; helping it to a full consciousness of the genial yet delicate homeliness it loved, for which it had fought so bravely, and was ready at any moment to fight anew, against man or the sea. Thomas de Keyser,[3] who understood better than any one else the kind of quaint new Atticism[4] which had found its way into the world over those waste salt marshes, wondering whether quite its finest type as he understood it could ever actually be seen there, saw it at last, in lively motion, in the person of Sebastian van Storck, and desired to paint his portrait. A little to his surprise, the young man declined the offer; not graciously, as was thought.

Holland, just then, was reposing on its laurels after its long contest with Spain,[5] in a short period of complete wellbeing, before troubles of another kind should set in. That a darker time might return again, was clearly enough felt by Sebastian the elder—a time like that of William the Silent,[6] with its insane civil animosities, which would demand similarly energetic personalities, and offer them similar opportunities. And then, it was part of his honest geniality of character to admire those who "get on" in the world. Himself had been, almost from boyhood, in contact with great affairs. A member of the States-General which had taken so hardly the kingly airs of Frederick Henry,[7] he had assisted at the Congress of Münster,[8] and figures conspicuously in Terburgh's picture[9] of that assembly, which had finally established Holland as a first-rate power. The heroism by which the national wellbeing had been achieved was still of recent memory—the air full of its reverberation, and great movement. There was a tradition to be maintained; the sword by no means resting in its sheath. The age was still fitted to evoke a generous ambition; and this son, from whose natural gifts there was so much to hope for, might play his part, at least as a diplomatist, if the present quiet continued. Had not the learned man said that his natural disposition would lead him out always upon practice? And in truth, the memory of that Silent hero had its fascination for the youth. When, about this time, Peter de Keyser,[10] Thomas's brother, unveiled at last his tomb of wrought bronze and marble in the *Nieuwe Kerk*[11] at Delft, the young Sebastian was one of a small company present, and relished much the cold and abstract simplicity of the monument, so conformable to the great, abstract, and unuttered force of the hero who slept beneath.

In complete contrast to all that is abstract or cold in art, the home of Sebastian, the family mansion of the Storcks—a house, the front of which still survives in one of those patient architectural pieces by Jan van der Heyde[12]—was, in its minute and busy wellbeing, like an epitome of Holland itself with all the good-fortune of its "thriving genius" reflected, quite spontaneously, in the national taste. The nation had learned to content itself with a religion which told little, or not at all, on the outsides of things. But we may fancy that something of the religious spirit had gone, according to the law of the transmutation of forces, into the scrupulous care for cleanliness, into the grave, old-world, conservative beauty of Dutch houses, which meant that the life people maintained in them was normally affectionate and pure.

The most curious florists of Holland were ambitious to supply the Burgomaster van Storck with the choicest products of their skill for the garden spread below the windows on either side of the portico, and along the central avenue of hoary beeches which led to it. Naturally this house, within a mile of the city of Haarlem, became a resort of the artists, then mixing freely in great society, giving and receiving hints as to the domestic picturesque. Creatures of leisure—of leisure on both sides—they were the appropriate complement of Dutch prosperity, as it was understood just then. Sebastian the elder could almost have wished his son to be one of them: it was the next best thing to being an influential publicist or statesman. The Dutch had just begun to see what a picture their country was—its canals, and *boomjis,*[13] and endless, broadly-lighted meadows, and thousands of miles of quaint water-side: and their painters, the first true masters of landscape for its own sake, were further informing them in the matter. They were bringing proof, for all who cared to see, of the wealth of colour there was all around them in this, supposably, sad land. Above all, they developed the Low-country taste for interiors. Those innumerable *genre* pieces[14] —conversation, music, play—were in truth the equivalent of novel-reading for that day; its own actual life, in its own proper circumstances, reflected in various degrees of idealisation, with no diminution of the sense of reality (that is to say) but with more and more purged and perfected delightfulness of interest. Themselves illustrating, as every student of their history knows, the good-fellowship of family life, it was the ideal of that life which these artists depicted; the ideal of home in a country where the preponderant interest of life, after all, could not well be out of doors. Of the earthy—genuine red earth of the old Adam[15]—it was an ideal very different from that which the sacred Italian painters had evoked from the life of Italy, yet, in its best types, was not without a kind of natural religiousness. And in the achievement of a type of beauty so national and vernacular, the votaries of purely Dutch art might well feel that the Italianisers, like Berghem, Boll, and Jan Weenix[16] went so far afield in vain.

The fine organisation and acute intelligence of Sebastian would have made him an effective connoisseur of the arts, as he showed by the justice of his remarks in those assemblies of the artists which his father so much loved. But in truth the arts were a matter he could but just tolerate. Why add, by a forced and artificial production, to the monotonous tide of competing, fleeting experience? Only, finding so much fine art actually about him, he was compelled (so to speak) to adjust himself to it; to ascertain and accept that in it which should least collide with, or might even carry forward a little, his own characteristic tendencies. Obviously somewhat jealous of his intellectual interests, he loved inanimate nature, it might have been thought, better than man. He cared nothing, indeed, for the warm sandbanks of Wynants,[17] nor for those eerie relics of the ancient Dutch woodland which survive in Hobbema and Ruysdael,[18] still less for the highly-coloured sceneries of the academic band at Rome, in spite of the escape they provide one into clear breadth of atmosphere. For though Sebastian van Storck refused to travel, he loved the distant—enjoyed the sense of things seen from a distance, carrying us, as on wide wings of space itself, far out of one's actual surrounding. His preference in the matter of art was, therefore, for those prospects *à vol d'oiseau*[19]—of the caged bird on the wing at last—of which Rubens[20] had the secret, and still more Philip de Koninck,[21] four of whose choicest works occupied the four walls of his chamber; visionary escapes, north, south, east, and west, into a wide-open though, it must be confessed, a somewhat sullen land. For the fourth of them he had exchanged with his mother a marvelously vivid Metsu,[22] lately bequeathed to him, in which she herself was presented. They were the sole ornaments he permitted himself. From the midst of the busy and busy-looking house, crowded with the furniture and the pretty little toys of many generations, a long passage led the rare visitor up a winding staircase, and (again at the end of a long passage) he found himself as if shut off from the whole talkative Dutch world, and in the embrace of that wonderful quiet which is also possible in Holland at its height all around him. It was here that Sebastian could yield himself, with the only sort of love he had ever felt, to the supremacy of his difficult thoughts.— A kind of *empty* place! Here, you felt, all had been mentally put to rights by the working-out of a long equation, which had zero is equal to zero for its result. Here one did, and perhaps felt, nothing; one only thought. Of living creatures only birds came there freely, the sea-birds especially, to attract and detain which there were all sorts of ingenious contrivances about the windows, such as one may see in the cottage sceneries of Jan Steen[23] and others. There was something, doubtless, of his passion for distance in this welcoming of the creatures of the air. An extreme simplicity in their manner of life was, indeed, characteristic of many a distinguished Hollander—William the Silent, Baruch de Spinosa,[24] the brothers de Witt.[25] But the simplicity of Sebastian van Storck was something different from that, and certainly nothing democratic. His mother thought him like one disembarrassing himself carefully, and little by little, of all impediments, habituating himself gradually to make shift with as little as possible, in preparation for a long journey.

The Burgomaster van Storck entertained a party of friends, consisting chiefly of his favourite artists, one summer evening. The guests were seen arriving on foot in the fine weather, some of them accompanied by their wives and daughters, against the light of the low sun, falling red on the old trees of the avenue and the faces of those who advanced along it:—Willem van Aelst, expecting to find hints for a flower-portrait in the exotics which would decorate the banqueting-room; Gerard Dow, to feed his eye, amid all that glittering luxury, on the combat between candle-light and the last rays of the departing sun; Thomas de Keyser, to catch by stealth the likeness of Sebastian the younger. Albert Cuyp was there, who, developing the latent gold in Rembrandt, had brought into his native Dordrecht a heavy wealth of sunshine, as exotic as those flowers or the eastern carpets on the Burgomaster's tables, with Hooch, the indoor Cuyp, and Willem van de Velde, who painted those shore-pieces with gay ships of war, such as he loved, for his patron's cabinet. Thomas de Keyser came in company with his brother Peter, his niece, and young Mr. Nicholas Stone[26] from England, pupil of that brother Peter, who afterwards married the niece. For the life of Dutch artists, too, was exemplary in matters of domestic relationship, its history telling many a cheering story of mutual faith in misfortune. Hardly less exemplary was the comradeship which they displayed among themselves, obscuring their own best gifts sometimes, one in the mere accessories of another man's work, so that they came together to-night with no fear of falling out, and spoiling the musical interludes of Madame van Storck in the large back parlour. A little way behind the other guests, three of them together, son, grandson, and the grandfather, moving slowly, came the Hondecoeters—Giles, Gybrecht, and Melchior.[27] They led the party before the house was entered, by fading light, to see the curious poultry of the Burgomaster go to roost; and it was almost night when the supper-room was reached at last. The occasion was an important one to Sebastian, and to others through him. For (was it the music of the duets? he asked himself next morning, with a certain distaste as he remembered it all, or the heady Spanish wines poured out so freely in those narrow but deep Venetian glasses?) on this evening he approached more nearly than he had ever yet done to Mademoiselle van Westrheene, as she sat there beside the *clavecin*[28] looking very ruddy and fresh in her white satin, trimmed with glossy crimson swansdown.

So genially attempered, so warm, was life become, in the land of which Pliny[29] had spoken as scarcely dry land at all. And, in truth, the sea which Sebastian so much loved, and with so great a satisfaction and sense of wellbeing in every hint of its nearness, is never far distant in Holland. Invading all places, stealing under one's feet, insinuating itself everywhere along an endless network of canals (by no means such formal channels as we understand by the name, but picturesque rivers, with sedgy banks and haunted by innumerable birds) its incidents present themselves oddly even in one's park or woodland walks; the ship in full sail appearing suddenly among the great trees or above the garden wall, where we had no suspicion of the presence of water. In the very conditions of life in such a country there was a standing force of pathos. The country itself shared the uncertainty of the individual human life; and there was pathos also in the con-

stantly renewed, heavily-taxed labour, necessary to keep the
native soil, fought for so unselfishly, there at all, with a warfare that must still be maintained when that other struggle
with the Spaniard was over. But though Sebastian liked to
breathe, so nearly, the sea and its influences, those were
considerations he scarcely entertained. In his passion for
Schwindsucht[30]—we haven't the word—he found it pleasant
to think of the resistless element which left one hardly a
foot-space amidst the yielding sand; of the old beds of lost
rivers, surviving now only as deeper channels in the sea; of
the remains of a certain ancient town, which within men's
memory had lost its few remaining inhabitants, and, with its
already empty tombs, dissolved and disappeared in the flood.

It happened, on occasion of an exceptionally low tide, that
some remarkable relics were exposed to view on the coast of
the island of Vleeland.[31] A countryman's waggon over-
taken by the tide, as he returned with merchandise from the
shore! you might have supposed, but for a touch of grace in
the construction of the thing—lightly wrought timber-work,
united and adorned by a multitude of brass fastenings, like
the work of children for their simplicity, while the rude, stiff
chair, or throne, set upon it, seemed to distinguish it as a
chariot of state. To some antiquarians it told the story of the
overwhelming of one of the chiefs of the old primeval people
of Holland, amid all his gala array, in a great storm. But it
was another view which Sebastian preferred; that this object
was sepulchral, namely, in its motive—the one surviving relic
of a grand burial, in the ancient manner, of a king or hero,
whose very tomb was wasted away.—*Sunt metis metae!*[32]
There came with it the odd fancy that he himself would like
to have been dead and gone as long ago, with a kind of envy
of those whose deceasing was so long since over.

On more peaceful days he would ponder Pliny's account of
those primeval forefathers, but without Pliny's contempt for
them. A cloyed Roman might despise their humble existence,
fixed by necessity from age to age, and with no desire of
change, as "the ocean poured in its flood twice a day, making
it uncertain whether the country was a part of the continent
or of the sea."[33] But for his part Sebastian found something
of poetry in all that, as he conceived what thoughts the old
Hollander might have had at his fishing, with nets themselves
woven of seaweed, waiting carefully for his drink on the
heavy rains, and taking refuge, as the flood rose, on the sand-

hills, in a little hut constructed but airily on tall stakes, conformable to the elevation of the highest tides, like a navigator, thought the learned writer, when the sea was risen, like a shipwrecked mariner when it was retired. For the fancy of Sebastian he lived with great breadths of calm light above and around him, influenced by, and, in a sense, living upon them, and surely might well complain, though to Pliny's so infinite surprise, on being made a Roman citizen.

And certainly Sebastian van Storck did not felicitate his people on the luck which, in the words of another old writer, "hath disposed them to so thriving a genius." Their restless ingenuity in making and maintaining dry land where nature had willed the sea, was even more like the industry of animals than had been that life of their forefathers. Away with that tetchy, feverish, unworthy agitation! with this and that, all too importunate, motive of interest! And then, "My son!" said his father, "be stimulated to action!" he, too, thinking of that heroic industry which had triumphed over nature precisely where the contest had been most difficult.

Yet, in truth, Sebastian was forcibly taken by the simplicity of a great affection, as set forth in an incident of real life' of which he heard just then. The eminent Grotius[34] being condemned to perpetual imprisonment, his wife determined to share his fate, alleviated only by the reading of books sent by friends. The books, finished, were returned in a great chest. In this chest the wife enclosed the husband, and was able to reply to the objections of the soldiers who carried it complaining of its weight, with a self-control, which she maintained till the captive was in safety, herself remaining to face the consequences; and there was a kind of absoluteness of affection in that, which attracted Sebastian for a while to ponder on the practical forces which shape men's lives. Had he turned, indeed, to a practical career it would have been less in the direction of the military or political life than of another form of enterprise popular with his countrymen. In the eager, gallant life of that age, if the sword fell for a moment into its sheath, they were for starting off on perilous voyages to the regions of frost and snow in search after that "North-Western passage,"[35] for the discovery of which the States-General had offered large rewards. Sebastian, in effect, found a charm in the thought of that still, drowsy, spellbound world of perpetual ice, as in art and life he could always tolerate the sea. Admiral-general of Holland, as painted by

Van der Helst, with a marine background by Backhuizen:[36] —at moments his father could fancy him so.

There was still another very different sort of character to which Sebastian would let his thoughts stray, without check, for a time. His mother, whom he much resembled outwardly, a Catholic from Brabant,[37] had had saints in her family, and from time to time the mind of Sebastian had been occupied on the subject of monastic life, its quiet, its negation. The portrait of a certain Carthusian prior,[38] which, like the famous statue of Saint Bruno, the first Carthusian, in the church of Santa Maria degli Angeli at Rome, could it have spoken, would have said, "Silence!" kept strange company with the painted visages of men of affairs. A great theological strife was then raging in Holland. Grave ministers of religion assembled sometimes, as in the painted scene by Rembrandt, in the Burgomaster's house, and once, not however in their company, came a renowned young Jewish divine, Baruch de Spinosa, with whom, most unexpectedly, Sebastian found himself in sympathy, meeting the young Jew's far-reaching thoughts half-way, to the confirmation of his own; and he did not know that his visitor, very ready with the pencil, had taken his likeness as they talked on the fly-leaf of his notebook. Alive to that theological disturbance in the air all around him, he refused to be moved by it, as essentially a strife on small matters, anticipating a vagrant regret which may have visited many other minds since, the regret, namely, that the old, pensive, use-and-wont Catholicism, which had accompanied the nation's earlier struggle for existence, and consoled it therein, had been taken from it. And for himself, indeed, what impressed him in that old Catholicism was a kind of lull in it—a lulling power—like that of the monotonous organ-music, which Holland, Catholic or not, still so greatly loves. But what he could not away with in the Catholic religion was its unfailing drift towards the concrete—the positive imageries of a faith, so richly beset with persons, things, historical incidents.

Rigidly logical in the method of his inferences, he attained the poetic quality only by the audacity with which he conceived the whole sublime extension of his premises. The contrast was a strange one between the careful, the almost petty fineness of his personal surroundings—all the elegant conventionalities of life, in that rising Dutch family—and the mortal coldness of a temperament, the intellectual tendencies of

which seemed to necessitate straightforward flight from all
that was positive. He seemed, if one may say so, in love with
death; preferring winter to summer; finding only a tranquillising influence in the thought of the earth beneath our feet
cooling down for ever from its old cosmic heat; watching
pleasurably how their colours fled out of things, and the long
sand-bank in the sea, which had been the rampart of a town,
was washed down in its turn. One of his acquaintance, a
penurious young poet, who, having nothing in his pockets
but the imaginative or otherwise barely potential gold of
manuscript verses, would have grasped so eagerly, had they
lain within his reach, at the elegant outsides of life, thought
the fortunate Sebastian, possessed of every possible opportunity of that kind, yet bent only on dispensing with it, certainly
a most puzzling and comfortless creature. A few only, half
discerning what was in his mind, would fain have shared his
intellectual clearness, and found a kind of beauty in this
youthful enthusiasm for an abstract theorem. Extremes meeting, his cold and dispassionate detachment from all that is
most attractive to ordinary minds came to have the impres-
siveness of a great passion. And for the most part, people had
loved him; feeling instinctively that somewhere there must be
the justification of his difference from themselves. It was like
being in love: or it was an intellectual malady, such as pleaded
for forbearance, like bodily sickness, and gave at times a
resigned and touching sweetness to what he did and said.
Only once, at a moment of the wild popular excitement which
at that period was easy to provoke in Holland, there was a
certain group of persons who would have shut him up as no
wellwisher to, and perhaps a plotter against, the common-
weal. A single traitor might cut the dykes in an hour, in the
interest of the English or the French. Or, had he already committed some treasonable act, who was so anxious to expose no
writing of his that he left his very letters unsigned, and there
were little stratagems to get specimens of his fair manuscript?
For with all his breadth of mystic intention, he was persistent,
as the hours crept on, to leave all the inevitable details of life
at least in order, in equation. And all his singularities appeared
to be summed up in his refusal to take his place in the life-
sized family group (*très distingué et très soigné*,[39] remarks
a modern critic of the work) painted about this time. His
mother expostulated with him on the matter:—she must
needs feel, a little icily, the emptiness of hope, and something

more than the due measure of cold in things for a woman of her age, in the presence of a son who desired but to fade out of the world like a breath—and she suggested filial duty. "Good mother," he answered, "there are duties towards the intellect also, which women can but rarely understand."

The artists and their wives were come to supper again, with the Burgomaster van Storck. Mademoiselle van Westrheene was also come, with her sister and mother. The girl was by this time fallen in love with Sebastian; and she was one of the few who, in spite of his terrible coldness, really loved him for himself. But though of good birth she was poor, while Sebastian could not but perceive that he had many suitors of his wealth. In truth, Madame van Westrheene, her mother, did wish to marry this daughter into the great world, and plied many arts to that end, such as "daughterful" mothers use. Her healthy freshness of mien and mind, her ruddy beauty, some showy presents that had passed, were of a piece with the ruddy colouring of the very house these people lived in; and for a moment the cheerful warmth that may be felt in life seemed to come very close to him,—to come forth, and enfold him. Meantime the girl herself taking note of this, that on a former occasion of their meeting he had seemed likely to respond to her inclination, and that his father would readily consent to such a marriage, surprised him on the sudden with those coquetries and importunities, all those little arts of love, which often succeed with men. Only, to Sebastian they seemed opposed to that absolute nature we suppose in love. And while, in the eyes of all around him to-night, this courtship seemed to promise him, thus early in life, a kind of quiet happiness, he was coming to an estimate of the situation, with strict regard to that ideal of a calm, intellectual difference, of which he was the sworn chevalier. Set in the cold, hard light of that ideal, this girl, with the pronounced personal views of her mother, and in the very effectiveness of arts prompted by a real affection, bringing the warm life they prefigured so close to him, seemed vulgar! And still he felt himself bound in honour; or judged from their manner that she and those about them thought him thus bound. He did not reflect on the inconsistency of the feeling of honour (living, as it does essentially, upon the concrete and minute detail of social relationship) for one who, on principle, set so slight a value on anything whatever that is merely relative in its character.

The guests, lively and late, were almost pledging the betrothed in the rich wine. Only Sebastian's mother knew; and at that advanced hour, while the company were thus intently occupied, drew away the Burgomaster to confide to him the misgiving she felt, grown to a great height just then. The young man had slipped from the assembly; but certainly not with Mademoiselle van Westrheene, who was suddenly withdrawn also. And she never appeared again in the world. Already, next day, with the rumour that Sebastian had left his home, it was known that the expected marriage would not take place. The girl, indeed, alleged something in the way of a cause on her part; but seemed to fade away continually afterwards, and in the eyes of all who saw her was like one perishing of wounded pride. But to make a clean breast of her poor girlish worldliness, before she became a *béguine*,[40] she confessed to her mother the receipt of the letter—the cruel letter that had killed her. And in effect, the first copy of this letter, written with a very deliberate fineness, rejecting her—accusing her, so natural, and simply loyal! of a vulgar coarseness of character—was found, oddly tacked on, as their last word, to the studious record of the abstract thoughts which had been the real business of Sebastian's life, in the room whither his mother went to seek him next day, littered with the fragments of the one portrait of him in existence.

The neat and elaborate manuscript volume, of which this letter formed the final page (odd transition! by which a train of thought so abstract drew its conclusion in the sphere of action) afforded at length to the few who were interested in him a much-coveted insight into the curiosity of his existence; and I pause just here to indicate in outline the kind of reasoning through which, making the "Infinite" his beginning and his end, Sebastian had come to think all definite forms of being, the warm pressure of life, the cry of nature itself, no more than a troublesome irritation of the surface of the one absolute mind, a passing vexatious thought or uneasy dream there, at its height of petulant importunity in the eager, human creature.

The volume was, indeed, a kind of treatise to be:—a hard, systematic, well-concatenated train of thought, still implicated in the circumstances of a journal. Freed from the accidents of that particular literary form with its unavoidable details of place and occasion, the theoretic strain would have been found mathematically continuous. The already so weary

Sebastian might perhaps never have taken in hand, or succeeded in, this detachment of his thoughts; every one of which, beginning with himself, as the peculiar and intimate apprehension of this or that particular day and hour, seemed still to protest against such disturbance, as if reluctant to part from those accidental associations of the personal history which had prompted it, and so become a purely intellectual abstraction.

The series began with Sebastian's boyish enthusiasm for a strange, fine saying of Doctor Baruch de Spinosa, concerning the Divine Love:—That whoso loveth God truly must not expect to be loved by him in return.[41] In mere reaction against an actual surrounding of which every circumstance tended to make him a finished egotist, that bold assertion defined for him the ideal of an intellectual disinterestedness, of a domain of unimpassioned mind, with the desire to put one's subjective side out of the way, and let pure reason speak.

And what pure reason affirmed in the first place, as the "beginning of wisdom," was that the world is but a thought, or a series of thoughts: that it exists, therefore, solely in mind. It showed him, as he fixed the mental eye with more and more of self-absorption on the phenomena of his intellectual existence, a picture or vision of the universe as actually the product, so far as he really knew it, of his own lonely thinking power—of himself, there, thinking: as being zero without him: and as possessing a perfectly homogeneous unity in that fact. "Things that have nothing in common with each other," said the axiomatic reason, "cannot be understood or explained by means of each other."[42] But to pure reason things discovered themselves as being, in their essence, thoughts:—all things, even the most opposite things, mere transmutations of a single power, the power of thought. All was but conscious mind. Therefore, all the more exclusively, he must minister to mind, to the intellectual power, submitting himself to the sole direction of that, whithersoever it might lead him. Everything must be referred to, and, as it were, changed into the terms of that, if its essential value was to be ascertained. "Joy," he said, anticipating Spinosa—that, for the attainment of which men are ready to surrender all beside—"is but the name of a passion in which the mind passes to a greater perfection or power of thinking; as grief is the name of the passion in which it passes to a less."[43]

Looking backward for the generative source of that creative power of thought in him, from his own mysterious intellectual being to its first cause, he still reflected, as one can but do, the enlarged pattern of himself into the vague region of hypothesis. In this way, some, at all events, would have explained his mental process. To him that process was nothing less than the apprehension, the revelation, of the greatest and most real of ideas—the true substance of all things. He, too, with his vividly-coloured existence, with this picturesque and sensuous world of Dutch art and Dutch reality all around that would fain have made him the prisoner of its colours, its genial warmth, its struggle for life, its selfish and crafty love, was but a transient perturbation of the one absolute mind; of which indeed, all finite things whatever, time itself, the most durable achievements of nature and man, and all that seems most like independent energy, are no more than petty accidents or affections. Theorem and corollary! Thus they stood:

"*There can be only one substance:* (corollary) it is the greatest of errors to think that the non-existent, the world of finite things seen and felt, really is: (theorem): *for, whatever is, is but in that:* (practical corollary): one's wisdom, therefore, consists in hastening, so far as may be, the action of those forces which tend to the restoration of equilibrium, the calm surface of the absolute, untroubled mind, to *tabula rasa*,[44] by the extinction in one's self of all that is but correlative to the finite illusion—by the suppression of ourselves."

In the loneliness which was gathering round him, and, oddly enough, as a somewhat surprising thing, he wondered whether there were, or had been, others possessed of like thoughts, ready to welcome any such as his veritable compatriots. And in fact he became aware just then, in readings difficult indeed, but which from their all-absorbing interest seemed almost like an illicit pleasure, a sense of kinship with certain older minds. The study of many an earlier adventurous theorist satisfied his curiosity as the record of daring physical adventure, for instance, might satisfy the curiosity of the healthy. It was a tradition—a constant tradition—that daring thought of his; an echo, or haunting recurrent voice of the human soul itself, and as such sealed with natural truth, which certain minds would not fail to heed; discerning also, if they were really loyal to themselves, its practical conclusion.—The one alone is: and all things beside are but its passing affections, which have no necessary or proper right to be.

As but such "accidents" or "affections," indeed, there might have been found, within the circumference of that one infinite creative thinker, some scope for the joy and love of the creature. There have been dispositions in which that abstract theorem has only induced a renewed value for the finite interests around and within us. Centre of heat and light, truly nothing has seemed to lie beyond the touch of its perpetual summer. It has allied itself to the poetical or artistic sympathy, which feels challenged to acquaint itself with and explore the various forms of finite existence all the more intimately, just because of that sense of one lively spirit circulating through all things—a tiny particle of the one soul, in the sunbeam, or the leaf. Sebastian van Storck, on the contrary, was determined, perhaps by some inherited satiety or fatigue in his nature, to the opposite issue of the practical dilemma. For him, that one abstract being was as the pallid Arctic sun, disclosing itself over the dead level of a glacial, a barren and absolutely lonely sea. The lively purpose of life had been frozen out of it. What he must admire, and love if he could, was "equilibrium," the void, the *tabula rasa*, into which, through all those apparent energies of man and nature, that in truth are but forces of disintegration, the world was really settling. And, himself a mere circumstance in a fatalistic series, to which the clay of the potter was no sufficient parallel, he could not expect to be "loved in return."[45] At first, indeed, he had a kind of delight in his thoughts—in the eager pressure forward, to whatsoever conclusion, of a rigid intellectual gymnastic, which was like the making of Euclid. Only, little by little, under the freezing influence of such propositions, the theoretic energy itself, and with it his old eagerness for truth, the care to track it from proposition to proposition, was chilled out of him. In fact, the conclusion was there already, and might have been foreseen, in the premises. By a singular perversity, it seemed to him that every one of those passing "affections"—he too, alas! at times—was for ever trying to be, to assert *itself*, to maintain its isolated and petty self, by a kind of practical lie in things; although through every incident of its hypothetic existence it had protested that its proper function was to die. Surely! those transient affections marred the freedom, the truth, the beatific calm, of the absolute selfishness, which could not, if it would, pass beyond the circumference of itself; to which, at times, with a fantastic sense of wellbeing, he was capable of a sort of fanatical devotion. And those, as he conceived, were his moments of genuine theoretic insight, in which, under the abstract "perpetual light," he died to self; while the intellect, after all, had attained a freedom of its own through the vigorous act which assured him that, as nature was but a thought of his, so himself also was but the passing thought of God.

No! rather a puzzle only, an anomaly, upon that one, white, unruffled consciousness! His first principle once recognised, all the rest, the whole array of propositions down to the heartless practical conclusion, must follow of themselves. Detachment: to hasten hence: to fold up one's whole self, as a vesture put aside: to anticipate, by such individual force as he could find in him, the slow disintegration by which nature herself is levelling the eternal hills:—here would be the secret of peace, of such dignity and truth as there could be in a world which after all was essentially an illusion. For Sebastian at least, the world and the individual alike had been divested of all effective purpose. The most vivid of finite objects, the dramatic episodes of Dutch history, the brilliant personalities which had found their parts to play in them, that golden art, surrounding us with an ideal world, beyond which the real world is discernible indeed, but etherealised by the medium through which it comes to one: all this, for most men so powerful a link to existence, only set him on the thought of escape—means of escape—into a formless and nameless infinite world, quite evenly grey. The very emphasis of those objects, their importunity to the eye, the ear, the finite intelligence, was but the measure of their distance from what really is. One's personal presence, the presence, such as it is, of the most incisive things and persons around us, could only lessen by so much, that which really is. To restore *tabula rasa*, then, by a continual effort at self-effacement! Actually proud at times of his curious, well-reasoned nihilism, he could but regard what is called the business of life as no better than a trifling and wearisome delay. Bent on making sacrifice of the rich existence possible for him, as he would readily have sacrificed that of other people, to the bare and formal logic of the answer to a query (never proposed at all to entirely healthy minds) regarding the remote conditions and tendencies of that existence, he did not reflect that if others had inquired as curiously as himself the world could never have come so far at all—that the fact of its having come so far was itself a weighty exception to his hypothesis. His odd devotion, soaring or sinking into fanaticism, into a kind of religious mania, with what was really a vehement assertion of his individual will, he had formulated duty as the principle to hinder as little as possible what he called the restoration of equilibrium, the restoration of the primary consciousness to itself—its relief from that uneasy, tetchy, unworthy dream of a world, made so ill, or dreamt so weakly—to forget, to be forgotten.

And at length this dark fanaticism, losing the support of his pride in the mere novelty of a reasoning so hard and dry, turned round upon him, as our fanaticism will, in black melancholy. The theoretic or imaginative desire to urge Time's creeping footsteps, was felt now as the physical fatigue which leaves the book or the letter unfinished, or finishes eagerly out of hand, for mere finishing's sake, unimportant business. Strange! that the presence to the mind of a meta-physical abstraction should have had this power over one so fortunately endowed for the reception of the sensible world. It could hardly have been so with him but for the concurrence of physical causes with the influences proper to a mere thought. The moralist, indeed, might have noted that a meaner kind of pride, the morbid fear of vulgarity, lent secret strength to the intellectual prejudice, which realised duty as the renunciation of all finite objects, the fastidious refusal to be or do any limited thing. But besides this it was legible in his own admissions from time to time, that the body, fol-lowing, as it does with powerful temperaments, the lead of mind and the will, the intellectual consumption (so to term it) had been concurrent with, had strengthened and been strengthened by, a vein of physical *phthisis*[46]—by a merely physical accident, after all, of his bodily constitution, such as might have taken a different turn, had another accident fixed his home among the hills instead of on the shore. Is it only the result of disease? he would ask himself sometimes with a sudden suspicion of his intellectual cogency—this per-suasion that myself, and all that surrounds me, are but a diminution of that which really is?—this unkindly melancholy?

The journal, with that "cruel" letter to Mademoiselle van Westrheene coming as the last step in the rigid process of theoretic deduction, circulated among the curious; and people

made their judgments upon it. There were some who held
that such opinions should be suppressed by law; that they
were, or might become, dangerous to society. Perhaps it was
the confessor of his mother who thought of the matter most
justly. The aged man smiled, observing how, even for minds
by no means superficial, the mere dress it wears alters the
look of a familiar thought; with a happy sort of smile, as he
added (reflecting that such truth as there was in Sebastian's
theory was duly covered by the propositions of his own creed,
and quoting Sebastian's favourite pagan wisdom from the lips
of Saint Paul) "in Him, we live, and move, and have our
being."[47]

Next day, as Sebastian escaped to the sea under the long,
monotonous line of wind-mills, in comparative calm of mind
—reaction of that pleasant morning from the madness of the
night before—he was making light, or trying to make light,
with some success, of his late distress. He would fain have
thought it a small matter, to be adequately set at rest for him
by certain well-tested influences of external nature, in a long
visit to the place he liked best: a desolate house, amid the
sands of the Helder, one of the old lodgings of his family,
property now, rather, of the sea-birds, and almost surrounded
by the encroaching tide, though there were still relics enough
of hardy, sweet things about it, to form what was to Sebastian
the most perfect garden in Holland. Here he could make
"equation" between himself and what was not himself, and set
things in order, in preparation towards such deliberate and
final change in his manner of living as circumstances so
clearly necessitated.

As he stayed in this place, with one or two silent serving
people, a sudden rising of the wind altered, as it might seem,
in a few dark, tempestuous hours, the entire world around
him. The strong wind changed not again for fourteen days,
and its effect was a permanent one; so that people might have
fancied that an enemy had indeed cut the dykes somewhere—
a pin-hole enough to wreck the ship of Holland, or at least
this portion of it, which underwent an inundation of the sea
the like of which had not occurred in that province for half a
century. Only, when the body of Sebastian was found, apparently not long after death, a child lay asleep, swaddled
warmly in his heavy furs, in an upper room of the old tower,
to which the tide was almost risen; though the building still
stood firmly, and still with the means of life in plenty. And it

was in the saving of this child, with a great effort, as certain circumstances seemed to indicate, that Sebastian had lost his life.

His parents were come to seek him, believing him bent on self-destruction, and were almost glad to find him thus. A learned physician, moreover, endeavoured to comfort his mother by remarking that in any case he must certainly have died ere many years were passed, slowly, perhaps painfully, of a disease then coming into the world; disease begotten by the fogs of that country—waters, he observed, not in their place, "above the firmament"[48]—on people grown somewhat over-delicate in their nature by the effects of modern luxury.

NOTES

1. Adrian van de Velde (1636–1672), Isaac van Ostade (1621–1649), both Dutch landscape painters.
2. Albert Cuyp (1620–1691), Dutch portrait and landscape painter.
3. Thomas de Keyser (1596–1667), Dutch portrait painter.
4. "Atticism": concern with ancient Greek culture.
5. "Long contest with Spain": eighty years up to 1648.
6. William the Silent (1533–1584), prince of Orange, greatest leader of the Dutch.
7. Frederick Henry (1583–1647), prince of Orange, youngest child of William the Silent, and the most accomplished general of his family.
8. Congress of Münster: in 1648 the Dutch made peace with Spain, at Munster, Germany.
9. Gerard Terburgh (Ter Borch) (1617–1681), Dutch portrait painter.
10. Peter de Keyser, mid-seventeenth-century Dutch architect and sculptor.
11. *Nieuwe Kerk:* "New Church."
12. Jan van der Heyde (1635–1686), Dutch painter who worked in England.
13. *Boomjis:* "trees."
14. *"Genre* pieces": realistic paintings of common scenes.
15. "Red earth of the old Adam": Pater alludes to the literal Hebrew meaning of Adam's name, "red earth."
16. Jan Weenix (1621–1660), Dutch painter who studied in Italy, and subsequently taught the Dutch painters Nicholas Berghem (Berchem) (1620–1683) and Cornelius Bol (mid-seventeenth century).

17. Jan Wynants (1625–1684), Dutch landscape painter.
18. Meindert Hobbema (1639–1709) and Jacob Ruysdael (1628–1682), also noted painters of Dutch landscape.
19. *"À vol d'oiseau":* "seen with a bird's-eye view."
20. Peter Paul Rubens (1577–1640), unsurpassed Flemish painter.
21. Philip de Koningh (1619–1681), Dutch history painter.
22. Gabriel Metsu (1630–1667), Dutch painter of common life-scenes.
23. Jan Steen (1626–1679), Dutch painter also known for exuberant scenes of common life.
24. Baruch de Spinosa (Benedict Spinoza, 1632–1677), renowned Dutch-Jewish metaphysician and moralist.
25. Cornelius de Witt (1623–1672) and John de Witt (1625–1672), Dutch political leaders.
26. These are all Dutch painters of reputation, except for Nicholas Stone (1586–1647), English sculptor and architect: Willem van Aelst (1620–1679); Gerhard Douw or Dow (1613–1675); Pieter de Hoogh (1643–1708); Willem Vandevelde (1610–1693).
27. The Hondecoeters were all known as painters of domestic fowls, through three generations: Giles (early seventeenth century); his son, Gysbrecht (1613–1653); and *his* son, Melchior (1636–1695).
28. *Clavecin:* "harpsichord."
29. Pliny the Elder, Roman historian (23–79 A.D.).
30. *Schwindsucht:* a strange word, meaning at once "consumption or phthisis" and also "renunciation or self-curtailment."
31. Vleeland: island at mouth of the Zuider Zee.
32. *Sunt metis metae:* "There are goals (limits) even for goals."
33. From Pliny's *Natural History* IV, 39.
34. Hugo Grotius (1583–1645), Dutch scholar and politician; sentenced, in 1619, to imprisonment for life, he escaped, in 1621, as Pater relates.
35. "North-Western passage": to Orient through America, object of an endless quest.
36. Bartholomew Van der Helst (1613–1670), Dutch portrait painter; Ludolph Backhuysen (1631–1708), Dutch painter of seascapes.
37. Brabant: region in north-central Belgium and southern Holland.
38. "Carthusian prior": the Carthusian order of monks was founded by St. Bruno (1030–1101) in 1084, in southeastern France.
39. *"Très distingué et très soigné":* "very distinguished and very carefully executed."
40. *"Béguine":* a quasi-nun, member of lay-sisterhood.
41. From Spinoza's *Ethics,* Part V, Proposition XIX.

42. From Spinoza's *Ethics,* Part I, Axiom V.
43. From Spinoza's *Ethics,* Part IV, Proposition XLII.
44. *Tabula rasa:* blank tablet.
45. "Loved in return": see note 41, above.
46. *Phthis:* consumption; see note 30, above.
47. From Acts 17:28.
48. From Genesis 1:7.

Denys L'Auxerrois*

Almost every people, as we know, has had its legend of a "golden age" and of its return—legends which will hardly be forgotten, however prosaic the world may become, while man himself remains the aspiring, never quite contented being he is. And yet in truth, since we are no longer children, we might well question the advantage of the return to us of a condition of life in which, by the nature of the case, the values of things would, so to speak, lie wholly on their surfaces, unless we could regain also the childish consciousness, or rather unconsciousness, in ourselves, to take all that adroitly and with the appropriate lightness of heart. The dream, however, has been left for the most part in the usual vagueness of dreams: in their waking hours people have been too busy to furnish it forth with details. What follows is a quaint legend, with detail enough, of such a return of a golden or poetically-gilded age (a denizen of old Greece[1] itself actually finding his way back again among men) as it happened in an ancient town of medieval France.

Of the French town, properly so called, in which the products of successive ages, not without lively touches of the present, are blended together harmoniously, with a beauty *specific*[2]—a beauty cisalpine and northern, yet at the same time quite distinct from the massive German picturesque of Ulm, or Freiburg, or Augsburg, and of which Turner has found the ideal in certain of his studies of the rivers of France,

* Published in *Macmillan's Magazine,* October, 1886; reprinted as the second Portrait in *Imaginary Portraits,* 1887.

a perfectly happy conjunction of river and town being of the essence of its physiognomy—the town of Auxerre is perhaps the most complete realisation to be found by the actual wanderer. Certainly, for picturesque expression it is the most memorable of a distinguished group of three in these parts,— Auxerre, Sens, Troyes,[3]—each gathered, as if with deliberate aim at such effect, about the central mass of a huge grey cathedral.

Around Troyes the natural picturesque is to be sought only in the rich, almost coarse, summer colouring of the Champagne country, of which the very tiles, the plaster and brick-work of its tiny villages and great, straggling, village-like farms have caught the warmth. The cathedral, visible far and wide over the fields seemingly of loose wild-flowers, itself a rich mixture of all the varieties of the Pointed style[4] down to the latest *Flamboyant*,[5] may be noticed among the greater French churches for breadth of proportions internally, and is famous for its almost unrivalled treasure of stained glass, chiefly of a florid, elaborate, later type, with much highly conscious artistic contrivance in design as well as in colour. In one of the richest of its windows, for instance, certain lines of pearly white run hither and thither, with delightful distant effect, upon ruby and dark blue. Approaching nearer you find it to be a Travellers' window, and those odd lines of white the long walking-staves in the hands of Abraham, Raphael, the Magi, and the other saintly patrons of journeys. The appropriate provincial character of the *bourgeoisie* of Champagne is still to be seen, it would appear, among the citizens of Troyes. Its streets, for the most part in timber and pargeting, present more than one unaltered specimen of the ancient *hôtel* or townhouse, with forecourt and garden in the rear; and its more devout citizens would seem even in their church-building to have sought chiefly to please the eyes of those occupied with mundane affairs and out of doors, for they have finished, with abundant outlay, only the vast, useless portals of their parish churches, of surprising height and lightness, in a kind of wildly elegant Gothic-on-stilts, giving to the streets of Troyes a peculiar air of the grotesque, as if in some quaint nightmare of the Middle Age.

At Sens, thirty miles away to the west, a place of far graver aspect, the name of Jean Cousin denotes a more chastened temper, even in these sumptuous decorations. Here all is cool and composed, with an almost English austerity. The first growth of the Pointed style in England—the hard "early English" of Canterbury—is indeed the creation of William, a master reared in the architectural school of Sens; and the severity of his taste might seem to have acted as a restraining power on all the subsequent changes of manner in this place—changes in themselves for the most part towards luxuriance. In harmony with the atmosphere of its great church is the cleanly quiet of the town, kept fresh by little channels of clear water circulating through its streets, derivatives of the rapid Vanne which falls just below into the Yonne. The Yonne, bending gracefully, link after link, through a never-ending rustle of poplar trees, beneath lowly vine-clad hills, with relics of delicate woodland here and there, sometimes close at hand, sometimes leaving an interval of broad meadow, has all the lightsome characteristics of French riverside scenery on a smaller scale than usual, and might pass for the child's fancy of a river, like the rivers of the old miniature-painters, blue, and full to a fair green margin. One notices along its course a greater proportion than elsewhere of still untouched old seignorial residences, larger or smaller. The range of old gibbous towns along its banks, expanding their gay quays upon the water-side, have a common character—Joigny, Villeneuve, Saint Julien-du-Sault—yet tempt us to tarry at each and examine its relics, old glass and the like, of the Renaissance or the Middle Age, for the acquisition of real though minor lessons on the various arts which have left themselves a central monument at Auxerre.—Auxerre! A slight ascent in the winding road! and you have before you the prettiest town in France—the broad framework of vineyard sloping upwards gently to the horizon, with distant white cottages inviting one to walk: the quiet curve of river below, with all the river-side details: the three great purple-tiled masses of Saint Germain, Saint Pierre, and the cathedral of Saint Étienne, rising out of the crowded houses with more than the usual abruptness and irregularity of French building. Here, that rare artist, the susceptible painter of architecture, if he understands the value alike of line and mass of broad masses and delicate lines, has "a subject made to his hand."

A veritable country of the vine, it presents nevertheless an expression peaceful rather than radiant. Perfect type of that happy mean between northern earnestness and the luxury of the south, for which we prize midland France, its physiognomy is not quite happy—attractive in part for its melancholy. Its most characteristic atmosphere is to be seen when the tide of light and distant cloud is travelling quickly over it, when rain is not far off, and every touch of art or of time on its old building is defined in clear grey. A fine summer ripens its grapes into a valuable wine; but in spite of that it seems always longing for a larger and more continuous allowance of the sunshine which is so much to its taste. You might fancy something querulous or plaintive in that rustling movement of the vine-leaves, as blue-frocked Jacques Bonhomme[6] finishes his day's labour among them.

To beguile one such afternoon when the rain set in early and walking was impossible, I found my way to the shop of an old dealer in bric-à-brac. It was not a monotonous display, after the manner of the Parisian dealer, of a stock-in-trade the like of which one has seen many times over, but a discriminate collection of real curiosities. One seemed to recognise a provincial school of taste in various relics of the housekeeping of the last century, with many a gem of earlier times from old churches and religious houses of the neighbourhood. Among them was a large and brilliant fragment of stained glass which might have come from the cathedral itself. Of the very finest quality in colour and design, it presented a figure not exactly conformable to any recognised ecclesiastical type; and it was clearly part of a series. On my eager inquiry for the remainder, the old man replied that no more of it was known, but added that the priest of a neighbouring village was the possessor of an entire set of tapestries, apparently intended for suspension in church, and designed to portray the whole subject of which the figure in the stained glass was a portion.

Next afternoon accordingly I repaired to the priest's house, in reality a little Gothic building, part perhaps of an ancient manor-house, close to the village church. In the front garden, flower-garden and *potager*[7] in one, the bees were busy among the autumn growths—many-coloured asters, bignonias, scarlet-beans, and the old-fashioned parsonage flowers. The courteous owner readily showed me his tapestries, some of which hung on the walls of his parlour and staircase by way of a background for the display of the other curiosities of which he was a collector. Certainly, those tapestries and the stained glass dealt with the same theme. In both were the same musical instruments—pipes, cymbals, long reed-like trumpets. The story, indeed included the building of an organ, just such an instrument, only on a larger scale, as was standing in the old priest's library, though almost soundless now, whereas in certain of the woven pictures the hearers appear as if transported, some of them shouting rapturously to the organ music. A sort of mad vehemence, prevails, indeed, throughout the delicate bewilderments of the whole series—giddy dances, wild animals leaping, above all perpetual wreathings of the vine, connecting, like some mazy arabesque, the various presentations of one oft-repeated figure, translated here out of the clear-coloured glass into the sadder, somewhat opaque and earthen hues of the silken threads. The figure was that of the organ-builder himself, a flaxen and flowery creature, sometimes wellnigh naked among the vine-leaves, sometimes muffled in skins against the cold, sometimes in the dress of a monk, but always with a strong impress of real character and incident from the veritable streets of Auxerre. What is it? Certainly, notwithstanding its grace, and wealth of graceful accessories, a suffering, tortured figure. With all the regular beauty of a pagan god, he has suffered after a manner of which we must suppose pagan gods incapable. It was as if one of those fair, triumphant beings had cast in his lot with the creatures of an age later than is own, people of larger spiritual capacity and assuredly of a larger capacity for melancholy. With this fancy in my mind, by the help of certain notes, which lay in the priest's curious library, upon the history of the works at the cathedral during the period of its finishing, and in repeated examination of the old tapestried designs, the story shaped itself at last.

Towards the middle of the thirteenth century[8] the cathedral of Saint Étienne was complete in its main outlines: what remained was the building of the great tower, and all that various labour of final decoration which it would take more than one generation to accomplish. Certain circumstances, however, not wholly explained, led to a somewhat rapid finishing, as it were out of hand, yet with a marvellous fulness at once and grace. Of the result much has perished, or been transferred elsewhere; a portion is still visible in sumptuous relics of stained windows, and, above all, in the reliefs which adorn the western portals, very delicately carved in a fine, firm stone from Tonnerre,[9] of which time has only browned the surface, and which, for early mastery in art, may be compared with the contemporary work of Italy. They come nearer than the art of that age was used to do to the expression of life; with a feeling for reality, in no ignoble form, caught, it might seem, from the ardent and full-veined existence then current in these actual streets and houses. Just then Auxerre had its turn in that political movement which broke out sympathetically, first in one, then in another of the towns of France, turning their narrow, feudal institutions into a free, communistic life—a movement of which those great centres of popular devotion, the French cathedrals, are in many instances the monument. Closely connected always with the assertion of individual freedom, alike in mind and manners, at Auxerre this political stir was associated also, as cause or effect, with the figure and character of a particular personage, long remembered. He was the very genius, it would appear, of that new, free, generous manner in art, active and potent as a living creature.

As the most skilful of the band of carvers worked there one day, with a labour he could never quite make equal to the vision within him, a finely-sculptured Greek coffin of stone, which had been made to serve for some later Roman funeral, was unearthed by the masons. Here, it might seem, the thing was indeed done, and art achieved, as far as regards those final graces, and harmonies of execution, which were precisely what lay beyond the hand of the medieval workman, who for his part had largely at command a seriousness of conception lacking in the old Greek. Within the coffin lay an object of a fresh and brilliant clearness among the ashes of the dead—a flask of lively green glass, like a great emerald. It might have been "the wondrous vessel of the Grail." Only, this object seemed to bring back no ineffable purity, but rather the riotous and earthy heat of old paganism itself. Coated within, and, as some were persuaded, still redolent with the tawny sediment of the Roman wine it had held so long ago, it was set aside for use at the supper which was shortly to celebrate the completion of the mason's work. Amid much talk of the great age of gold, and some random expressions of hope that it might return again, fine old wine of Auxerre was sipped in small glasses from the precious flask as supper ended. And, whether or not the opening of the buried vessel had anything to do with it, from that time a sort of golden age seemed indeed to be reigning there for a while, and the triumphant completion of the great church was contemporary with a series of remarkable wine seasons. The vintage of those years was long remembered. Fine and abundant wine was to be found stored up even in poor men's cottages; while a new beauty, a gaiety, was abroad, as all the conjoint arts branched out exuberantly in a reign of quiet, delighted labour, at the prompting, as it seemed, of the singular being who came suddenly and oddly to Auxerre to be the centre of so pleasant a period, though in truth he made but a sad ending.

A peculiar usage long perpetuated itself at Auxerre. On Easter Day the canons, in the very centre of the great church, played solemnly at ball. Vespers being sung, instead of conducting the bishop to his palace, they proceeded in order into the nave, the people standing in two long rows to watch. Girding up their skirts a little way, the whole body of clerics awaited their turn in silence, while the captain of the singing-boys cast the ball into the air, as high as he might, along the vaulted roof of the central aisle to be caught by any boy who could, and tossed again with hand or foot till it passed on to the portly chanters, the chaplains, the canons themselves, who finally played out the game with all the decorum of an ecclesiastical ceremony. It was just then, just as the canons took the ball to themselves so gravely, that Denys—Denys l'Auxerrois, as he was afterwards called—appeared for the first time. Leaping in among the timid children, he made the thing really a game. The boys played like boys, the men almost like madmen, and all with a delightful glee which became contagious, first in the clerical body, and then among the spectators. The aged Dean of the Chapter, Protonotary of his Holiness, held up his purple skirt a little higher, and stepping from the ranks with an amazing levity, as if suddenly relieved of his burden of eighty years, tossed the ball with his foot to the venerable capitular Homilist, equal to the occasion. And then, unable to stand inactive any longer, the laity carried on the game among themselves, with shouts of not too boisterous amusement; the sport continuing till the flight of the ball could no longer be traced along the dusky aisles.

Though the home of his childhood was but a humble one—one of those little cliff-houses cut out in the low chalky hill-side, such as are still to be found with inhabitants in certain districts of France—there were some who connected his birth with the story of a beautiful country girl,[10] who, about eighteen years before, had been taken from her own people, not unwillingly, for the pleasure of the Count of Auxerre. She had wished indeed to see the great lord, who had sought her privately, in the glory of his own house; but, terrified by the strange splendours of her new abode and manner of life, and the anger of the true wife, she had fled suddenly from the place during the confusion of a violent storm, and in her flight given birth prematurely to a child. The child, a singularly fair one, was found alive, but the mother dead, by lightning-stroke as it seemed, not far from her lord's chamber-door, under the shelter of a ruined ivy-clad tower. Denys himself certainly was a joyous lad enough. At the cliff-side cottage, nestling actually beneath the vineyards, he came to be an unrivalled gardener, and, grown to manhood, brought his produce to market, keeping a stall in the great cathedral square for the sale of melons and pomegranates, all manner of seeds and flowers (*omnia speciosa camporum*), honey also, wax tapers, sweetmeats hot from the frying-pan, rough home-made pots and pans from the little pottery in the wood, loaves baked by the aged woman in whose house he lived. On that Easter Day he had entered the great church for the first time, for the purpose of seeing the game.

And from the very first, the women who saw him at his business, or watering his plants in the cool of the evening, idled for him.[11] The men who noticed the crowd of women at his stall, and how even fresh young girls from the country, seeing him for the first time, always loitered there, suspected —who could tell what kind of powers? hidden under the white veil of that youthful form; and pausing to ponder the matter, found themselves also fallen into the snare. The sight of him made old people feel young again. Even the sage monk Hermes, devoted to study and experiment, was unable to keep the fruit-seller out of his mind, and would fain have discovered the secret of his charm, partly for the friendly purpose of explaining to the lad himself his perhaps more than natural gifts with a view to their profitable cultivation.

It was a period, as older men took note, of young men and their influence. They took fire, no one could quite explain how, as if at his presence, and asserted a wonderful amount of volition, of insolence, yet as if with the consent of their elders, who would themselves sometimes lose their balance, a little comically. That revolution in the temper and manner of individuals concurred with the movement then on foot at Auxerre, as in other French towns, for the liberation of the *commune* from its old feudal superiors. Denys they called *Frank*, among many other nicknames. Young lords prided themselves on saying that labour should have its ease, and were almost prepared to take freedom, plebeian freedom (of course duly decorated, at least with wild-flowers) for a bride. For in truth Denys at his stall was turning the grave, slow movement of politic heads into a wild social license, which for a while made life like a stage-play. He first led those long processions, through which by and by "the little people," the discontented, the despairing, would utter their minds. One man engaged with another in talk in the marketplace; a new influence came forth at the contact; another and then another adhered; at last a new spirit was abroad everywhere. The hot nights were noisy with swarming troops of dishevelled women and youths with red-stained limbs and faces, carrying their lighted torches over the vine-clad hills, or rushing down the streets, to the horror of timid watchers, towards the cool spaces by the river. A shrill music, a laughter at all things, was everywhere. And the new spirit repaired even to church to take part in the novel offices of the Feast of Fools. Heads flung back in ecstasy—the morning sleep among the vines, when the fatigue of the night was over—dew-drenched garments—the serf lying at his ease at last: the artists, then so numerous at the place, caught what they could, something, at least, of the richness, the flexibility of the visible aspects of life, from all this. With them the life of seeming idleness, to which Denys was conducting the youth of Auxerre so pleasantly, counted but as the cultivation, for their due service to man, of delightful natural things. And the powers of nature concurred. It seemed there would be winter no more. The planet Mars drew nearer to the earth than usual, hanging in the low sky like a fiery red lamp. A massive but well-nigh lifeless vine on the wall of the cloister, allowed to remain there only as a curiosity on account of its immense age, in that *great* season, as it was long after called, clothed itself with fruit once more. The culture of the grape greatly increased. The sunlight fell for the first time on many a spot of deep woodland cleared for vine-growing; though Denys, a lover of trees, was careful to leave a stately specimen of forest growth here and there.

When his troubles came, one characteristic that had seemed most amiable in his prosperity was turned against him—a fondness for oddly grown or even misshapen, yet potentially happy, children; for odd animals also: he sympathised with them all, was skilful in healing their maladies, saved the hare in the chase, and sold his mantle to redeem a lamb from the butcher. He taught the people not to be afraid of the strange, ugly creatures which the light of the moving torches drew from their hiding-places, nor think it a bad omen that they approached. He tamed a veritable wolf to keep him company like a dog.[12] It was the first of many ambiguous circumstances about him, from which, in the minds of an increasing number of people, a deep suspicion and hatred began to define itself. The rich *bestiary*, then compiling in the library of the great church, became, through his assistance, nothing less than a garden of Eden—the garden of Eden grown wild. The owl alone he abhorred.[13] A little later, almost as if in revenge, alone of all animals it clung to him, haunting him persistently among the dusky stone towers, when grown gentler than ever he dared not kill it. He moved unhurt in the famous *ménagerie* of the castle, of which the common people were so much afraid, and let out the lions, themselves timid prisoners enough, through the streets during the fair. The incident suggested to the somewhat barren penmen of the day a "morality" adapted from the old pagan books—a stage-play in which the God of Wine should return in triumph from the East. In the cathedral square the pageant was presented, amid an intolerable noise of every kind of pipe-music, with Denys in the chief part, upon a gaily-painted chariot, in soft silken raiment, and, for headdress, a strange elephant-scalp with gilded tusks.

And that unrivalled fairness and freshness of aspect:— how did he alone preserve it untouched, through the wind and heat? In truth, it was not by magic, as some said, but by a natural simplicity in his living. When that dark season of his troubles arrived he was heard begging querulously one wintry night, "Give me wine, meat; dark wine and brown meat!"— come back to the rude door of his old home in the cliff-side. Till that time the great vine-dresser himself drank only water; he had lived on spring-water and fruit. A lover of fertility in all its forms, in what did but suggest it, he was curious and penetrative concerning the habits of water, and had the secret of the divining-rod. Long before it came, he could detect the scent of rain from afar, and would climb with delight to the great scaffolding on the unfinished tower to watch its coming over the thirsty vineland, till it rattled on the great tiled roof of the church below; and then, throwing off his mantle, allow it to bathe his limbs freely, clinging firmly against the tempestuous wind among the carved imageries of dark stone.

It was on his sudden return after a long journey (one of many inexplicable disappearances), coming back changed somewhat, that he ate flesh for the first time, tearing the hot, red morsels with his delicate fingers in a kind of wild greed. He had fled to the south from the first forbidding days of a hard winter which came at last. At the great seaport of Marseilles he had trafficked with sailors from all parts of the world, from Arabia and India, and bought their wares, exposed now for sale, to the wonder of all, at the Easter fair—richer wines and incense than had been known in Auxerre, seeds of marvellous new flowers, creatures wild and tame, new pottery painted in raw gaudy tints, the skins of animals, meats fried with unheard-of condiments. His stall formed a strange, unwonted patch of colour, found suddenly displayed in the hot morning.

The artists were more delighted than ever, and frequented his company in the little manorial habitation, deserted long since by its owners and haunted, so that the eyes of many looked evil upon it, where he had taken up his abode, attracted, in the first instance, by its rich though neglected garden, a tangle of every kind of creeping, vine-like plant. Here, surrounded in abundance by the pleasant materials of his trade, the vine-dresser as it were turned pedant and kept school for the various artists, who learned here an art supplementary to their own,—that gay magic, namely (art or trick) of his existence, till they found themselves grown into a kind of aristocracy, like veritable *gens fleur-de-lisés*, as they worked together for the decoration of the great church and a hundred other places beside. And yet a darkness had grown upon him. The kind creature had lost something of his gentleness. Strange motiveless misdeeds had happened; and, at a loss for other causes, not the envious only would fain have traced the blame to Denys. He was making the younger world mad. Would he make himself Count of Auxerre? The lady Ariane, deserted by her former lover,[14] had looked kindly upon him; was ready to make him son-in-law to the old count her father, old and not long for this world. The wise monk Hermes bethought him of certain old readings in which the Wine-god, whose part Denys had played so well, had his contrast, his dark or antipathetic side; was like a double creature, of two natures, difficult or impossible to harmonise. And in truth the much-prized wine of Auxerre has itself but a fugitive charm, being apt to sicken and turn gross long before the bottle is empty, however carefully sealed; as it goes indeed, at its best, by hard names, among those who grow it, such as *Chainette* and *Migraine*.

A kind of degeneration, of coarseness—the coarseness of satiety, and shapeless, battered-out appetite—with an almost savage taste for carnivorous diet, had come over the company. A rumour went abroad of certain women who had drowned, in mere wantonness, their new-born babes. A girl with child was found hanged by her own act in a dark cellar. Ah! if Denys also had not felt himself mad! But when the guilt of a murder, committed with a great vine-axe far out among the vineyards, was attributed vaguely to him, he could but wonder whether it had been indeed thus, and the shadow of a fancied crime abode with him. People turned against their favorite, whose former charms must now be counted only as the fascinations of witchcraft. It was as if the wine poured out for them had soured in the cup. The golden age had indeed come back for a while:—golden was it, or gilded only, after all? and they were too sick, or at least too serious, to carry through their parts in it. The monk Hermes was whimsically reminded of that *after-thought* in pagan poetry, of a Wine-god who had been in hell.[15] Denys certainly, with all his flaxen fairness about him, was manifestly a sufferer. At first he thought of departing secretly to some other place. Alas! his wits were too far gone for certainty of success in the attempt. He feared to be brought back a prisoner. Those fat years were over. It was a time of scarcity. The working people might not eat and drink of the good things they had helped to store away. Tears rose in the eyes of needy children, of old or weak people like children, as they woke up again and again to sunless, frost-bound, ruinous mornings; and the little hungry creatures went prowling after scattered hedge-nuts or dried vine-tendrils. Mysterious, dark rains prevailed throughout the summer. The great offices of Saint John were fumbled through in a sudden darkness of unseasonable storm, which greatly damaged the carved ornaments of the church, the bishop reading his mid-day Mass by the light of the little candle at his book. And then, one night, the night which seemed literally to have swallowed up the shortest day in the year, a plot was contrived by certain persons to take Denys as he went and kill him privately for a sorcerer. He could hardly tell how he escaped, and found himself safe in his earliest home, the cottage in the cliff-side, with such a big fire as he delighted in burning upon the hearth. They made a little feast as well as they could for the beautiful hunted creature, with abundance of waxlights.

And at last the clergy bethought themselves of a remedy for this evil time. The body of one of the patron saints had lain neglected somewhere under the flagstones of the sanctuary. This must be piously exhumed, and provided with a shrine worthy of it. The goldsmiths, the jewellers and lapidaries, set diligently to work, and no long time after, the shrine, like a little cathedral with portals and tower complete, stood ready, its chiselled gold framing panels of rock crystal, on the great altar. Many bishops arrived, with King Lewis the Saint himself accompanied by his mother, to assist at the search for and disinterment of the sacred relics. In their presence, the Bishop of Auxerre, with vestments of deep red in honour of the relics, blessed the new shrine, according to the office *De benedictione capsarum pro reliquiis*. The pavement of the choir, removed amid a surging sea of lugubrious chants, all persons fasting, discovered as if it had been a battlefield of mouldering human remains. Their odour rose plainly above the plentiful clouds of incense, such as was used in the king's private chapel. The search for the Saint himself continued in vain all day and far into the night. At last from a little narrow chest, into which the remains had been almost crushed together, the bishop's red-gloved hands drew the dwindled body, shrunken inconceivably, but still with every feature of the face traceable in a sudden oblique ray of ghastly dawn.

That shocking sight, after a sharp fit as though a demon were going out of him, as he rolled on the turf of the cloister to which he had fled alone from the suffocating church, where the crowd still awaited the Procession of the relics and the Mass *De reliquiis quae continentur in Ecclesiis*, seemed indeed to have cured the madness of Denys, but certainly did not restore his gaiety. He was left a subdued, silent, melancholy creature. Turning now, with an odd revulsion of feeling, to gloomy objects, he picked out a ghastly shred from the common bones on the pavement to wear about his neck, and in a little while found his way to the monks of Saint Germain, who gladly received him into their workshop, though secretly, in fear of his foes.

The busy tribe of variously gifted artists, labouring rapidly at the many works on hand for the final embellishment of the cathedral of St. Étienne, made those conventual buildings just then cheerful enough to lighten a melancholy, heavy even as that of our friend Denys. He took his place among the workmen, a conventual novice; a novice also as to whatever concerns any actual handicraft. He could but compound sweet incense for the sanctuary. And yet, again by merely visible presence, he made himself felt in all the varied exercise around him of those arts which address themselves first of all to sight. Unconsciously he defined a peculiar manner, alike of feeling and expression, to those skilful hands at work day by day with the chisel, the pencil, or the needle, in many an enduring form of exquisite fancy. In three successive phases or fashions might be traced, especially in the carved work, the humours he had determined. There was first wild gaiety, exuberant in a wreathing of life-like imageries, from which nothing really present in nature was excluded. That, as the soul of Denys darkened, had passed into obscure regions of the satiric, the grotesque and coarse. But from this time there was manifest, with no loss of power or effect, a well-assured seriousness, somewhat jealous and exclusive, not so much in the selection of the material on which the arts were to work, as in the precise sort of expression that should be induced upon it. It was as if the gay old pagan world had been *blessed* in some way; with effects to be seen most clearly in the rich miniature work of the manuscripts of the capitular library,— a marvellous Ovid especially, upon the pages of which those old loves and sorrows seemed to come to life again in medieval costume, as Denys, in cowl now with tonsured head, leaned over the painter, and led his work, by a kind of visible sympathy, often unspoken, rather than by any formal comment.

Above all, there was a desire abroad to attain the instruments of a freer and more various sacred music than had been in use hitherto—a music that might express the whole compass of souls now grown to manhood. Auxerre, indeed, then as afterwards, was famous for its liturgical music. It was Denys, at last, to whom the thought occurred of combining in a fuller tide of music all the instruments then in use. Like the Wine-god of old, he had been a lover and patron especially of the music of the pipe, in all its varieties. Here, too, there had been evident those three fashions or "modes:"— first, the simple and pastoral, the homely note of the pipe, like the piping of the wind itself from off the distant fields; then, the wild, savage din, that had cost so much to quiet people, and driven excitable people mad. Now he would compose all this to sweeter purposes; and the building of the first organ became like the book of his life: it expanded to the full compass of his nature, in its sorrow and delight. In long, enjoyable days of wind and sun by the river-side, the seemingly half-witted "brother" sought and found the needful varieties of reed. The carpenters, under his instruction, set up the great wooden passages for the thunder; while the little pipes of pasteboard simulated the sound of the human voice singing to the victorious notes of the long metal trumpets. At times this also, as people heard night after night those wandering sounds, seemed like the work of a madman, though they awoke sometimes in wonder at snatches of a new, an unmistakable new music. It was the triumph of all the various modes of the power of the pipe, tamed, ruled, united. Only, on the painted shutters of the organ-case Apollo with his lyre in his hand, as lord of the strings, seemed to look askance on the music of the reed, in all the jealousy with which he put Marsyas to death so cruelly.[16]

Meantime, the people, even his enemies, seemed to have forgotten him. Enemies, in truth, they still were, ready to take his life should the opportunity come; as he perceived when at last he ventured forth on a day of public ceremony. The bishop was to pronounce a blessing upon the foundations of a new bridge, designed to take the place of the ancient Roman bridge which, repaired in a thousand places, had hitherto served for the chief passage of the Yonne. It was as if the disturbing of that time-worn masonry let out the dark spectres of departed times. Deep down, at the core of the central pile, a painful object was exposed—the skeleton of a child, placed there alive, it was rightly surmised, in the superstitious belief that, by way of vicarious substitution, its death would secure the safety of all who should pass over. There were some who found themselves, with a little surprise, looking round as if for a similar pledge of security in their new undertaking. It was just then that Denys was seen plainly, standing, in all essential features precisely as of old, upon one of the great stones prepared for the foundation of the new building. For a moment he felt the eyes of the people upon him full of that strange humour, and with characteristic alertness, after a rapid gaze over the grey city in its broad green framework of vineyards, best seen from this spot, flung himself down into the water and disappeared from view where the stream flowed most swiftly below a row of flour-mills. Some indeed fancied they had seen him emerge again safely on the deck of one of the great boats, loaded with grapes and wreathed triumphantly with flowers like a floating garden, which were then bringing down the vintage from the country; but generally the people believed their strange enemy now at last departed for ever. Denys in truth was at work again in peace at the cloister, upon his house of reeds and pipes. At times his fits came upon him again; and when they came, for his cure he would dig eagerly, turned sexton now, digging by choice, graves for the dead in the various churchyards of the town. There were those who had seen him thus employed (that form seeming still to carry something of real sun-gold upon it) peering into the darkness, while his tears fell sometimes among the grim relics his mattock had disturbed.

In fact, from the day of the exhumation of the body of the Saint in the great church, he had had a wonderful curiosity for such objects, and one wintry day bethought him of removing the body of his mother from the unconsecrated ground in which it lay, that he might bury it in the cloister, near the spot where he was now used to work. At twilight he came over the frozen snow. As he passed through the stony barriers of the place the world around seemed curdled to the centre—all but himself, fighting his way across it, turning now and then right-about from the persistent wind, which dealt so roughly with his blond hair and the purple mantle whirled about him. The bones, hastily gathered, he placed, awefully but without ceremony, in a hollow space prepared secretly within the grave of another.

Meantime the winds of his organ were ready to blow; and with difficulty he obtained grace from the Chapter for a trial of its powers on a notable public occasion, as follows. A singular guest was expected at Auxerre. In recompense for some service rendered to the Chapter in times gone by, the Sire de Chastellux had the hereditary dignity of a canon of the church. On the day of his reception he presented himself at the entrance of the choir in surplice and amice, worn over the military habit. The old count of Chastellux was lately dead, and the heir had announced his coming, according to custom, to claim his ecclesiastical privilege. There had been long feud between the houses of Chastellux and Auxerre; but on this happy occasion an offer of peace came with a proposal for the hand of the Lady Ariane.

The goodly young man arrived, and, duly arrayed, was received into his stall at vespers, the bishop assisting. It was then that the people heard the music of the organ, rolling over them for the first time, with various feelings of delight. But the performer on and author of the instrument was forgotten in his work, and there was no re-instatement of the former favorite. The religious ceremony was followed by a civic festival, in which Auxerre welcomed its future lord. The festival was to end at nightfall with a somewhat rude popular pageant, in which the person of Winter would be hunted blindfold through the streets. It was the sequel to that earlier stage-play of the *Return from the East* in which Denys had been the central figure. The old forgotten player saw his part before him, and, as if mechanically, fell again into the chief place, monk's dress and all. It might restore his popularity: who could tell? Hastily he donned the ashen-grey mantle, the rough haircloth about the throat, and went through the preliminary matter. And it happened that a point of the haircloth scratched his lip deeply, with a long trickling of blood upon the chin. It was as if the sight of blood transported the spectators with a kind of mad rage, and suddenly revealed to them the truth. The pretended hunting of the unholy creature became a real one, which brought out, in rapid increase, men's evil passions. The soul of Denys was already at rest, as his body, now borne along in front of the crowd, was tossed hither and thither, torn at last limb from limb.[17] The men stuck little shreds of his flesh, or, failing that, of his torn raiment, into their caps; the women lending their long hairpins for the purpose. The monk Hermes sought in vain next day for any remains of the body of his friend. Only, at nightfall, the heart of Denys was brought to him by a stranger, still entire. It must long since have mouldered into dust under the stone, marked with a cross, where he buried it in a dark corner of the cathedral aisle.

So the figure in the stained glass explained itself. To me, Denys seemed to have been a real resident at Auxerre. On days of a certain atmosphere, when the trace of the Middle Age comes out, like old marks in the stones in rainy weather, I seemed actually to have seen the tortured figure there—to have met Denys l'Auxerrois in the streets.

NOTES

1. "A denizen of old Greece": Dionysus or Bacchus, god of
   intoxication and release; behind this curious story is Heine's
   tale, "The Gods in Exile." There is a large-scale study of
   Dionysus in Pater's *Greek Studies*, which deserves careful
   contrast to Nietzsche's *The Birth of Tragedy*. Pater never
   mentions Nietzsche, yet may have read him.
2. "Specific": in the sense of belonging to a species.
3. These are towns in Champagne, roughly one hundred miles
   to the southeast of Paris.
4. "The Pointed style" is Gothic.
5. In "flamboyant" architecture, the ornamentation is rich
   enough to shroud the structure.
6. "Jacques Bonhomme" is a traditional name for the archetypal
   French peasant.
7. *Potager:* vegetable garden.
8. The middle of the thirteenth century is one of Pater's peculiar
   placements of the start of the Renaissance.
9. About twenty miles to the east of Auxerre.
10. The "beautiful country girl" is a version of Semele, mother of
    Dionysus by Zeus, who destroyed her by lightning bolt.
11. Women traditionally are more drawn to the worship of
    Dionysus.
12. Dionysus, attended by many beasts, came to be associated
    with the sacrifice of a wolf.
13. The owl, associated with the wisdom of Pallas Athena, is a
    natural enemy of Dionysus.
14. The association is with Ariadne, who turned to Dionysus
    when she was abandoned by Theseus.
15. In *Greek Studies*, Pater noted the association of Dionysus
    with Persephone, Queen of Hades, in later Greek legend.
16. The organ is associated here with Pan's pipes, evoking the
    story of the satyr Marsyas, flayed to death by Apollo for
    daring to compete with him. This prefigures the fate of
    Denys–Dionysus, another traditional opponent of Apollo.
17. This is the *sparagmos*, the Dionysian rending-apart that Pater
    takes from later Orphic tradition.

from *Appreciations*

Style

Since all progress of mind consists for the most part in differentiation, in the resolution of an obscure and complex object into its component aspects, it is surely the stupidest of losses to confuse things which right reason has put asunder, to lose the sense of achieved distinctions, the distinction between poetry and prose, for instance, or, to speak more exactly, between the laws and characteristic excellences of verse and prose composition. On the other hand, those who have dwelt most emphatically on the distinction between prose and verse, prose and poetry, may sometimes have been tempted to limit the proper functions of prose too narrowly; and this again is at least false economy, as being, in effect, the renunciation of a certain means or faculty, in a world where after all we must needs make the most of things. Critical efforts to limit art *a priori*,[1] by anticipations regarding the natural incapacity of the material with which this or that artist works, as the sculptor with solid form, or the prose-writer with the ordinary language of men, are always liable to be discredited by the facts of artistic production; and while prose is actually found to be a coloured thing with Bacon, picturesque with Livy and Carlyle, musical with Cicero and Newman, mystical and intimate with Plato and Michelet and Sir Thomas Browne, exalted or florid, it may be, with Milton and Taylor,[2] it will be useless to protest that it can be nothing at all, except something very tamely and narrowly confined to mainly practical ends—a kind of "good roundhand;" as useless as the protest that poetry might not touch prosaic subjects as with Wordsworth, or an abstruse matter as with Browning, or treat contemporary life nobly as with Tennyson. In subordination to one

essential beauty in all good literary style, in all literature as a
fine art, as there are many beauties of poetry so the
beauties of prose are many, and it is the business of criticism
to estimate them as such; as it is good in the criticism of
verse to look for those hard, logical, and quasi-prosaic excellences which that too has, or needs. To find in the poem,
amid the flowers, the allusions, the mixed perspectives, of
Lycidas for instance,[3] the thought, the logical structure:—
how wholesome! how delightful! as to identify in prose what
we call the poetry, the imaginative power, not treating it as
out of place and a kind of vagrant intruder, but by way of an
estimate of its rights, that is, of its achieved powers, there.

Dryden, with the characteristic instinct of his age, loved to
emphasise the distinction between poetry and prose, the protest against their confusion with each other, coming with
somewhat diminished effect from one whose poetry was so
prosaic. In truth, his sense of prosaic excellence affected his
verse rather than his prose, which is not only fervid, richly
figured, poetic, as we say, but vitiated, all unconsciously, by
many a scanning line.[4] Setting up correctness, that humble
merit of prose, as the central literary excellence, he is really
a less correct writer than he may seem, still with an imperfect mastery of the relative pronoun.[5] It might have been
foreseen that, in the rotations of mind, the province of poetry
in prose would find its assertor; and, a century after Dryden,
amid very different intellectual needs, and with the need
therefore of great modifications in literary form, the range of
the poetic force in literature was effectively enlarged by
Wordsworth. The true distinction between prose and poetry
he regarded as the almost technical or accidental one of the
absence or presence of metrical beauty, or, say! metrical
restraint; and for him the opposition came to be between
verse and prose of course;[6] but, as the essential dichotomy in
this matter, between imaginative and unimaginative writing,
parallel to De Quincey's distinction between "the literature of
power and the literature of knowledge,"[7] in the former of
which the composer gives us not fact, but his peculiar sense
of fact, whether past or present.

Dismissing then, under sanction of Wordsworth, that
harsher opposition of poetry to prose, as savouring in fact of
the arbitrary psychology of the last century, and with it the
prejudice that there can be but one only beauty of prose style,
I propose here to point out certain qualities of all literature

as a fine art, which, if they apply to the literature of fact, apply still more to the literature of the imaginative sense of fact, while they apply indifferently to verse and prose, so far as either is really imaginative—certain conditions of true art in both alike, which conditions may also contain in them the secret of the proper discrimination and guardianship of the peculiar excellences of either.

The line between fact and something quite different from external fact is, indeed, hard to draw. In Pascal,[8] for instance, in the persuasive writers generally, how difficult to define the point where, from time to time, argument which, if it is to be worth anything at all, must consist of facts or groups of facts, becomes a pleading—a theorem no longer, but essentially an appeal to the reader to catch the writer's spirit, to think with him, if one can or will—an expression no longer of fact but of his sense of it, his peculiar intuition of a world, prospective, or discerned below the faulty conditions of the present, in either case changed somewhat from the actual world. In science, on the other hand, in history so far as it conforms to scientific rule, we have a literary domain where the imagination may be thought to be always an intruder. And as, in all science, the functions of literature reduce themselves eventually to the transcribing of fact, so all the excellences of literary form in regard to science are reducible to various kinds of painstaking; this good quality being involved in all "skilled work" whatever, in the drafting of an act of parliament, as in sewing. Yet here again, the writer's sense of fact, in history especially, and in all those complex subjects which do but lie on the borders of science, will still take the place of fact, in various degrees. Your historian, for instance, with absolutely truthful intention, amid the multitude of facts presented to him must needs select, and in selecting assert something of his own humour, something that comes not of the world without but of a vision within. So Gibbon[9] moulds his unwieldy material to a preconceived view. Livy, Tacitus, Michelet, moving full of poignant sensibility amid the records of the past, each, after his own sense, modifies—who can tell where and to what degree?—and becomes something else than a transcriber; each, as he thus modifies, passing into the domain of art proper. For just in proportion as the writer's aim, consciously or unconsciously, comes to be the transcribing, not of the world, not of mere fact, but of his sense of it, he becomes an artist, his work *fine* art; and good art (as I

hope ultimately to show) in proportion to the truth of his
presentment of that sense; as in those humbler or plainer
functions of literature also, truth—truth to bare fact, there—
is the essence of such artistic quality as they may have. Truth!
there can be no merit, no craft at all, without that. And further, all beauty is in the long run only *fineness* of truth, or
what we call expression, the finer accommodation of speech
to that vision within.

—The transcript of his sense of fact rather than the fact,
as being preferable, pleasanter, more beautiful to the writer
himself. In literature, as in every other product of human
skill, in the moulding of a bell or a platter for instance,
wherever this sense asserts itself, wherever the producer
so modifies his work as, over and above its primary use or
intention, to make it pleasing (to himself, of course, in the
first instance) there, "fine" as opposed to merely serviceable
art, exists. Literary art, that is, like all art which is in any
way imitative or reproductive of fact—form, or colour, or
incident—is the representation of such fact as connected with
soul, of a specific personality, in its preferences, its volition
and power.

Such is the matter of imaginative or artistic literature—this
transcript, not of mere fact, but of fact in its infinite variety,
as modified by human preference in all its infinitely varied
forms. It will be good literary art not because it is brilliant or
sober, or rich, or impulsive, or severe, but just in proportion
as its representation of that sense, that soul-fact, is true,
verse being only one department of such literature, and imaginative prose, it may be thought, being the special art of the
modern world. That imaginative prose should be the special
and opportune art of the modern world results from two
important facts about the latter: first, the chaotic variety and
complexity of its interests, making the intellectual issue, the
really master currents of the present time incalculable—a
condition of mind little susceptible of the restraint proper to
verse form, so that the most characteristic verse of the nineteenth century has been lawless verse;[10] and secondly, an all-
pervading naturalism,[11] a curiosity about everything whatever as it really is, involving a certain humility of attitude,
cognate to what must, after all, be the less ambitious form of
literature. And prose thus asserting itself as the special and
privileged artistic faculty of the present day, will be, however
critics may try to narrow its scope, as varied in its excellence

as humanity itself reflecting on the facts of its latest experience—an instrument of many stops, meditative, observant, descriptive, eloquent, analytic, plaintive, fervid. Its beauties will be not exclusively "pedestrian": it will exert, in due measure, all the varied charms of poetry, down to the rhythm which, as in Cicero, or Michelet, or Newman, at their best, gives its musical value to every syllable.*

The literary artist is of necessity a scholar, and in what he proposes to do will have in mind, first of all, the scholar and the scholarly conscience—the male conscience in this matter, as we must think it, under a system of education which still to so large an extent limits real scholarship to men. In his self-criticism, he supposes always that sort of reader who will go (full of eyes) warily, considerately, though without consideration for him, over the ground which the female conscience traverses so lightly, so amiably. For the material in which he works is no more a creation of his own than the sculptor's marble. Product of a myriad various minds and contending tongues, compact of obscure and minute association, a language has its own abundant and often recondite laws, in the habitual and summary recognition of which scholarship consists. A writer, full of a matter he is before all things anxious to express, may think of those laws, the limitations of vocabulary, structure, and the like, as a restriction, but if a real artist will find in them an opportunity. His punctilious observance of the proprieties of his medium will diffuse through all he writes a general air of sensibility, of refined usage. *Exclusiones debitæ naturæ*—the exclusions, or rejections, which nature demands—we know how large a part these play, according to Bacon,[12] in the science of nature. In a somewhat changed sense, we might say that the art of the scholar is summed up in the observance of those rejections demanded by the nature of his medium, the material he must use. Alive to the value of an atmosphere in which every term finds its utmost degree of expression, and with all the jealousy of a

* Mr. Saintsbury, in his *Specimens of English Prose, from Malory to Macaulay,* has succeeded in tracing, through successive English prose-writers, the tradition of that severer beauty in them, of which this admirable scholar of our literature is known to be a lover. *English Prose, from Mandeville to Thackeray,* more recently "chosen and edited" by a younger scholar, Mr. Arthur Galton, of New College, Oxford, a lover of our literature at once enthusiastic and discreet, aims at a more various illustration of the eloquent powers of English prose, and is a delightful companion. (Pater's own note.)

lover of words, he will resist a constant tendency on the part of the majority of those who use them to efface the distinctions of language, the facility of writers often reinforcing in this respect the work of the vulgar. He will feel the obligation not of the laws only, but of those affinities, avoidances, those mere preferences, of his language, which through the associations of literary history have become a part of its nature, prescribing the rejection of many a neology,[13] many a license, many a gipsy phrase which might present itself as actually expressive. His appeal, again, is to the scholar, who has great experience in literature, and will show no favour to short-cuts, or hackneyed illustration, or an affectation of learning designed for the unlearned. Hence a contention, a sense of self-restraint and renunciation, having for the susceptible reader the effect of a challenge for minute consideration; the attention of the writer, in every minutest detail, being a pledge that it is worth the reader's while to be attentive too, that the writer is dealing scrupulously with his instrument, and therefore, indirectly, with the reader himself also, that he has the science of the instrument he plays on, perhaps, after all, with a freedom which in such case will be the freedom of a master.

For meanwhile, braced only by those restraints, he is really vindicating his liberty in the making of a vocabulary, an entire system of composition, for himself, his own true manner; and when we speak of the manner of a true master we mean what is essential in his art. Pedantry being only the scholarship of *le cuistre*[14] (we have no English equivalent) he is no pedant, and does but show his intelligence of the rules of language in his freedoms with it, addition or expansion, which like the spontaneities of manner in a well-bred person will still further illustrate good taste.—The right vocabulary! Translators have not invariably seen how all-important that is in the work of translation, driving for the most part at idiom or construction; whereas, if the original be first-rate, one's first care should be with its elementary particles, Plato, for instance, being often reproducible by an exact following, with no variation in structure, of word after word, as the pencil follows a drawing under tracing-paper, so only each word or syllable be not of false colour, to change my illustration a little.

Well! that is because any writer worth translating at all has winnowed and searched through his vocabulary, is conscious of the words he would select in systematic reading of a dictionary, and still more of the words he would reject were the dictionary other than Johnson's;[15] and doing this with his peculiar sense of the world ever in view, in search of an instrument for the adequate expression of that, he begets a vocabulary faithful to the colouring of his own spirit, and in the strictest sense original. That living authority which language needs lies, in truth, in its scholars, who recognising always that every language possesses a genius, a very fastidious genius, of its own, expand at once and purify its very elements, which must needs change along with the changing thoughts of living people. Ninety years ago, for instance, great mental force, certainly, was needed by Wordsworth,[16] to break through the consecrated poetic associations of a century, and speak the language that was his, that was to become in a measure the language of the next generation. But he did it with the tact of a scholar also. English, for a quarter of a century past, has been assimilating the phraseology of pictorial art; for half a century, the phraseology of the great German metaphysical movement of eighty years ago; in part also the language of mystical theology: and none but pedants will regret a great consequent increase of its resources. For many years to come its enterprise may well lie in the naturalisation of the vocabulary of science, so only it be under the eye of a sensitive scholarship—in a liberal naturalisation of the ideas of science too, for after all the chief stimulus of good style is to possess a full, rich, complex matter to grapple with. The literary artist, therefore, will be well aware of physical science; science also attaining, in its turn, its true literary ideal. And then, as the scholar is nothing without the historic sense, he will be apt to restore not really obsolete or really worn-out words, but the finer edge of words still is use: *ascertain, communicate, discover*—words like these it has been part of our "business" to misuse.[17] And still, as language was made for man, he will be no authority for correctnesses which, limiting freedom of utterance, were yet but accidents in their origin; as if one vowed not to say "*its*," which ought to have been in Shakespeare; "*his*" and "*hers*," for inanimate objects, being but a barbarous and really inexpressive survival.[18] Yet we have known many things like this. Racy Saxon monosyllables, close to us as touch and sight, he will intermix readily with those long, savoursome, Latin words, rich in "second intention." In this late day certainly, no critical process can be conducted reasonably without eclecticism. Of such eclecticism we have a justifying example in one of the first poets of our time. How illustrative of monosyllabic effect, of sonorous Latin, of the phraseology of science, of metaphysic, of colloquialism even, are the writings of Tennyson; yet with what a fine, fastidious scholarship throughout!

A scholar writing for the scholarly, he will of course leave something to the willing intelligence of his reader. "To go preach to the first passer-by," says Montaigne,[19] "to become tutor to the ignorance of the first I meet, is a thing I abhor;" a thing, in fact, naturally distressing to the scholar, who will therefore ever be shy of offering uncomplimentary assistance to the reader's wit. To really strenuous minds there is a pleasurable stimulus in the challenge for a continuous effort on their part, to be rewarded by securer and more intimate grasp of the author's sense. Self-restraint, a skilful economy of means, *ascêsis*,[20] that too has a beauty of its own; and for the reader supposed there will be an æsthetic satisfaction in that frugal closeness of style which makes the most of a word, in the exaction from every sentence of a precise relief, in the just spacing out of word to thought, in the logically filled space connected always with the delightful sense of difficulty overcome.

Different classes of persons, at different times, make, of course, very various demands upon literature. Still, scholars, I suppose, and not only scholars, but all disinterested lovers of books, will always look to it, as to all other fine art, for a refuge, a sort of cloistral refuge, from a certain vulgarity in the actual world. A perfect poem like *Lycidas*, a perfect fiction like *Esmond*,[21] the perfect handling of a theory like Newman's *Idea of a University*, has for them something of the uses of a religious "retreat." Here, then, with a view to the central need of a select few, those "men of a finer thread" who have formed and maintain the literary ideal, everything, every component element, will have undergone exact trial, and, above all, there will be no uncharacteristic or tarnished or vulgar decoration, permissible ornament being for the most part structural, or necessary. As the painter in his picture, so the artist in his book, aims at the production by honourable artifice of a peculiar atmosphere. "The artist," says Schiller,[22] "may be known rather by what he *omits*"; and in literature, too, the true artist may be best recognised by his tact of omission. For to the grave reader words too are grave; and the ornamental world, the figure, the accessory form or colour or reference, is rarely content to die to thought precisely at the right moment, but will inevitably linger awhile, stirring a long "brainwave" behind it of perhaps quite alien associations.

Just there, it may be, is the detrimental tendency of the sort of scholarly attentiveness of mind I am recommending. But the true artist allows for it. He will remember that, as the very word ornament indicates what is in itself non-essential, so the "one beauty" of all literary style is of its very essence, and independent, in prose and verse alike, of all removable decoration; that it may exist in its fullest lustre, as in Flaubert's *Madame Bovary*, for instance, or in Stendhal's *Le Rouge et Le Noir*,[23] in a composition utterly unadorned, with hardly a single suggestion of visibly beautiful things. Parallel, allusion, the allusive way generally, the flowers in the garden:—he knows the narcotic force of these upon the negligent intelligence to which any *diversion*, literally, is welcome, any vagrant intruder, because one can go wandering away with it from the immediate subject. Jealous, if he have a really quickening motive within, of all that does not hold directly to that, of the facile, the otiose, he will never depart from the strictly pedestrian process, unless he gains a ponderable something thereby. Even assured of its congruity, he will still question its serviceableness. Is it worth while, can we afford, to attend to just that, to just that figure or literary reference, just then?—Surplusage! he will dread that, as the runner on his muscles. For in truth all art does but consist in the removal of surplusage, from the last finish of the gemengraver blowing away the last particle of invisible dust, back to the earliest divination of the finished work to be, lying somewhere, according to Michelangelo's fancy, in the roughhewn block of stone.

And what applies to figure or flower must be understood of all other accidental or removable ornaments of writing whatever; and not of specific ornament only, but of all that latent colour and imagery which language as such carries in it. A lover of words for their own sake, to whom nothing about them is unimportant, a minute and constant observer of their physiognomy, he will be on the alert not only for obviously mixed metaphors of course, but for the metaphor that is mixed in all our speech, though a rapid use may involve no cognition of it. Currently recognising the incident, the colour, the physical elements or particles in words like *absorb*, *consider*, *extract*, to take the first that occur, he will avail himself of them, as further adding to the resources of expression. The elementary particles of language will be realised as colour and light and shade through his scholarly living in the full sense of them. Still opposing the constant degradation of language by those who use it carelessly, he will not treat coloured glass as if it were clear; and while half the world is using figure unconsciously, will be fully aware not only of all that latent figurative texture in speech, but of the vague, lazy, half-formed personification—a rhetoric, depressing, and worse than nothing, because it has no really rhetorical motive—which plays so large a part there, and, as in the case of more ostentatious ornament, scrupulously exact of it, from syllable to syllable, its precise value.

So far I have been speaking of certain conditions of the literary art arising out of the medium or material in or upon which it works, the essential qualities of language and its aptitudes for contingent ornamentation, matters which define scholarship as science and good taste respectively. They are both subservient to a more intimate quality of good style: more intimate, as coming nearer to the artist himself. The otiose, the facile, surplusage: why are these abhorrent to the true literary artist, except because, in literary as in all other art, structure is all-important, felt, or painfully missed, everywhere?—that architectural conception of work, which foresees the end in the beginning and never loses sight of it, and in every part is conscious of all the rest, till the last sentence does but, with undiminished vigour, unfold and justify the first—a condition of literary art, which, in contradistinction to another quality of the artist himself, to be spoken of later, I shall call the necessity of *mind* in style.

An acute philosophical writer, the late Dean Mansel[24] (a writer whose works illustrate the literary beauty there may be in closeness, and with obvious repression or economy of a fine rhetorical gift) wrote a book, of fascinating precision in a very obscure subject, to show that all the technical laws of logic are but means of securing, in each and all of its apprehensions, the unity, the strict identity with itself, of the apprehending mind. All the laws of good writing aim at a similar unity or identity of the mind in all the processes by which the word is associated to its import. The term is right, and has its essential beauty, when it becomes, in a manner, what it signifies, as with the names of simple sensations. To give the phrase, the sentence, the structural member, the entire composition, song, or essay, a similar unity with its subject and with itself:—style is in the right way when it tends towards that. All depends upon the original unity, the vital wholeness and identity, of the initiatory apprehension or view. So much is true of all art, which therefore requires always its logic, its comprehensive reason—insight, foresight, retrospect, in simultaneous action—true, most of all, of the literary art, as being of all the arts most closely cognate to the abstract intelligence. Such logical coherency may be evidenced not merely in the lines of composition as a whole, but in the choice of a single word, while it by no means interferes with, but may even prescribe, much variety, in the building of the sentence for instance, or in the manner, argumentative, descriptive, discursive, of this or that part or member of the entire design. The blithe, crisp sentence, decisive as a child's expression of its needs, may alternate with the long-contending, victoriously intricate sentence; the sentence, born with the integrity of a single word, relieving the sort of sentence in which, if you look closely, you can see much contrivance, much adjustment, to bring a highly qualified matter into compass at one view. For the literary architecture, if it is to be rich and expressive, involves not only foresight of the end in the beginning, but also development or growth of design, in the process of execution, with many irregularities, surprises, and afterthoughts; the contingent as well as the necessary being subsumed under the unity of the whole. As truly, to the lack of such architectural design, of a single, almost visual, image, vigorously informing an entire, perhaps very intricate, composition, which shall be austere, ornate, argumentative, fanciful, yet true from first to last to that vision within, may be attributed those weaknesses of conscious or unconscious repetition of word, phrase, motive, or member of the whole matter, indicating, as Flaubert was aware, an original structure in thought not organically complete. With such foresight, the actual conclusion will most often get itself written out of hand, before, in the more obvious sense, the work is finished. With some strong and leading sense of the world, the tight hold of which secures true *composition* and not mere loose accretion, the literary artist, I suppose, goes on considerately, setting joint to joint, sustained by yet restraining the productive ardour, retracing the negligences of his first sketch, repeating his steps only that he may give the reader a sense of secure and restful progress, readjusting mere assonances even, that they may soothe the reader, or at least not interrupt him on his way; and then, somewhere before the end comes, is burdened, inspired, with his conclusion, and betimes delivered of it, leaving off, not in weariness and because he finds *himself* at an end, but in all the freshness of volition. His work now structurally complete, with all the accumulating effect of secondary shades of meaning, he finishes the whole up to the just proportion of that ante-penultimate conclusion, and all becomes expressive. The house he has built is rather a body he has informed. And so it happens, to its greater credit, that the better interest even of a narrative to be recounted, a story to be told, will often be in its second reading. And though there are instances of great writers who have been no artists, an unconscious tact sometimes directing work in which we may detect, very pleasurably, many of the effects of conscious art, yet one of the greatest pleasures of really good prose literature is in the critical tracing out of that conscious artistic structure, and the pervading sense of it as we read. Yet of poetic literature too; for, in truth, the kind of constructive intelligence here supposed is one of the forms of the imagination.

That is the special function of mind, in style. Mind and soul:—hard to ascertain philosophically, the distinction is real enough practically, for they often interfere, are sometimes in conflict, with each other. Blake, in the last century, is an instance of preponderating soul, embarrassed, at a loss, in an era of preponderating mind. As a quality of style, at all events, soul is a fact, in certain writers—the way they have of absorbing language, of attracting it into the peculiar spirit they are of, with a subtlety which makes the actual result seem like some inexplicable inspiration. By mind, the literary artist reaches us, through static and objective indications of design in his work, legible to all. By soul, he reaches us, somewhat capriciously perhaps, one and not another, through vagrant sympathy and a kind of immediate contact. Mind we cannot choose but approve where we recognise it; soul may repel us, not because we misunderstand it. The way in which theological interests sometimes avail themselves of language is perhaps the best illustration of the force I mean to indicate generally in literature, by the word *soul*. Ardent religious persuasion may exist, may make its way, without finding any equivalent heat in language: or, again, it may enkindle words to various degrees, and when it really takes hold of them doubles its force. Religious history presents many remarkable instances in which, through no mere phrase-worship, an unconscious literary tact has, for the sensitive, laid open a privileged pathway from one to another. "The altar-fire," people say, "has touched those lips!" The Vulgate, the English Bible, the English Prayer-Book, the writings of Swedenborg, the Tracts for the Times:[25]—there, we have instances of widely different and largely diffused phases of religious feeling in operation as soul in style. But something of the same kind acts with similar power in certain writers of quite other than theological literature, on behalf of some wholly personal and peculiar sense of theirs. Most easily illustrated by theological literature, this quality lends to profane writers a kind of religious influence. At their best, these writers become, as we say sometimes, "prophets"; such character depending on the effect not merely of their matter, but of their matter as allied to, in "electric affinity" with, peculiar form, and working in all cases by an immediate sympathetic contact, on which account it is that it may be called soul, as opposed to mind, in style. And this too is a faculty of choosing and rejecting what is congruous or otherwise, with a drift towards unity—unity of atmosphere here, as there of design —soul securing colour (or perfume, might we say?) as mind secures form, the latter being essentially finite, the former vague or infinite, as the influence of a living person is practically infinite. There are some to whom nothing has any real interest, or real meaning, except as operative in a given person; and it is they who best appreciate the quality of soul in literary art. They seem to know a *person*, in a book, and make way by intuition: yet, although they thus enjoy the completeness of a personal information, it is still a characteristic of soul, in this sense of the word, that it does but suggest what can never be uttered, not as being different from, or more obscure than, what actually gets said, but as containing that plenary substance of which there is only one phase or facet in what is there expressed.

If all high things have their martyrs, Gustave Flaubert might perhaps rank as the martyr of literary style. In his printed correspondence, a curious series of letters, written in his twenty-fifth year, records what seems to have been his one other passion—a series of letters which, with its fine casuistries, its firmly repressed anguish, its tone of harmonious grey, and the sense of disillusion in which the whole matter ends, might have been, a few slight changes supposed, one of his own fictions. Writing to Madame X.[26] certainly he does display, by "taking thought" mainly, by constant and delicate pondering, as in his love for literature, a heart really moved, but still more, and as the pledge of that emotion, a loyalty to his work. Madame X., too, is a literary artist, and the best gifts he can send her are precepts of perfection in art, counsels for the effectual pursuit of that better love. In his love-letters it is the pains and pleasures of art he insists on, its solaces: he communicates secrets, reproves, encourages, with a view to that. Whether the lady was dissatisfied with such divided or indirect service, the reader is not enabled to see; but sees that, on Flaubert's part at least, a living person could be no rival of what was, from first to last, his leading passion, a somewhat solitary and exclusive one.

> I must scold you (he writes) for one thing, which shocks, scandalises me, the small concern, namely, you show for art just now. As regards glory be it so: there, I approve. But for art!—the one thing in life that is good and real—can you compare with it an earthly love?—prefer the adoration of a relative beauty to the *cultus* of the true beauty? Well! I tell you the truth. That is the one thing good in me: the one thing I have, to me estimable. For yourself, you blend with the beautiful a heap of alien things, the useful, the agreeable, what not?—
>
> The only way not to be unhappy is to shut yourself up in art, and count everything else as nothing. Pride takes the place of all beside when it is established on a large basis. Work! God wills it. That, it seems to me, is clear.—
>
> I am reading over again the *Æneid*, certain verses of which I repeat to myself to satiety. There are phrases there which stay in one's head, by which I find myself beset, as with those musical airs which are for ever returning, and cause you pain, you love them so much. I observe that I no longer laugh much, and am no longer depressed. I am ripe. You talk of my serenity, and envy me. It may well surprise you. Sick, irritated, the prey a thousand times a day of cruel pain, I continue my labour like a true working-man, who, with sleeves turned up, in the sweat of his brow, beats away at his anvil, never troubling himself whether it rains or blows, for hail or thunder. I was not like that formerly. The change has taken place naturally, though my will has counted for something in the matter.—
>
> Those who write in good style are sometimes accused of a neglect of ideas, and of the moral end, as if the end of the

physician were something else than healing, of the painter than painting—as if the end of art were not, before all else, the beautiful.

What, then, did Flaubert understand by beauty, in the art he pursued with so much fervour, with so much self-command? Let us hear a sympathetic commentator:[27]—

> Possessed of an absolute belief that there exists but one way of expressing one thing, one word to call it by, one adjective to qualify, one verb to animate it, he gave himself to super-human labour for the discovery, in every phrase, of that word, that verb, that epithet. In this way, he believed in some mysterious harmony of expression, and when a true word seemed to him to lack euphony still went on seeking another, with invincible patience, certain that he had not yet got hold of the *unique* word. . . . A thousand preoccupations would beset him at the same moment, always with this desperate certitude fixed in his spirit: Among all the expressions in the world, all forms and turns of expression, there is but *one*— one form, one mode—to express what I want to say.

The one word for the one thing, the one thought, amid the multitude of words, terms, that might just do: the problem of style was there!—the unique word, phrase, sentence, paragraph, essay, or song, absolutely proper to the single mental presentation or vision within. In that perfect justice, over and above the many contingent and removable beauties with which beautiful style may charm us, but which it can exist without, independent of them yet dexterously availing itself of them, omnipresent in good work, in function at every point, from single epithets to the rhythm of a whole book, lay the specific, indispensable, very intellectual, beauty of literature, the possibility of which constitutes it a fine art.

One seems to detect the influence of a philosophic idea there, the idea of a natural economy, of some pre-existent adaptation, between a relative, somewhere in the world of thought, and its correlative, somewhere in the world of language—both alike, rather, somewhere in the mind of the artist, desiderative, expectant, inventive—meeting each other with the readiness of "soul and body reunited," in Blake's rapturous design;[28] and, in fact, Flaubert was fond of giving his theory philosophical expression.—

There are no beautiful thoughts (he would say) without beautiful forms, and conversely. As it is impossible to extract from a physical body the qualities which really constitute it—colour, extension, and the like—without reducing it to a hollow abstraction, in a word, without destroying it; just so it is impossible to detach the form from the idea, for the idea only exists by virtue of the form.

All the recognised flowers, the removable ornaments of literature (including harmony and ease in reading aloud, very carefully considered by him) counted, certainly; for these too are part of the actual value of what one says. But still, after all, with Flaubert, the search, the unwearied research, was not for the smooth, or winsome, or forcible word, as such, as with false Ciceronians,[29] but quite simply and honestly, for the word's adjustment to its meaning. The first condition of this must be, of course, to know yourself, to have ascertained your own sense exactly. Then, if we suppose an artist, he says to the reader,—I want you to see precisely what I see. Into the mind sensitive to "form," a flood of random sounds, colours, incidents, is ever penetrating from the world without, to become, by sympathetic selection, a part of its very structure, and, in turn, the visible vesture and expression of that other world it sees so steadily within, nay, already with a partial conformity thereto, to be refined, enlarged, corrected, at a hundred points; and it is just there, just at those doubtful points that the function of style, as tact or taste, intervenes. The unique term will come more quickly to one than another, at one time than another, according also to the kind of matter in question. Quickness and slowness, ease and closeness alike, have nothing to do with the artistic character of the true word found at last. As there is a charm of ease, so there is also a special charm in the signs of discovery, of effort and contention towards a due end, as so often with Flaubert himself—in the style which has been pliant, as only obstinate, durable metal can be, to the inherent perplexities and recusancy of a certain difficult thought.

If Flaubert had not told us, perhaps we should never have guessed how tardy and painful his own procedure really was, and after reading his confession may think that his almost endless hesitation had much to do with diseased nerves. Often, perhaps, the felicity supposed will be the product of a happier, a more exuberant nature than Flaubert's. Aggravated, certainly, by a morbid physical condition, that anxiety in "seeking the phrase," which gathered all the other small *ennuis*[30] of a really quiet existence into a kind of battle, was connected with his lifelong contention against facile poetry, facile art—art, facile and flimsy; and what constitutes the true artist is not the slowness or quickness of the process, but the absolute success of the result. As with those labourers in the parable,[31] the prize is independent of the mere length of the actual day's work. "You talk," he writes, odd, trying lover, to Madame X.——

> "You talk of the exclusiveness of my literary tastes. That might have enabled you to divine what kind of a person I am in the matter of love. I grow so hard to please as a literary artist, that I am driven to despair. I shall end by not writing another line."

"Happy," he cries, in a moment of discouragement at that patient labour, which for him, certainly, was the condition of a great success——

> Happy those who have no doubts of themselves! who lengthen out, as the pen runs on, all that flows forth from their brains. As for me, I hesitate, I disappoint myself, turn round upon myself in despite: my taste is augmented in proportion as my natural vigour decreases, and I afflict my soul over some dubious word out of all proportion to the pleasure I get from a whole page of good writing. One would have to live two centuries to attain a true idea of any matter whatever. What Buffon said is a big blasphemy: genius is not long-continued patience. Still, there is some truth in the statement, and more than people think, especially as regards our own day. Art! art! art! bitter deception! phantom that glows with light, only to lead one on to destruction.

Again——

> I am growing so peevish about my writing. I am like a man whose ear is true but who plays falsely on the violin: his fingers refuse to reproduce precisely those sounds of which he has the inward sense. Then the tears come rolling down from the poor scraper's eyes and the bow falls from his hand.

Coming slowly or quickly, when it comes, as it came with so much labour of mind, but also with so much lustre, to

Gustave Flaubert, this discovery of the word will be, like all artistic success and felicity, incapable of strict analysis: effect of an intuitive condition of mind, it must be recognised by like intuition on the part of the reader, and a sort of immediate sense. In every one of those masterly sentences of Flaubert there was, below all mere contrivance, shaping and after-thought, by some happy instantaneous concourse of the various faculties of the mind with each other, the exact apprehension of what was *needed* to carry the meaning. And that it fits with absolute justice will be a judgment of immediate sense in the appreciative reader. We all feel this in what may be called inspired translation. Well! all language involves translation from inward to outward. In literature, as in all forms of art, there are the absolute and the merely relative or accessory beauties; and precisely in that exact proportion of the term to its purpose is the absolute beauty of style, prose or verse. All the good qualities, the beauties, of verse also, are such, only as precise expression.

In the highest as in the lowliest literature, then, the one indispensable beauty is, after all, truth:—truth to bare fact in the latter, as to some personal sense of fact, diverted some-what from men's ordinary sense of it, in the former: truth there as accuracy, truth here as expression, that finest and most intimate form of truth, the *vraie vérité*.[32] And what an eclectic principle this really is! employing for its one sole purpose—that absolute accordance of expression to idea—all other literary beauties and excellences whatever: how many kinds of style it covers, explains, justifies, and at the same time safeguards! Scott's facility, Flaubert's deeply pondered evocation of "the phrase," are equally good art. Say what you have to say, what you have a will to say, in the simplest, the most direct and exact manner possible, with no surplusage:— there, is the justification of the sentence so fortunately born, "entire, smooth, and round," that it needs no punctuation, and also (that is the point!) of the most elaborate period, if it be right in its elaboration. Here is the office of ornament: here also the purpose of restraint in ornament. As the expo-nent of truth, that austerity (the beauty, the function, of which in literature Flaubert understood so well) becomes not the correctness or purism of the mere scholar, but a secur-ity against the otiose, a jealous exclusion of what does not really tell towards the pursuit of relief, of life and vigour in the portraiture of one's sense. License again, the making free with rule, if it be indeed, as people fancy, a habit of genius, flinging aside or transforming all that opposes the liberty of beautiful production, will be but faith to one's own meaning. The seeming baldness of *Le Rouge et Le Noir* is nothing in itself; the wild ornament of *Les Misérables* is nothing in itself; and the restraint of Flaubert, amid a real natural opulence, only redoubled beauty—the phrase so large and so precise at the same time, hard as bronze, in service to the more perfect adaptation of words to their matter. Afterthoughts, retouchings, finish, will be of profit only so far as they too really serve to bring out the original, initiative, generative, sense in them.

In this way, according to the well-known saying, "The style is the man,"[33] complex or simple, in his individuality, his plenary sense of what he really has to say, his sense of the world; all cautions regarding style arising out of so many natural scruples as to the medium through which alone he can expose that inward sense of things, the purity of this medium, its laws or tricks of refraction: nothing is to be left there which might give conveyance to any matter save that. Style in all its varieties, reserved or opulent, terse, abundant, musical, stimulant, academic, so long as each is really characteristic or expressive, finds thus its justification, the sumptuous good taste of Cicero being as truly the man himself, and not another, justified, yet insured inalienably to him, thereby, as would have been his portrait by Raffaelle, in full consular splendour, on his ivory chair.

A relegation, you may say perhaps—a relegation of style to the subjectivity, the mere caprice, of the individual, which must soon transform it into mannerism. Not so! since there is, under the conditions supposed, for those elements of the man, for every lineament of the vision within, the one word, the one acceptable word, recognisable by the sensitive, by others "who have intelligence" in the matter, as absolutely as ever anything can be in the evanescent and delicate region of human language. The style, the manner, would be the man, not in his unreasoned and really uncharacteristic caprices, involuntary or affected, but in absolutely sincere apprehension of what is most real to him. But let us hear our French guide again.—

Styles (says Flaubert's commentator), *Styles*, as so many peculiar moulds, each of which bears the mark of a particular writer, who is to pour into it the whole content of his ideas, were no part of his theory. What he believed in was *Style:* that is to say, a certain absolute and unique manner of expressing a thing, in all its intensity and colour. For him the *form* was the work itself. As in living creatures, the blood, nourishing the body, determines its very contour and external aspect, just so, to his mind, the *matter,* the basis, in a work of art, imposed, necessarily, the unique, the just expression, the measure, the rhythm—the *form* in all its characteristics.

If the style be the man, in all the colour and intensity of a veritable apprehension, it will be in a real sense "impersonal."

I said, thinking of books like Victor Hugo's *Les Misérables,* that prose literature was the characteristic art of the nineteenth century, as others, thinking of its triumphs since the youth of Bach, have assigned that place to music. Music and prose literature are, in one sense, the opposite terms of art; the art of literature presenting to the imagination, through the intelligence, a range of interests, as free and various as those which music presents to it through sense. And certainly the tendency of what has been here said is to bring literature too under those conditions, by conformity to which music takes rank as the typically perfect art. If music be the ideal of all art whatever, precisely because in music it is impossible to distinguish the form from the substance or matter, the subject from the expression, then, literature, by finding its specific excellence in the absolute correspondence of the term to its import, will be but fullfilling the condition of all artistic quality in things everywhere, of all good art.

Good art, but not necessarily great art; the distinction between great art and good art depending immediately, as regards literature at all events, not on its form, but on the matter, Thackeray's *Esmond,* surely, is greater art than *Vanity Fair,* by the greater dignity of its interests. It is on the quality of the matter it informs or controls, its compass, its variety, its alliance to great ends, or the depth of the note of revolt, or the largeness of hope in it, that the greatness of literary art depends, as *The Divine Comedy, Paradise Lost, Les Misérables, The English Bible,* are great art. Given the conditions I have tried to explain as constituting good art;— then, if it be devoted further to the increase of men's happiness, to the redemption of the oppressed, or the enlargement of our sympathies with each other, or to such presentment of new or old truth about ourselves and our relation to the world as may ennoble and fortify us in our sojourn here, or immediately, as with Dante, to the glory of God, it will be also great art; if, over and above those qualities I summed up as mind and soul—that colour and mystic perfume, and that reasonable structure, it has something of the soul of humanity in it, and finds its logical, its architectural place, in the great structure of human life.[34]

1888

NOTES

1. "To limit art *a priori*": this is a Ruskinian protest against an Arnoldian approach; the *a priori* or presumptive view would rule out that interpenetration of the arts that is crucial for Ruskin and Pater. As in "The School of Giorgione," Pater sees all the arts as undergoing an *Anders-streben,* a reach toward the otherness of a rival medium, which here becomes the reach of prose toward poetry.
2. Jules Michelet (1798–1874), French historian; Sir Thomas Browne (1605–1682), author of the *Religio Medici,* and Jeremy Taylor (1613–1667), English divine and writer of ornate prose; Pater regards these as part of his own literary ancestry.
3. The appreciation of "the mixed perspectives" of Milton's pastoral elegy, *Lycidas* (1638) is notable here, but is also Ruskinian.
4. "A scanning line": when prose gives the impression of having *unconsciously* become verse; Pater is correct that Dryden suffers this lapse, but so does Pater, rather too frequently.
5. Oddly enough, this is a fault of Pater as well as of Dryden; both frequently make us hunt for antecedents. In any case, Dryden confessed more than once that he had not attained "correctness."
6. Wordsworth's "Preface" to *Lyrical Ballads* (1798).
7. Thomas De Quincey (1785–1859), another of Pater's prime precursors, made the useful distinction between "the literature of power and the literature of knowledge" in his essay on "The Poetry of Pope." See his *Works,* ed. David Masson, 1897, vol. XI, p. 59.
8. Blaise Pascal (1623–1662), the great French theologian and polemicist, was the subject of one of Pater's last essays.
9. Edward Gibbon (1737–1794), whose *The Decline and Fall of the Roman Empire* (1776–1788) molded its material to a preconceived view not wholly unacceptable to Pater.

10. "Lawless verse": perhaps Pater is thinking of experiments in free or freer verse, like those of Coleridge, Heine, Whitman, and various French Symbolists, but more likely he means "lawless" by the stricter canons of the Enlightenment literary mind, whether in later seventeenth-century France or earlier eighteenth-century England. "Lawless" verse would thus include the major work of Goethe, Wordsworth, Hugo, and of all their followers.

11. This "all-pervading naturalism" finds a particular instance in Pater's "Conclusion" to *The Renaissance*.

12. Francis Bacon, *Novum Organum,* Second Book of Aphorisms, no. XVIII.

13. "Neology": a coinage or new word.

14. *Le cuistre:* from the Latin for "cook," and so this word intimates a lower sort of competence; a *cuistre* is thus a narrow-minded pedant.

15. Samuel Johnson's *Dictionary of the English Language* (1755).

16. This reflects Wordsworth's remarks in his "Preface" to the second edition of the *Lyrical Ballads* (1800).

17. *"Ascertain, communicate, discover":* Pater presumably meant the loss of the sharper meanings of these words: "ascertain" = to make definitely known; "communicate" = to give to another as a partaker; "discover" = to betray, or show unconsciously.

18. Shakespeare, like most Elizabethans, uses *his* for *it,* a masculine rather than a neuter possessive.

19. From Montaigne's essay "Of the Art of Conversing."

20. This is Pater's version of *askesis* again, as in the "Preface" to *The Renaissance* and, later, in his work on the Greeks.

21. Thackeray's novel, *The History of Henry Esmond* (1852), was greatly admired by Pater.

22. Friedrich von Schiller (1759–1805), German dramatist, poet, æsthetician, friend of Goethe.

23. Marie Henri Beyle, "Stendhal" (1783–1842), is classified as a Romantic in Pater's "Postscript" to *Appreciations*.

24. H. L. Mansel, Dean of St. Paul's, who published *Prolegomena Logica* in 1851.

25. The Vulgate is St. Jerome's fourth-century Latin translation of the Bible. Emanuel Swedenborg (1688–1772) founded the New Church, on the opaque basis of his visionary writings. The *Tracts for the Times* (1833–1841) were composed by Newman, Pusey, and other revivalists of the Oxford Movement.

26. Madame X was Flaubert's great love, Madame Louise Colet.

27. The "sympathetic commentator" was Flaubert's disciple, the short-story writer Guy de Maupassant.

28. Blake's design is one of his illustrations for Robert Blair's long poem, *The Grave* (Design X , "The Re-Union of Soul and Body").

29. *Ciceronians:* highly overt stylists.
30. *Ennuis:* tediums.
31. The parable is Matthew 20:1–16.
32. *Vraie vérité:* "true truth."
33. Buffon's famous adage.
34. It is not possible to reconcile wholly this final paragraph of "Style" either with the rest of the essay, or with the greater part of Pater's writings. A profound anxiety, primarily societal, is at work here, and causes him to falsify his critical vision, at least in part.

Wordsworth

Some English critics at the beginning of the present century had a great deal to say concerning a distinction, of much importance, as they thought, in the true estimate of poetry, between the *Fancy*, and another more powerful faculty—the *Imagination*.[1] This metaphysical distinction, borrowed originally from the writings of German philosophers, and perhaps not always clearly apprehended by those who talked of it, involved a far deeper and more vital distinction, with which indeed all true criticism more or less direct has to do, the distinction, namely, between higher and lower degrees of intensity in the poet's perception of his subject, and in his concentration of himself upon his work.[2] Of those who dwelt upon the metaphysical distinction between the Fancy and the Imagination, it was Wordsworth who made the most of it,[3] assuming it as the basis for the final classification of his poetical writings; and it is in these writings that the deeper and more vital distinction, which, as I have said, underlies the metaphysical distinction, is most needed, and may best be illustrated.

For nowhere is there so perplexed a mixture as in Wordsworth's own poetry, of work touched with intense and individual power, with work of almost no character at all. He has much conventional sentiment, and some of that insincere poetic diction, against which his most serious critical efforts were directed: the reaction in his political ideas, consequent on the excesses of 1795, makes him, at times, a mere declaimer on moral and social topics; and he seems, sometimes, to force an unwilling pen, and write by rule. By making the most of these blemishes it is possible to obscure the true æsthetic value of his work, just as his life also, a life of much quiet delicacy and independence, might easily be placed in a false focus, and made to appear a somewhat tame theme in illustration of the more obvious parochial virtues. And those who wish to understand his influence, and experience his peculiar savour, must bear with patience the presence of an alien element in Wordsworth's work, which never coalesced with what is really delightful in it, nor underwent his special power. Who that values his writings most has not felt the intrusion there, from time to time, of something tedious and prosaic? Of all poets equally great, he would gain most by a skilfully made anthology. Such a selection would show, in truth, not so much what he was, or to himself or others seemed to be, as what, by the more energetic and fertile quality in his writings, he was ever tending to become. And the mixture in his work, as it actually stands, is so perplexed, that one fears to miss the least promising composition even, lest some precious morsel should be lying hidden within—the few perfect lines, the phrase, the single word perhaps, to which he often works up mechanically through a poem, almost the whole of which may be tame enough. He who thought that in all creative work the larger part was *given* passively, to the recipient mind, who waited so dutifully upon the gift, to whom so large a measure was sometimes given, had his times also of desertion and relapse; and he has permitted the impress of these too to remain in his work. And this duality there—the fitfulness with which the higher qualities manifest themselves in it, gives the effect in his poetry of a power not altogether his own, or under his control, which comes and goes when it will, lifting or lowering a matter, poor in itself; so that that old fancy which made the poet's art an enthusiasm, a form of divine possession, seems almost literally true of him.

This constant suggestion of an absolute duality between higher and lower moods, and the work done in them, stimulating one always to look below the surface, makes the reading of Wordsworth an excellent sort of training towards the things of art and poetry. It begets in those, who, coming across him in youth, can bear him at all, a habit of reading between the lines, a faith in the effect of concentration and collectedness of mind in the right appreciation of poetry, an expectation of things, in this order, coming to one by means of a right discipline of the temper as well as of the intellect.[4] He meets us with the promise that he has much, and something very peculiar, to give us, if we will follow a certain difficult way, and seems to have the secret of a special and privileged state of mind. And those who have undergone his influence, and followed this difficult way, are like people who have passed through some initiation, a *disciplina arcani*,[5] by submitting to which they become able constantly to distinguish in art, speech, feeling, manners, that which is organic, animated, expressive, from that which is only conventional, derivative, inexpressive.

But although the necessity of selecting these precious morsels for oneself is an opportunity for the exercise of Wordsworth's peculiar influence, and induces a kind of just criticism and true estimate of it, yet the purely literary product would have been more excellent, had the writer himself purged away that alien element. How perfect would have been the little treasury, shut between the covers of how thin a book! Let us suppose the desired separation made, the electric thread untwined, the golden pieces, great and small, lying apart together.* What are the peculiarities of this residue? What special sense does Wordsworth exercise, and what instincts does he satisfy? What are the subjects and the motives which in him excite the imaginative faculty? What are the qualities in things and persons which he values, the impression and sense of which he can convey to others, in an extraordinary way?

An intimate consciousness of the expression of natural things, which weighs, listens, penetrates, where the earlier mind passed roughly by, is a large element in the complexion of modern poetry.[6] It has been remarked as a fact in mental history again and again. It reveals itself in many forms; but is strongest and most attractive in what is strongest and most attractive in modern literature. It is exemplified, almost equally, by writers as unlike each other as Senancour[7] and Théophile Gautier:[8] as a singular chapter in the history of the human

---

* Since this essay was written, such selections have been made, with excellent taste, by Matthew Arnold and Professor Knight. (Pater's own note.)

mind, its growth might be traced from Rousseau[9] to Chateaubriand, from Chateaubriand to Victor Hugo: it has doubtless some latent connexion with those pantheistic theories[10] which locate an intelligent soul in material things, and have largely exercised men's minds in some modern systems of philosophy: it is traceable even in the graver writings of historians: it makes as much difference between ancient and modern landscape art,[11] as there is between the rough masks of any early mosaic and a portrait by Reynolds or Gainsborough. Of this new sense, the writings of Wordsworth are the central and elementary expression: he is more simply and entirely occupied with it than any other poet, though there are fine expressions of precisely the same thing in so different a poet as Shelley. There was in his own character a certain contentment, a sort of inborn religious placidity, seldom found united with a sensibility so mobile as his, which was favourable to the quiet, habitual observation of inanimate, or imperfectly animate, existence. His life of eighty years is divided by no very profoundly felt incidents: its changes are almost wholly inward, and it falls into broad, untroubled, perhaps somewhat monotonous spaces. What it most resembles is the life of one of those early Italian or Flemish painters, who, just because their minds were full of heavenly visions, passed, some of them, the better part of sixty years in quiet, systematic industry. This placid life matured a quite unusual sensibility, really innate in him, to the sights and sounds of the natural world—the flower and its shadow on the stone, the cuckoo and its echo.[12] The poem of *Resolution and Independence* is a storehouse of such records: for its fulness of imagery it may be compared to Keats's *Saint Agnes' Eve*.[13] To read one of his longer pastoral poems for the first time, is like a day spent in a new country: the memory is crowded for a while with its precise and vivid incidents—

> The pliant harebell swinging in the breeze
> On some grey rock;—[14]
>
> The single sheep and the one blasted tree
> And the bleak music from that old stone wall;—[15]
>
> In the meadows and the lower ground
> Was all the sweetness of a common dawn;—[16]
>
> And that green corn all day is rustling in thine ears.[17]

Clear and delicate at once, as he is in the outlining of visible imagery, he is more clear and delicate still, and finely scrupulous, in the noting of sounds; so that he conceives of noble sound as even moulding the human countenance to nobler types, and as something actually "profaned" by colour, by visible form, or image.[18] He has a power likewise of realising, and conveying to the consciousness of the reader, abstract and elementary impressions—silence, darkness, absolute motionlessness: or, again, the whole complex sentiment of a particular place, the abstract expression of desolation in the long white road, of peacefulness in a particular folding of the hills.[19] In the airy building of the brain, a special day or hour even, comes to have for him a sort of personal identity, a spirit or angel given to it, by which, for its exceptional insight, or the happy light upon it, it has a presence in one's history, and acts there, as a separate power or accomplishment; and he has celebrated in many of his poems the "efficacious spirit," which, as he says, resides in these "particular spots" of time.[20]

It is to such a world, and to a world of congruous meditation thereon, that we see him retiring in his but lately published poem of *The Recluse*—taking leave, without much count of costs, of the world of business, of action and ambition, as also of all that for the majority of mankind counts as sensuous enjoyment.*

---

* In Wordsworth's prefatory advertisement to the first edition of *The Prelude*, published in 1850, it is stated that that work was intended to be introductory to *The Recluse;* and that *The Recluse,* if completed, would have consisted of three parts. The second part is "The Excursion." The third part was only planned; but the first book of the first part was left in manuscript by Wordsworth—though in manuscript, it is said, in no great condition of forwardness for the printers. This book, now for the first time printed *in extenso* (a very noble passage from it found place in that prose advertisement to *The Excursion*), is included in the latest edition of Wordsworth by Mr. John Morley. It was well worth adding to the poet's great bequest to English literature. A true student of his work, who has formulated for himself what he supposes to be the leading characteristics of Wordsworth's genius, will feel, we think, lively interest in testing them by the various fine passages in what is here presented for the first time. Let the following serve for a sample:—

> Thickets full of songsters, and the voice
> Of lordly birds, an unexpected sound
> Heard now and then from morn to latest eve,
> Admonishing the man who walks below
> Of solitude and silence in the sky:—

And so it came about that this sense of a life in natural objects, which in most poetry is but a rhetorical artifice, is with Wordsworth the assertion of what for him is almost literal fact. To him every natural object seemed to possess more or less of a moral or spiritual life, to be capable of a companionship with man, full of expression, of inexplicable affinities and delicacies of intercourse.[21] An emanation,[22] a particular spirit, belonged, not to the moving leaves or water only, but to the distant peak of the hills arising suddenly, by some change of perspective, above the nearer horizon,[23] to the passing space of light across the plain, to the lichened Druidic stone even, for a certain weird fellowship in it with the moods of men.[24] It was like a "survival,"[25] in the peculiar intellectual temperament of a man of letters at the end of the eighteenth century, of that primitive condition, which some philosophers have traced in the general history of human culture, wherein all outward objects alike, including even the works of men's hands, were believed to be endowed with animation, and the world was "full of souls"—that mood in which the old Greek gods were first begotten, and which had many strange aftergrowths.[26]

In the early ages, this belief, delightful as its effects on poetry often are, was but the result of a crude intelligence. But, in Wordsworth, such power of seeing life, such perception of a soul, in inanimate things, came of an exceptional susceptibility to the impressions of eye and ear, and was, in its essence, a kind of sensuousness. At least, it is only in a

---

These have we, and a thousand nooks of earth
Have also these, but nowhere else is found,
Nowhere (or is it fancy?) can be found
The one sensation that is here; 'tis here,
Here as it found its way into my heart
In childhood, here as it abides by day,
By night, here only; or in chosen minds
That take it with them hence, where'er they go.
—'Tis, but I cannot name it, 'tis the sense
Of majesty, and beauty, and repose,
A blended holiness of earth and sky,
Something that makes this individual spot,
This small abiding-place of many men,
A termination, and a last retreat,
A centre, come from wheresoe'er you will.
A whole without dependence or defect,
Made for itself, and happy in itself,
Perfect contentment, Unity entire.

(Pater's own note.)

temperament exceptionally susceptible on the sensuous side, that this sense of the expressiveness of outward things comes to be so large a part of life. That he awakened "a sort of thought in sense," is Shelley's just estimate of this element in Wordsworth's poetry.[27]

And it was through nature, thus ennobled by a semblance of passion and thought, that he approached the spectacle of human life.[28] Human life, indeed, is for him, at first, only an additional, accidental grace[29] on an expressive landscape. When he thought of man, it was of man as in the presence and under the influence of these effective natural objects, and linked to them by many associations. The close connexion of man with natural objects, the habitual association of his thoughts and feelings with a particular spot of earth, has sometimes seemed to degrade those who are subject to its influence, as if it did but reinforce that physical connexion of our nature with the actual lime and clay of the soil, which is always drawing us nearer to our end. But for Wordsworth, these influences tended to the dignity of human nature, because they tended to tranquillise it. By raising nature to the level of human thought he gives it power and expression: he subdues man to the level of nature, and gives him thereby a certain breadth and coolness and solemnity. The leech-gatherer on the moor,[30] the woman "stepping westward,"[31] are for him natural objects, almost in the same sense as the aged thorn,[32] or the lichened rock on the heath.[33] In this sense the leader of the "Lake School," in spite of an earnest preoccupation with man, his thoughts, his destiny, is the poet of nature. And of nature, after all, in its modesty. The English lake country has, of course, its grandeurs. But the peculiar function of Wordsworth's genius, as carrying in it a power to open out the soul of apparently little or familiar things, would have found its true test had he become the poet of Surrey,[34] say! and the prophet of its life. The glories of Italy and Switzerland, though he did write a little about them, had too potent a material life of their own to serve greatly his poetic purpose.[35]

Religious sentiment, consecrating the affections and natural regrets of the human heart, above all, that pitiful awe and care for the perishing human clay, of which relic-worship is but the corruption, has always had much to do with localities, with the thoughts which attach themselves to actual scenes and places.[36] Now what is true of it everywhere, is

truest of it in those secluded valleys where one generation
after another maintains the same abiding-place; and it was on
this side, that Wordsworth apprehended religion most strongly.
Consisting, as it did so much, in the recognition of local
sanctities, in the habit of connecting the stones and trees of a
particular spot of earth with the great events of life, till the
low walls, the green mounds, the half-obliterated epitaphs
seemed full of voices,[87] and a sort of natural oracles, the very
religion of these people of the dales appeared but as another
link between them and the earth, and was literally a religion
of nature. It tranquillised them by bringing them under the
placid rule of traditional and narrowly localised observances.
"Grave livers," they seemed to him, under this aspect, with
stately speech, and something of that natural dignity of manners, which underlies the highest courtesy.[38]

And, seeing man thus as a part of nature, elevated and
solemnised in proportion as his daily life and occupations
brought him into companionship with permanent natural
objects, his very religion forming new links for him with the
narrow limits of the valley, the low vaults of his church, the
rough stones of his home, made intense for him now with
profound sentiment, Wordsworth was able to appreciate passion in the lowly. He chooses to depict people from humble
life, because, being nearer to nature than others, they are on
the whole more impassioned, certainly more direct in their
expression of passion, than other men: it is for this direct
expression of passion, that he values their humble words. In
much that he said in exaltation of rural life, he was but
pleading indirectly for that sincerity, that perfect fidelity to
one's own inward presentations, to the precise features of the
picture within, without which any profound poetry is impossible. It was not for their tameness, but for this passionate
sincerity, that he chose incidents and situations from common life, "related in a selection of language really used by
men."[39] He constantly endeavours to bring his language near
to the real language of men: to the real language of men,
however, not on the dead level of their ordinary intercourse,
but in select moments of vivid sensation, when this language
is winnowed and ennobled by excitement. There are poets
who have chosen rural life as their subject, for the sake of its
passionless repose, and times when Wordsworth himself extols
the mere calm and dispassionate survey of things as the highest aim of poetical culture. But it was not for such passionless

calm that he preferred the scenes of pastoral life; and the meditative poet, sheltering himself, as it might seem, from the agitations of the outward world, is in reality only clearing the scene for the great exhibitions of emotion, and what he values most is the almost elementary expression of elementary feelings.

And so he has much for those who value highly the concentrated presentment of passion, who appraise men and women by their susceptibility to it, and art and poetry as they afford the spectacle of it. Breaking from time to time into the pensive spectacle of their daily toil, their occupations near to nature, come those great elementary feelings, lifting and solemnising their language and giving it a natural music. The great, distinguishing passion came to Michael by the sheepfold, to Ruth by the wayside, adding these humble children of the furrow to the true aristocracy of passionate souls.[40] In this respect, Wordsworth's work resembles most that of George Sand, in those of her novels which depict country life.[41] With a penetrative pathos, which puts him in the same rank with the masters of the sentiment of pity in literature, with Meinhold[42] and Victor Hugo, he collects all the traces of vivid excitement which were to be found in that pastoral world—the girl who rung her father's knell; the unborn infant feeling about its mother's heart;[43] the instinctive touches of children;[44] the sorrows of the wild creatures, even—their home-sickness, their strange yearnings; the tales of passionate regret that hang by a ruined farm-building, a heap of stones, a deserted sheepfold;[45] that gay, false, adventurous, outer world, which breaks in from time to time to bewilder and deflower these quiet homes;[46] not "passionate sorrow"[47] only, for the overthrow of the soul's beauty, but the loss of, or carelessness for personal beauty[48] even, in those whom men have wronged—their pathetic wanness; the sailor "who, in his heart, was half a shepherd on the stormy seas";[49] the wild woman teaching her child to pray for her betrayer;[50] incidents like the making of the shepherd's staff, or that of the young boy laying the first stone of the sheepfold;[51]—all the pathetic episodes of their humble existence, their longing, their wonder at fortune, their poor pathetic pleasures, like the pleasures of children, won so hardly in the struggle for bare existence; their yearning towards each other, in their darkened houses, or at their early toil. A sort of biblical depth and solemnity hangs over this strange, new, passionate, pastoral world, of which he first raised the image, and the reflection of which some of our best modern fiction has caught from him.[52]

He pondered much over the philosophy of his poetry, and reading deeply in the history of his own mind, seems at times to have passed the borders of a world of strange speculations, inconsistent enough, had he cared to note such inconsistencies, with those traditional beliefs, which were otherwise the object of his devout acceptance. Thinking of the high value he set upon customariness, upon all that is habitual, local, rooted in the ground, in matters of religious sentiment, you might sometimes regard him as one tethered down to a world, refined and peaceful indeed, but with no broad outlook, a world protected, but somewhat narrowed, by the influence of received ideas. But he is at times also something very different from this, and something much bolder. A chance expression is overheard and placed in a new connexion,[53] the sudden memory of a thing long past occurs to him, a distant object is relieved for a while by a random gleam of light—accidents turning up for a moment what lies below the surface of our immediate experience—and he passes from the humble graves and lowly arches of "the little rock-like pile" of a Westmoreland church,[54] on bold trains of speculative thought, and comes, from point to point, into strange contact with thoughts which have visited, from time to time, far more venturesome, perhaps errant, spirits.

He had pondered deeply, for instance, on those strange reminiscences and forebodings, which seem to make our lives stretch before and behind us, beyond where we can see or touch anything, or trace the lines of connexion. Following the soul, backwards and forwards, on these endless ways, his sense of man's dim, potential powers became a pledge to him, indeed, of a future life, but carried him back also to that mysterious notion of an earlier state of existence—the fancy of the Platonists—the old heresy of Origen.[55] It was in this mood that he conceived those oft-reiterated regrets for a half-ideal childhood, when the relics of Paradise still clung about the soul—a childhood, as it seemed, full of the fruits of old age, lost for all, in a degree, in the passing away of the youth of the world, lost for each one, over again, in the passing away of actual youth. It is this ideal childhood which he celebrates in his famous *Ode on the Recollections of Child-*

hood, and some other poems which may be grouped around it, such as the lines on *Tintern Abbey*, and something like what he describes was actually truer of himself than he seems to have understood; for his own most delightful poems were really the instinctive productions of earlier life, and most surely for him, "the first diviner influence of this world"[56] passed away, more and more completely, in his contact with experience.

Sometimes as he dwelt upon those moments of profound, imaginative power, in which the outward object appears to take colour and expression, a new nature almost, from the prompting of the observant mind, the actual world would, as it were, dissolve and detach itself, flake by flake, and he himself seemed to be the creator, and when he would the destroyer, of the world in which he lived—that old isolating thought of many a brain-sick mystic of ancient and modern times.

At other times, again, in those periods of intense susceptibility, in which he appeared to himself as but the passive recipient of external influences, he was attracted by the thought of a spirit of life in outward things, a single, all-pervading mind in them, of which man, and even the poet's imaginative energy, are but moments—that old dream of the *anima mundi*, the mother of all things and their grave, in which some had desired to lose themselves, and others had become indifferent to the distinctions of good and evil.[57] It would come, sometimes, like the sign of the *macrocosm* to Faust in his cell:[58] the network of man and nature was seen to be pervaded by a common, universal life: a new, bold thought lifted him above the furrow, above the green turf of the Westmoreland churchyard, to a world altogether different in its vagueness and vastness, and the narrow glen was full of the brooding power of one universal spirit.[59]

And so he has something, also, for those who feel the fascination of bold speculative ideas, who are really capable of rising upon them to conditions of poetical thought. He uses them, indeed, always with a very fine apprehension of the limits within which alone philosophical imaginings have any place in true poetry; and using them only for poetical purposes, is not too careful even to make them consistent with each other. To him, theories which for other men bring a world of technical diction, brought perfect form and expression, as in those two lofty books of *The Prelude*, which describe the decay and the restoration of Imagination and Taste.[60] Skirting the borders of this world of bewildering heights and depths, he got but the first exciting influence of it, that joyful enthusiasm which great imaginative theories prompt, when the mind first comes to have an understanding of them; and it is not under the influence of these thoughts that his poetry becomes tedious or loses its blithness. He keeps them, too, always within certain ethical bounds, so that no word of his could offend the simplest of those simple souls which are always the largest portion of mankind. But it is, nevertheless, the contact of these thoughts, the speculative boldness in them, which constitutes, at least for some minds, the secret attraction of much of his best poetry—the sudden passage from lowly thoughts and places to the majestic forms of philosophical imagination, the play of these forms over a world so different, enlarging so strangely the bounds of its humble churchyards, and breaking such a wild light on the graves of christened children.[61]

And these moods always brought with them faultless expression. In regard to expression, as with feeling and thought, the duality of the higher and lower moods was absolute. It belonged to the higher, the imaginative mood, and was the pledge of its reality, to bring the appropriate language with it. In him, when the really poetical motive worked at all, it united, with absolute justice, the word and the idea; each, in the imaginative flame, becoming inseparably one with the other, by that fusion of matter and form, which is the characteristic of the highest poetical expression. His words are themselves thought and feeling; not eloquent, or musical words merely, but that sort of creative language which carries the reality of what it depicts, directly, to the consciousness.

The music of mere metre performs but a limited, yet a very peculiar and subtly ascertained function, in Wordsworth's poetry. With him, metre is but an additional grace, accessory to that deeper music of words and sounds, that moving power, which they exercise in the nobler prose no less than in formal poetry. It is a sedative to that excitement, an excitement sometimes almost painful, under which the language, alike of poetry and prose, attains a rhythmical power, independent of metrical combination, and dependent rather on some subtle adjustment of the elementary sounds of words themselves to the image or feeling they convey. Yet some of his pieces, pieces prompted by a sort of half-playful mysticism, like the *Daffodils* and *The Two April Mornings*, are distinguished by a certain quaint gaiety of metre, and rival by their perfect execution, in this respect, similar pieces among our own Elizabethan, or contemporary French poetry. And those who take up these poems after an interval of months, or years perhaps, may be surprised at finding how well old favourites wear, how their strange, inventive turns of diction or thought still send through them the old feeling of surprise. Those who lived about Wordsworth were all great lovers of the older English literature, and oftentimes there came out in him a noticeable likeness to our earlier poets. He quotes unconsciously, but with new power of meaning, a clause from one of Shakespeare's sonnets; and, as with some other men's most famous work, the *Ode on the Recollections of Childhood* had its anticipator.* He drew something too from the unconscious mysticism of the old English language itself, drawing out the inward significance of its racy idiom, and the not wholly unconscious poetry of the language used by the simplest people under strong excitement—language, therefore, at its origin.

The office of the poet is not that of the moralist, and the first aim of Wordsworth's poetry is to give the reader a peculiar kind of pleasure. But through his poetry, and through this pleasure in it, he does actually convey to the reader an extraordinary wisdom in the things of practice. One lesson, if men must have lessons, he conveys more clearly than all, the supreme importance of contemplation in the conduct of life.

Contemplation—impassioned contemplation—that, is with Wordsworth the end-in-itself, the perfect end. We see the majority of mankind going most often to definite ends, lower or higher ends, as their own instincts may determine; but the end may never be attained, and the means not be quite the right means, great ends and little ones alike being, for the most part, distant, and the ways to them, in this dim world, somewhat vague. Meantime, to higher or lower ends, they move too often with something of a sad countenance, with hurried and ignoble gait, becoming, unconsciously, something like thorns, in their anxiety to bear grapes; it being possible for people, in the pursuit of even great ends, to

* Henry Vaughan, in *The Retreat*. (Pater's own note.)

become themselves thin and impoverished in spirit and temper, thus diminishing the sum of perfection in the world, at
its very sources. We understand this when it is a question of
mean, or of intensely selfish ends—of Grandet, or Javert.[62]
We think it bad morality to say that the end justifies the
means, and we know how false to all higher conceptions of
the religious life is the type of one who is ready to do evil
that good may come. We contrast with such dark, mistaken
eagerness, a type like that of Saint Catherine of Siena, who
made the means to her ends so attractive, that she has
won for herself an undying place in the *House Beautiful*,[63]
not by her rectitude of soul only, but by its "fairness"—by
those quite different qualities which commend themselves to
the poet and the artist.

Yet, for most of us, the conception of means and ends
covers the whole of life, and is the exclusive type or figure
under which we represent our lives to ourselves. Such a figure, reducing all things to machinery, though it has on its
side the authority of that old Greek moralist who has fixed
for succeeding generations the outline of the theory of right
living, is too like a mere picture or description of men's lives
as we actually find them, to be the basis of the higher ethics.
It covers the meanness of men's daily lives, and much of the
dexterity and the vigour with which they pursue what may
seem to them the good of themselves or of others; but not
the intangible perfection of those whose ideal is rather in
being than in *doing*—not those *manners* which are, in the
deepest as in the simplest sense, *morals*, and without which
one cannot so much as offer a cup of water to a poor man
without offence—not the part of "antique Rachel," sitting in
the company of Beatrice;[64] and even the moralist might well
endeavour rather to withdraw men from the too exclusive
consideration of means and ends, in life.

Against this predominance of machinery in our existence,
Wordsworth's poetry, like all great art and poetry, is a continual protest. Justify rather the end by the means, it seems
to say: whatever may become of the fruit, make sure of the
flowers and the leaves. It was justly said, therefore, by one
who had meditated very profoundly on the true relation of
means to ends in life, and on the distinction between what is
desirable in itself and what is desirable only as machinery,
that when the battle which he and his friends were wag-
ing had been won, the world would need more than ever

those qualities which Wordsworth was keeping alive and nourishing.*

That the end of life is not action but contemplation—*being* as distinct from *doing*—a certain disposition of the mind: is, in some shape or other, the principle of all the higher morality. In poetry, in art, if you enter into their true spirit at all, you touch this principle, in a measure: these, by their very sterility, are a type of beholding for the mere joy of beholding. To treat life in the spirit of art, is to make life a thing in which means and ends are identified: to encourage such treatment, the true moral significance of art and poetry. Wordsworth, and other poets who have been like him in ancient or more recent times, are the masters, the experts, in this art of impassioned contemplation. Their work is, not to teach lessons, or enforce rules, or even to stimulate us to noble ends; but to withdraw the thoughts for a little while from the mere machinery of life, to fix them, with appropriate emotions, on the spectacle of those great facts in man's existence which no machinery affects, "on the great and universal passions of men, the most general and interesting of their occupations, and the entire world of nature,"—on "the operations of the elements and the appearances of the visible universe, on storm and sunshine, on the revolutions of the seasons, on cold and heat, on loss of friends and kindred, on injuries and resentments, on gratitude and hope, on fear and sorrow."[65] To witness this spectacle with appropriate emotions is the aim of all culture; and of these emotions poetry like Wordsworth's is a great nourisher and stimulant. He sees nature full of sentiment and excitement; he sees men and women as parts of nature, passionate, excited, in strange grouping and connexion with the grandeur and beauty of the natural world:—images, in his own words, "of man suffering, amid awful forms and powers."[66]

Such is the figure of the more powerful and original poet, hidden away, in part, under those weaker elements in Wordsworth's poetry, which for some minds determine their entire character; a poet somewhat bolder and more passionate than might at first sight be supposed, but not too bold for

* See an interesting paper, by Mr. John Morley, on "The Death of Mr. Mill," *Fortnightly Review,* June 1873. (Pater's own note.)

true poetical taste; an unimpassioned writer, you might sometimes fancy, yet thinking the chief aim, in life and art ailke,
to be a certain deep emotion; seeking most often the great
elementary passions in lowly places; having at least this
condition of all impassioned work, that he aims always at an
absolute sincerity of feeling and diction, so that he is the true
forerunner of the deepest and most passionate poetry of our
own day; yet going back also, with something of a protest
against the conventional fervour of much in the poetry popular in his own time, to those older Engligh poets, whose
unconscious likeness often comes out in him.

1874

NOTES

1. This distinction between the Fancy and the Imagination was
   made most notably by Coleridge in Chapter IV ff. of his
   Biographia Literaria. Leigh Hunt followed Coleridge in his
   book entitled *Imagination and Fancy*.
2. The emphasis upon *perception* here, and on the concentration of the poet's self, suggest Ruskin rather than Coleridge.
3. See Wordsworth's "Preface" of 1815, where too much unfortunately is made of this distinction.
4. This "right discipline of the temper as well as of the intellect"
   suggests Pater's psychological and moral notion of *askesis*,
   "half ethic, half physical" as he says in "Emerald Uthwart."
5. *Disciplina arcani:* arcane or secret discipline.
6. The influence of Ruskin is evident here, particularly in his
   tracing of the differences between ancient and modern landscape.
7. Etienne Pivert de Senancour (1770–1846), French novelist
   and moralist, wrote the epistolary romance, *Obermann,*
   greatly overrated by Matthew Arnold, with his customary
   bad judgment, who confounded the sentimental naturalism of
   Senancour with the finer visions of Goethe and Wordsworth.
8. Théophile Gautier (1811–1872), French man-of-letters,
   passed from an early High Romanticism to a polemical
   Aestheticism. Pater must be thinking of Gautier's earlier
   poetry.
9. Jean-Jacques Rousseau (1712–1778), Swiss-French visionary,
   is the true father of High Romanticism and its visionary
   naturalism, as Pater accurately implies here. François René,
   Vicomte de Chateaubriand (1768–1848), French diplomat,

romancer, and Christian polemicist, Pater sees (again accurately) as a major link between Rousseau and Hugo, the apotheosis of High Romanticism.

10. These pantheistic theories are presumably Schelling's; here as elsewhere Pater seems impatient with them, as he has a characteristic British empirical bias in metaphysics.

11. Though Pater declines to mention Ruskin here, as elsewhere, because of the anxieties-of-influence induced by Ruskin in him, the reference is certainly to *Modern Painters.*

12. See Wordsworth's "To the Cuckoo."

13. A strange judgment for Pater to have made, as "Resolution and Independence" is not a very Keatsian poem.

14. *The Prelude,* Book X.

15. *The Prelude,* Book XII.

16. *The Prelude,* Book IV.

17. "The Pet Lamb."

18. *The Prelude,* Book II.

19. *The Prelude,* Books I and II.

20. *The Prelude,* Book XII.

21. *The Prelude,* Book III.

22. *The Excursion,* Book IX, opening.

23. *The Prelude,* Book I.

24. *Guilt and Sorrow,* st. XIV.

25. "Survival": Pater uses this word in a consciously peculiar sense here, probably Viconian.

26. In *Plato and Platonism,* Pater was to link both Wordsworth and Shelley to the traditions of animism.

27. See Shelley's *Peter Bell the Third,* Part IV, where Shelley credits Wordsworth with "wakening a sort of thought in sense."

28. *The Prelude,* Book VIII.

29. *The Prelude,* Book VIII.

30. "Resolution and Independence."

31. "Stepping Westward."

32. "The Thorn."

33. "Resolution and Independence," IX.

34. That is, if like Pater he had been raised in the Surrey landscape.

35. *Descriptive Sketches; The Prelude,* Book VI.

36. Compare two Wordsworthian chapters of Pater's *Marius the Epicurean,* XXI and XXVI.

37. *The Excursion,* Book V.

38. "Resolution and Independence," XIV.

39. "Preface" to *Lyrical Ballads.*

40. "Michael" and "Ruth," where the great passion is self-destructive, almost apocalyptic hope, as it is in *The Ruined Cottage.*

41. George Sand (Amandine Aurore Lucie Dupin, 1804–1876), French novelist; Pater refers to her pastoral books, such as *La Petite Fadette.*
42. Johann Wilhelm Meinhold (1797–1851), German theologian and romancer, who may be thought of as Pater's version of Arnold's Senancour, since Pater overpraises him again in the "Postscript" on "Romanticism" in *Appreciations.*
43. "The Thorn," XIII.
44. "Her Eyes Are Wild," IV.
45. *The Ruined Cottage;* "Michael."
46. Propably "Ruth" or "Michael."
47. *The Prelude,* Book VII.
48. "Her Eyes Are Wild," VII.
49. "The Brothers."
50. "Her Eyes Are Wild," VIII.
51. "Michael."
52. It is difficult to know which novelists Pater means here, though we can justify his insight as being a prophecy of Hardy and Lawrence. But he *may* mean George Eliot, or even George Meredith.
53. Throughout *The Excursion,* Books II and III.
54. *The Prelude,* Book VII.
55. Origen (185-253), Alexandrian heterodox Christian theologian, who propounded the heresy of the pre-existence of the soul.
56. *The Prelude,* Book XII.
57. This dream of the *anima mundi* influenced Yeats in his highly Paterian *Per Amica Silentia Lunae.*
58. At the opening of Goethe's *Faust,* Part I.
59. *The Excursion,* Book VI.
60. Books XII and XIII.
61. *The Excursion,* Book VI.
62. Grandet is the heroic old man of Balzac's *Eugénie Grandet;* Javert is the remorseless, hunting policeman of Hugo's *Les Misérables.*
63. The *House Beautiful* is developed in the "Postscript" on "Romanticism." Its literary source is in John Bunyan's *The Pilgrim's Progress,* where Christian rests in it, and is able to see the Delectable Mountains from it.
64. See Dante's *Purgatorio,* XXVII, 105.
65. See the "Preface" to the Second Edition of *Lyrical Ballads.*
66. *The Prelude,* Book VIII.

Coleridge

Forms of intellectual and spiritual culture sometimes exercise their subtlest and most artful charm when life is already passing from them. Searching and irresistible as are the changes of the human spirit on its way to perfection, there is yet so much elasticity of temper that what must pass away sooner or later is not disengaged all at once, even from the highest order of minds. Nature, which by one law of development evolves ideas, hypotheses, modes of inward life, and represses them in turn, has in this way provided that the earlier growth should propel its fibres into the later, and so transmit the whole of its forces in an unbroken continuity of life. Then comes the spectacle of the reserve of the elder generation exquisitely refined by the antagonism of the new. That current of new life chastens them while they contend against it. Weaker minds fail to perceive the change: the clearest minds abandon themselves to it. To feel the change everywhere, yet not abandon oneself to it, is a situation of difficulty and contention. Communicating, in this way, to the passing stage of culture, the charm of what is chastened, high-strung, athletic, they yet detach the highest minds from the past, by pressing home its difficulties and finally proving it impossible. Such has been the charm of many leaders of lost causes in philosophy and in religion. It is the special charm of Coleridge, in connexion with those older methods of philosophic inquiry, over which the empirical philosophy of our day has triumphed.

Modern thought is distinguished from ancient by its cultivation of the "relative" spirit in place of the "absolute." Ancient philosophy sought to arrest every object in an eternal outline, to fix thought in a necessary formula, and the varieties of life in a classification by "kinds," or *genera*. To the modern spirit nothing is, or can be rightly known, except relatively and under conditions. The philosophical conception of the relative has been developed in modern times through the influence of the sciences of observation. Those sciences reveal types of life evanescing into each other by inexpressible refinements of change. Things pass into their opposites by accumulation of undefinable quantities. The growth of those sciences consists in a continual analysis of facts of rough and general observation into groups of facts more precise and minute. The faculty for truth is recognised as a power of distinguishing and fixing delicate and fugitive detail. The moral world is ever in contact with the physical, and the relative spirit has invaded moral philosophy from the ground of the inductive sciences. There it has started a new analysis of the relations of body and mind, good and evil, freedom and necessity. Hard and abstract moralities are yielding to a more exact estimate of the subtlety and complexity of our life. Always, as an organism increases in perfection, the conditions of its life become more complex. Man is the most complex of the products of nature. Character merges into temperament: the nervous system refines itself into intellect. Man's physical organism is played upon not only by the physical conditions about it, but by remote laws of inheritance, the vibration of long-past acts reaching him in the midst of the new order of things in which he lives. When we have estimated these conditions he is still not yet simple and isolated; for the mind of the race, the character of the age, sway him this way or that through the medium of language and current ideas. It seems as if the most opposite statements about him were alike true: he is so receptive, all the influences of nature and of society ceaselessly playing upon him, so that every hour in his life is unique, changed altogether by a stray word, or glance, or touch. It is the truth of these relations that experience gives us, not the truth of eternal outlines ascertained once for all, but a world of fine gradations and subtly linked conditions, shifting intricately as we ourselves change —and bids us, by a constant clearing of the organs of observation and perfecting of analysis, to make what we can of these. To the intellect, the critical spirit, just these subtleties of effect are more precious than anything else. What is lost in precision of form is gained in intricacy of expression. It is no vague scholastic abstraction that will satisfy the speculative instinct in our modern minds. Who would change the colour or curve of a roseleaf for that οὐσία ἀχρώματος, ἀσχημάτιστος, ἀναφὴς—that colourless, formless, intangible, being —Plato put so high?[1] For the true illustration of the speculative temper is not the Hindoo mystic, lost to sense, understanding, individuality, but one such as Goethe, to whom every moment of life brought its contribution of experimental, individual knowledge; by whom no touch of the world of form, colour, and passion was disregarded.

Now the literary life of Coleridge was a disinterested struggle against the relative spirit. With a strong native bent towards the tracking of all questions, critical or practical, to first principles, he is ever restlessly scheming to "apprehend the absolute," to affirm it effectively, to get it acknowledged. It was an effort, surely, an effort of sickly thought, that saddened his mind, and limited the operation of his unique poetic gift.

So what the reader of our own generation will least find in Coleridge's prose writings is the excitement of the literary sense. And yet, in those grey volumes, we have the larger part of the production of one who made way ever by a charm, the charm of voice, of aspect, of language, above all by the intellectual charm of new, moving, luminous ideas. Perhaps the chief offence in Coleridge is an excess of seriousness, a seriousness arising not from any moral principle, but from a misconception of the perfect manner. There is a certain shade of unconcern, the perfect manner of the eighteenth century, which may be thought to mark complete culture in the handling of abstract questions. The humanist, the possessor of that complete culture, does not "weep" over the failure of "a theory of the quantification of the predicate," nor "shriek" over the fall of a philosophical formula. A kind of humour is, in truth, one of the conditions of the just mental attitude, in the criticism of bypast stages of thought. Humanity cannot afford to be too serious about them, any more than a man of good sense can afford to be too serious in looking back upon his own childhood. Plato, whom Coleridge claims as the first of his spiritual ancestors, Plato, as we remember him, a true humanist, holds his theories lightly, glances with a somewhat blithe and naive inconsequence from one view to another, not anticipating the burden of importance "views" will one day have for men. In reading him one feels how lately it was that Crœsus thought it a paradox to say that external prosperity was not necessarily happiness.[2] But on Coleridge lies the whole weight of the sad reflection that has since come into the world, with which for us the air is full, which the "children in the market-place" repeat to each other.

His very language is forced and broken lest some saving formula should be lost—*distinctities, enucleation, pentad of operative Christianity*; he has a whole armoury of these terms, and expects to turn the tide of human thought by fixing the sense of such expressions as "reason," "understanding," "idea." Again, he lacks the jealousy of a true artist in excluding all associations that have no colour, or charm, or gladness in them; and everywhere allows the impress of a somewhat inferior theological literature.

"I was driven from life in motion to life in thought and sensation:" so Coleridge sums up his childhood, with its delicacy, its sensitiveness, and passion. But at twenty-five he was exercising a wonderful charm, and had already defined for himself his peculiar line of intellectual activity. He had an odd, attractive gift of conversation, or rather of monologue, as Madame de Staël[3] observed of him, full of *bizarreries*,[4] with the rapid alternations of a dream, and here or there an unexpected summons into a world strange to the hearer, abounding in images drawn from a sort of divided imperfect life, the consciousness of the opium-eater, as of one to whom the external world penetrated only in part, and, blent with all this, passages of deep obscurity, precious, if at all, only for their musical cadence, echoes in Coleridge of the eloquence of those older English writers of whom he was so ardent a lover. And all through this brilliant early manhood we may discern the power of the "Asiatic" temperament,[5] of that voluptuousness, which is connected perhaps with his appreciation of the intimacy, the almost mystical communion of touch, between nature and man. "I am much better," he writes, "and my new and tender health is all over me like a voluptuous feeling." And whatever fame, or charm, or life-inspiring gift he has had as a speculative thinker, is the vibration of the interest he excited then, the propulsion into years which clouded his early promise of that first buoyant, irresistible, self-assertion. So great is even the indirect power of a sincere effort towards the ideal life, of even a temporary escape of the spirit from routine.

In 1798 he visited Germany, then, the only half-known, "promised land," of the metaphysical, the "absolute," philosophy. A beautiful fragment of this period remains, describing a spring excursion to the Brocken. His excitement still vibrates in it. Love, all joyful states of mind, are self-expressive: they loosen the tongue, they fill the thoughts with sensuous images, they harmonise one with the world of sight. We hear of the "rich graciousness and courtesy" of Coleridge's manner, of the white and delicate skin, the abundant black hair, the full, almost animal lips—that whole physiognomy of the dreamer, already touched with narcotism. One says, of the beginning of one of his Unitarian sermons: "His voice rose like a stream of rich, distilled perfumes;" another, "He talks like an angel, and does—nothing!"

The *Aids to Reflection, The Friend, The Biographia Literaria:* those books came from one whose vocation was in the world of the imagination, the theory and practice of poetry. And yet, perhaps, of all books that have been influential in modern times, they are furthest from artistic form—bundles of notes; the original matter inseparably mixed up with that borrowed from others; the whole, just that mere preparation for an artistic effect which the finished literary artist would be careful one day to destroy. Here, again, we have a trait profoundly characteristic of Coleridge. He sometimes attempts to reduce a phase of thought, subtle and exquisite, to conditions too rough for it. He uses a purely speculative gift for direct moral edification. Scientific truth is a thing fugitive, relative, full of fine gradations: he tries to fix it in absolute formulas. The *Aids to Reflection, The Friend,* are efforts to propagate the volatile spirit of conversation into the less ethereal fabric of a written book; and it is only here or there that the poorer matter becomes vibrant, is really lifted by the spirit.

De Quincey said of him that "he wanted better bread than can be made with wheat:"[6] Lamb, that from childhood he had "hungered for eternity."[7] Yet the faintness, the continuous dissolution, whatever its cause, which soon supplanted the buoyancy of his first wonderful years, had its own consumptive refinements, and even brought, as to the "Beautiful Soul" in *Wilhelm Meister,*[8] a faint religious ectasy—that "singing in the sails" which is not of the breeze.[9] Here again is one of his occasional notes:—

"In looking at objects of nature while I am thinking, as at yonder moon, dim-glimmering through the window-pane, I seem rather to be seeking, as it were asking, a symbolical language for something within me, that already and for ever exists, than observing anything new. Even when the latter is the case, yet still I have always an obscure feeling, as if that new phenomenon were the dim awaking of a forgotten or hidden truth of my inner nature. While I was preparing the pen to make this remark, I lost the train of thought which had led me to it."

What a distemper of the eye of the mind! What an almost bodily distemper there is in that!

Coleridge's intellectual sorrows were many; but he had one singular intellectual happiness. With an inborn taste for transcendental philosophy, he lived just at the time when that philosophy took an immense spring in Germany, and connected itself with an impressive literary movement. He had the good luck to light upon it in its freshness, and introduce it to his countrymen. What an opportunity for one reared on the colourless analytic English philosophies of the last century, but who feels an irresistible attraction towards bold metaphysical synthesis! How rare are such occasions of intellectual contentment! This transcendental philosophy, chiefly as systematised by the mystic Schelling,[10] Coleridge applied with an eager, unwearied subtlety, to the questions of theology, and poetic or artistic criticism. It is in his theory of poetry, of art, that he comes nearest to principles of permanent truth and importance: that is the least fugitive part of his prose work. What, then, is the essence of his philosophy of art—of imaginative production?

Generally, it may be described as an attempt to reclaim the world of art as a world of fixed laws, to show that the creative activity of genius and the simplest act of thought are but higher and lower products of the laws of a universal logic. Criticism, feeling its own inadequacy in dealing with the greater works of art, is sometimes tempted to make too much of those dark and capricious suggestions of *genius*, which even the intellect possessed by them is unable to explain or recall. It has seemed due to the half-sacred character of those works to ignore all analogy between the productive process by which they had their birth, and the simpler processes of mind. Coleridge, on the other hand, assumes that the highest phases of thought must be more, not less, than the lower, subject to law.

With this interest, in the *Biographia Literaria*, he refines Schelling's "Philosophy of Nature" into a theory of art. "There can be no plagiarism in philosophy," says Heine:—*Es giebt kein Plagiat in der Philosophie*,[11] in reference to the charge brought against Schelling of unacknowledged borrowing from Bruno;[12] and certainly that which is common to Coleridge and Schelling and Bruno alike is of far earlier origin than any of them. Schellingism, the "Philosophy of Nature," is indeed a constant tradition in the history of thought: it embodies a permanent type of the speculative temper. That mode of conceiving nature as a mirror or reflex of the intelligence of man may be traced up to the first beginnings of Greek speculation. There are two ways of envisaging those aspects of nature which seem to bear the impress of reason or intelligence. There is the deist's way, which regards them merely as marks of design, which separates the informing mind from its result in nature, as the mechanist from the machine; and there is the pantheistic way, which identifies the two, which regards nature itself as the living energy of an intelligence of the same kind as though vaster in scope than the human. Partly through the influence of mythology, the Greek mind became early possessed with the conception of nature as living, thinking, almost speaking to the mind of man. This unfixed poetical prepossession, reduced to an abstract form, petrified into an idea, is the force which gives unity of aim to Greek philosophy. Little by little, it works out the substance of the Hegelian formula: "Whatever is, is according to reason: whatever is according to reason, that is." Experience, which has gradually saddened the earth's colours for us, stiffened its motions, withdrawn from it some blithe and debonair presence, has quite changed the character of the science of nature, as we understand it. The "positive" method, in truth, makes very little account of marks of intelligence in nature: in its wider view of phenonema, it sees that those instances are a minority, and may rank as happy coincidences: it absorbs them in the larger conception of universal mechanical law. But the suspicion of a mind latent in nature, struggling for release, and intercourse with the intellect of man through true ideas, has never ceased to haunt a certain class of minds. Started again and again in successive periods by enthusiasts on the antique pattern, in each case the thought may have seemed paler and more fantastic amid the growing consistency and sharpness of outline of other and more positive forms of knowledge. Still, wherever the speculative instinct has been united with a certain poetic inwardness of temperament, as in Bruno, in Schelling, there that old Greek conception, like some seed floating in the air, has taken root and sprung up anew. Coleridge, thrust inward upon himself, driven from "life in thought and sensation" to life in thought only, feels already, in his dark London school, a thread of the Greek mind on this matter vibrating strongly in him. At fifteen he is discoursing on Plotinus,[18] as in later years he reflects from Schelling that flitting intellectual tradition. He supposes a subtle, sympathetic co-ordination between the ideas of the human reason and the laws of the natural world. Science, the real knowledge of that natural world, is to be attained, not by observation, experiment, analysis, patient generalisation, but by the evolution or recovery of those ideas directly from within, by a sort of Platonic "recollection"; every group of observed facts remaining an enigma until the appropriate idea struck upon them from the mind of a Newton, or a Cuvier,[14] the genius in whom sympathy with the universal reason becomes entire. In the next place, he conceives that this reason or intelligence in nature becomes reflective, or self-conscious. He fancies he can trace, through all the simpler forms of life, fragments of an eloquent prophesy about the human mind. The whole of nature he regards as a development of higher forms out of the lower, through shade after shade of systematic change. The dim stir of chemical atoms towards the axis of crystal form, the trance-like life of plants, the animal troubled by strange irritabilities, are stages which anticipate consciousness. All through the ever-increasing movement of life that was shaping itself; every successive phase of life, in its unsatisfied susceptibilities, seeming to be drawn out of its own limits by the more pronounced current of life on its confines, the "shadow of approaching humanity" gradually deepening, the latent intelligence winning a way to the surface. And at this point the law of development does not lose itself in caprice: rather it becomes more constraining and incisive. From the lowest to the very highest acts of the conscious intelligence, there is another series of refining shades. Gradually the mind concentrates itself, frees itself from the limitations of the particular, the individual, attains a strange power of modifying and centralising what it receives from without, according to the pattern of an inward ideal. At last, in imaginative genius, ideas become effective: the intelligence of nature, all its discursive elements now connected and justified, is clearly reflected; the interpretation of its latent purposes being embodied in the great central products of creative art. The secret of creative genius would be an exquisitely purged sympathy with nature, with the reasonable soul antecedent there. Those associative conceptions of the imagination, those eternally fixed types of action and passion, would come, not so much from the conscious invention of the artist, as from his self-surrender to the suggestions of an abstract reason or ideality in things: they would be evolved by the stir of nature itself, realising the highest reach of its dormant reason: they would have a kind of prevenient necessity to rise at some time to the surface of the human mind.

It is natural that Shakespeare should be the favourite illustration of such criticism, whether in England or Germany. The first suggestion in Shakespeare is that of capricious detail, of a waywardness that plays with the parts careless of the impression of the whole; what supervenes is the constraining unity of effect, the ineffaceable impression, of Hamlet or Macbeth. His hand moving freely is curved round as if by some law of gravitation from within: an energetic unity or identity makes itself visible amid an abounding variety. This unity or identity Coleridge exaggerates into something like the identity of a natural organism, and the associative act which effected it into something closely akin to the primitive power of nature itself. "In the Shakespearian drama," he says, "there is a vitality which grows and evolves itself from within."

Again—

He, too, worked in the spirit of nature, by evolving the germ from within, by the imaginative power, according to the idea. For as the power of seeing is to light, so is an idea in mind to a law in nature. They are correlatives which suppose each other.

Again—

The organic form is innate: it shapes, as it develops, itself from within, and the fulness of its development is one and the same with the perfection of its outward form. Such as the life is, such is the form. Nature, the prime, genial artist, inexhaustible in diverse powers, is equally inexhaustible in forms: each exterior is the physiognomy of the being within, and even such is the appropriate excellence of Shakespeare, himself a nature humanised, a genial understanding, directing self-consciously a power and an implicit wisdom deeper even than our consciousness.

In this late age we are become so familiarised with the greater works of art as to be little sensitive of the act of creation in them: they do not impress us as a new presence in the world. Only sometimes, in productions which realise immediately a profound influence and enforce a change in taste, we are actual witnesses of the moulding of an unforeseen type by some new principle of association; and to that phenomenon Coleridge wisely recalls our attention. What makes his view a one-sided one is, that in it the artist has become almost a mechanical agent: instead of the most luminous and self-possessed phase of consciousness, the associative act in art or poetry is made to look like some blindly organic process of assimilation. The work of art is likened to a living organism. That expresses truly the sense of a self-delighting, independent life which the finished work of art gives us: it hardly figures the process by which such work was produced. Here there is no blind ferment of lifeless elements towards the realisation of a type. By exquisite analysis the artist attains clearness of idea; then, through many stages of refining, clearness of expression. He moves slowly over his work, calculating the tenderest tone, and restraining the subtlest curve, never letting hand or fancy move at large, gradually enforcing flaccid spaces to the higher degree of expressiveness. The philosophic critic, at least, will value, even in works of imagination, seemingly the most intuitive, the power of the understanding in them, their logical process of construction, the spectacle of a supreme intellectual dexterity which they afford.

Coleridge's prose writings on philosophy, politics, religion, and criticism, were, in truth, but one element in a whole lifetime of endeavours to present the then recent metaphysics of Germany to English readers, as a legitimate expansion of the older, classical and native masters of what has been variously called the *a priori*, or absolute, or spiritual, or Platonic, view of things. His criticism, his challenge for recognition in the concrete, visible, finite work of art, of the dim, unseen, comparatively infinite, soul or power of the artist, may well be remembered as part of the long pleading of German culture for the things "behind the veil."[15] To introduce that spiritual philosophy, as represented by the more transcendental parts of Kant,[16] and by Schelling, into all subjects, as a system of reason in them, one and ever identical with itself, however various the matter through which it was diffused, became with him the motive of an unflagging enthusiasm, which seems to have been the one thread of continuity in a life otherwise singularly wanting in unity of purpose, and in which he was certainly far from uniformly at his best. Fragmentary and obscure, but often eloquent, and always at once earnest and ingenious, those writings, supplementing his remarkable gift of conversation, were directly and indirectly influential, even on some the furthest removed from Coleridge's own masters; on John Stuart Mill, for instance, and some of the earlier writers of the "high-church" school. Like his verse, they display him also in two other characters—as a student of words, and as a psychologist, that is, as a more minute observer or student than other men of the phenomena of mind. To note the recondite associations of words, old or new; to expound the logic, the reasonable soul, of their various uses; to recover the interest of older writers who had had a phraseology of their own—this was a vein of inquiry allied to his undoubted gift of tracking out and analysing curious modes of thought. A quaint fragment of verse on *Human Life* might serve to illustrate his study of the earlier English philosophical poetry.[17] The latter gift, that power of the "subtle-souled psychologist," as Shelley calls him,[18] seems to have been connected with some tendency to disease in the physical temperament, something of a morbid want of balance in those parts where the physical and intellectual elements mix most closely together, with a kind of languid visionariness, deep-seated in the very constitution of the "narcotist," who had quite a gift for "plucking the poisons of self-harm," and which the actual habit of taking opium, accidentally acquired, did but reinforce. This morbid languor of nature, connected both with his fitfulness of purpose and his rich delicate dreaminess, qualifies Coleridge's poetic composition even more than his prose; his verse, with the exception of his avowedly political poems, being, unlike that of the "Lake School," to which in some respects he belongs, singularly unaffected by any moral, or professional, or personal effort or ambition,—"written," as he says, "after the more violent emotions of sorrow, to give him pleasure, when perhaps nothing else could;" but coming thus, indeed, very close to his own most intimately personal characteristics, and having a certain languidly soothing grace or cadence, for its most fixed quality, from first to last. After some Platonic soliloquy on a flower opening on a fine day in February, he goes on—

> Dim similitudes
> Weaving in mortal strains, I've stolen one hour
> From anxious self, life's cruel taskmaster!
> And the warm wooings of this sunny day
> Tremble along my frame and harmonise
> The attempered organ, that even saddest thoughts
> Mix with some sweet sensations, like harsh tunes
> Played deftly on a sweet-toned instrument.[19]

The expression of two opposed, yet allied, elements of sensibility in these lines, is very true to Coleridge:—the grievous agitation, the grievous listlessness, almost never entirely relieved, together with a certain physical voluptuousness. He has spoken several times of the scent of the bean-field in the air:—the tropical touches in a chilly climate; his is a nature that will make the most of these, which finds a sort of caress in such things. *Kubla Khan*, the fragment of a poem actually composed in some certainly not quite healthy sleep, is perhaps chiefly of interest as showing, by the mode of its composition, how physical, how much of a diseased or valetudinarian temperament, in its moments of relief, Coleridge's happiest gift really was; and side by side with *Kubla Khan* should be read, as Coleridge placed it, the *Pains of Sleep*, to illustrate that retarding physical burden in his temperament, that "unimpassioned grief,"[20] the source of which lay so near the source of those pleasures. Connected also with this, and again in contrast with Wordsworth, is the limited quantity of his poetical performance, as he himself regrets so eloquently in the lines addressed to Wordsworth after his recitation of *The Prelude*. It is like some exotic plant, just managing to blossom a little in the somewhat un-english air of Coleridge's own south-western birthplace,[21] but never quite well there.

In 1798 he joined Wordsworth in the composition of a volume of poems—the *Lyrical Ballads*. What Wordsworth then wrote already vibrates with that blithe impulse which carried him to final happiness and self-possession. In Coleridge we feel already that faintness and obscure dejection which clung like some contagious damp to all his work. Wordsworth was to be distinguished by a joyful and penetrative conviction of the existence of certain latent affinities between nature and the human mind, which reciprocally gild the mind and nature with a kind of "heavenly alchemy."

> My voice proclaims
> How exquisitely the individual mind
> (And the progressive powers, perhaps, no less
> Of the whole species) to the external world
> Is fitted; and how exquisitely, too,
> The external world is fitted to the mind;
> And the creation, by no lower name
> Can it be called, which they with blended might
> Accomplish.[22]

In Wordsworth this took the form of an unbroken dreaming over the aspects and transitions of nature—a reflective, though altogether unformulated, analysis of them.

There are in Coleridge's poems expressions of this conviction as deep as Wordsworth's. But Coleridge could never have abandoned himself to the dream, the vision, as Wordsworth did, because the first condition of such abandonment must be an unvexed quietness of heart. No one can read the *Lines composed above Tintern* without feeling how potent the physical element was among the conditions of Wordsworth's genius —"felt in the blood and felt along the heart."[23]

> My whole life I have lived in quiet thought![24]

The stimulus which most artists require of nature he can renounce. He leaves the ready-made glory of the Swiss mountains that he may reflect glory on a mouldering leaf. He loves best to watch the floating thistledown, because of its hint at an unseen life in the air. Coleridge's temperament, ἀεί ἐν σφοδρᾷ ὀρέξει,[25] with its faintness, its grieved dejection, could never have been like that.

> My genial spirits fail;
> And what can these avail
> To lift the smothering weight from off my breast?
> It were a vain endeavour,
> Though I should gaze for ever
> On that green light that lingers in the west:
> I may not hope from outward forms to win
> The passion and the life whose fountains are within.[26]

Wordsworth's flawless temperament, his fine mountain atmosphere of mind, that calm, sabbatic, mystic, wellbeing which De Quincey,[27] a little cynically, connected with worldly (that is to say, pecuniary) good fortune, kept his conviction of a latent intelligence in nature within the limits of sentiment or instinct, and confined it to those delicate and subdued shades of expression which alone perfect art allows. In Coleridge's sadder, more purely intellectual, cast of genius, what with Wordsworth was sentiment or instinct became a philosophical idea, or philosophical formula, developed, as much as possible, after the abstract and metaphysical fashion of the transcendental schools of Germany.

The period of Coleridge's residence at Nether Stowey, 1797–1798, was for him the *annus mirabilis*.[28] Nearly all the chief works by which his poetic fame will live were then composed or planned. What shapes itself for criticism as the main phenomenon of Coleridge's poetic life, is not, as with most true poets, the gradual development of a poetic gift, determined, enriched, retarded, by the actual circumstances of the poet's life, but the sudden blossoming, through one short season, of such a gift already perfect in its kind, which thereafter deteriorates as suddenly, with something like premature old age. Connecting this phenomenon with the leading motive of his prose writings, we might note it as the deterioration of a productive or creative power into one merely metaphysical or discursive. In his unambitious conception of his function as a poet, and in the very limited quantity of his poetical performance, as I have said, he was a contrast to his friend Wordsworth. That friendship with Wordsworth, the chief "developing" circumstance of his poetic life, comprehended a very close intellectual sympathy; and in such association chiefly, lies whatever truth there may be in the popular classification of Coleridge as a member of what is called the "Lake School." Coleridge's philosophical speculations do really turn on the ideas which underlay Wordsworth's poetical practice. His prose works are one long explanation of all that is involved in that famous distinction between the Fancy and the Imagination. Of what is understood by both writers as the imaginative quality in the use of poetic figures, we may take some words of Shakespeare as an example.—

My cousin Suffolk,
My soul shall thine keep company to heaven:
Tarry, sweet soul, for mine, then fly abreast.[29]

The complete infusion here of the figure into the thought, so vividly realised, that, though birds are not actually mentioned, yet the sense of their flight, conveyed to us by the single word "abreast," comes to be more than half of the thought itself:—this, as the expression of exalted feeling, is an instance of what Coleridge meant by Imagination. And this sort of identification of the poet's thought, of himself, with the image or figure which serves him, is the secret, sometimes, of a singularly entire realisation of that image, such as makes these lines of Coleridge, for instance, "imaginative"—

> Amid the howl of more than wintry storms,
> The halcyon hears the voice of vernal hours
> Already on the wing.[30]

There are many such figures both in Coleridge's verse and prose. He has, too, his passages of that sort of impassioned contemplation on the permanent and elementary conditions of nature and humanity, which Wordsworth held to be the essence of a poet;[31] as it would be his proper function to awaken such contemplation in other men—those "moments," as Coleridge says, addressing him—

> Moments awful,
> Now in thy inner life, and now abroad,
> When power streamed from thee, and thy soul received
> The light reflected, as a light bestowed.[32]

The entire poem from which these lines are taken, "composed on the night after Wordsworth's recitation of a poem on the growth of an individual mind," is, in its high-pitched strain of meditation, and in the combined justice and elevation of its philosophical expression—

> high and passionate thoughts
> To their own music chanted;[33]

wholly sympathetic with *The Prelude*, which it celebrates, and of which the subject is, in effect, the generation of the spirit of the "Lake poetry." The *Lines to Joseph Cottle* have the same philosophically imaginative character; the *Ode to Dejection* being Coleridge's most sustained effort of this kind.

It is in a highly sensitive apprehension of the aspects of external nature that Coleridge identifies himself most closely with one of the main tendencies of the "Lake School"; a tendency instinctive, and no mere matter of theory, in him as in Wordsworth. That record of the

> green light
> Which lingers in the west,

and again, of

> the western sky,
> And its peculiar tint of yellow green,[34]

which Byron found ludicrously untrue, but which surely needs no defence, is a characteristic example of a singular watchfulness for the minute fact and expression of natural scenery pervading all he wrote—a closeness to the exact physiognomy of nature, having something to do with that idealistic philosophy which sees in the external world no mere concurrence of mechanical agencies, but an animated body, informed and made expressive, like the body of man, by an indwelling intelligence. It was a tendency, doubtless, in the air, for Shelley too is affected by it, and Turner,[35] with the school of landscape which followed him. "I had found," Coleridge tells us,

> That outward forms, the loftiest, still receive
> Their finer influence from the world within;
> Fair ciphers of vague import, where the eye
> Traces no spot, in which the heart may read
> History and prophecy: . . .[36]

and this induces in him no indifference to actual colour and form and process, but such minute realism as this—

> The thin grey cloud is spread on high,
> It covers but not hides the sky.
> The moon is behind and at the full;
> And yet she looks both small and dull;

or this, which has a touch of "romantic" weirdness—

> Nought was green upon the oak
> But moss and rarest misletoe:

or this—

> There is not wind enough to twirl
> The one red leaf, the last of its clan,
> That dances as often as dance it can,
> Hanging so light, and hanging so high,
> On the topmost twig that looks up at the sky:[37]

or this, with a weirdness, again, like that of some wild French etcher—

> Lo! the new-moon winter-bright!
> And overspread with phantom light
> (With swimming phantom light o'erspread,
> But rimmed and circled with a silver thread)
> I see the old moon in her lap, foretelling
> The coming on of rain and squally blast.[38]

He has a like imaginative apprehension of the silent and unseen processes of nature, its "ministries" of dew and frost, for instance; as when he writes, in April—

> A balmy night! and though the stars be dim,
> Yet let us think upon the vernal showers
> That gladden the green earth, and we shall find
> A pleasure in the dimness of the stars.[39]

Of such imaginative treatment of landscape there is no better instance than the description of *The Dell*, in *Fears in Solitude*—

> A green and silent spot amid the hills,
> A small and silent dell! O'er stiller place
> No singing skylark ever poised himself—
>   But the dell,
> Bathed by the mist is fresh and delicate
> As vernal cornfield, or the unripe flax
> When, through its half-transparent stalks, at eve,
> The level sunshine glimmers with green light:—
>
>   The gust that roared and died away
> To the distant tree—
>   heard and only heard
> In this low dell, bowed not the delicate grass.[40]

This curious insistence of the mind on one particular spot, till it seems to attain actual expression and a sort of soul in

it—a mood so characteristic of the "Lake School"—occurs in
an earnest political poem, "written in April 1798, during the
alarm of an invasion"; and that silent dell is the background
against which the tumultuous fears of the poet are in strong
relief, while the quiet sense of the place, maintained all
through them, gives a true poetic unity to the piece. Good
political poetry—political poetry that shall be permanently
moving—can, perhaps, only be written on motives which, for
those they concern, have ceased to be open questions, and are
really beyond argument; while Coleridge's political poems are
for the most part on open questions. For although it was a
great part of his intellectual ambition to subject political questions to the action of the fundamental ideas of his philosophy,
he was nevertheless an ardent partisan, first on one side,
then on the other, of the actual politics proper to the end of
the last and the beginning of the present century, where there
is still room for much difference of opinion. Yet *The Destiny
of Nations*, though formless as a whole, and unfinished, presents many traces of his most elevated manner of speculation,
cast into that sort of imaginative philosophical expression, in
which, in effect, the language itself is inseparable from, or
essentially a part of, the thought. *France, an Ode*, begins with
a famous apostrophe to Liberty—

> Ye Clouds! that far above me float and pause,
>   Whose pathless march no mortal may control!
> Ye Ocean-waves! that wheresoe'er ye roll,
> Yield homage only to eternal laws!
> Ye Woods! that listen to the night-bird's singing,
>   Midway the smooth and perilous slope reclined,
> Save when your own imperious branches swinging,
>   Have made a solemn music of the wind!
> Where like a man beloved of God,
> Through glooms which never woodman trod,
>   How oft, pursuing fancies holy,
> My moonlight way o'er flowering weeds I wound,
> Inspired, beyond the guess of folly,
> By each rude shape and wild unconquerable sound!
> O ye loud Waves! and O ye Forests high!
>   And O ye Clouds that far above me soar'd!
> Thou rising Sun! thou blue rejoicing Sky!
> Yea, everything that is and will be free!
> Bear witness for me, wheresoe'er ye be,
> With what deep worship I have still adored
>   The spirit of divinest liberty.

And the whole ode, though, after Coleridge's way, not quite equal to that *exordium*,[41] is an example of strong national sentiment, partly in indignant reaction against his own earlier sympathy with the French Republic, inspiring a composition which, in spite of some turgid lines, really justifies itself as poetry, and has that true unity of effect which the ode requires. Liberty, after all his hopes of young France, is only to be found in nature:—

> Thou speedest on thy subtle pinions,
> The guide of homeless winds, and playmate of the waves![42]

In his changes of political sentiment, Coleridge was associated with the "Lake School"; and there is yet one other very different sort of sentiment in which he is one with that school, yet all himself, his sympathy, namely, with the animal world. That was a sentiment connected at once with the love of outward nature in himself and in the "Lake School," and its assertion of the natural affections in their simplicity; with the homeliness and pity, consequent upon that assertion. The *Lines to a Young Ass*, tethered—

> Where the close-eaten grass is scarcely seen,
> While sweet around her waves the tempting green,

which had seemed merely whimsical in their day, indicate a vein of interest constant in Coleridge's poems, and at its height in his greatest poems—in *Christabel*, where it has its effect, as it were antipathetically, in the vivid realisation of the serpentine element in Geraldine's nature; and in *The Ancient Mariner*, whose fate is interwoven with that of the wonderful bird, at whose blessing of the water-snakes the curse for the death of the albatross passes away, and where the moral of the love of all creatures, as a sort of religious duty, is definitely expressed.

Christabel, though not printed till 1816, was written mainly in the year 1797: *The Rhyme of the Ancient Mariner* was printed as a contribution to the *Lyrical Ballads* in 1798; and these two poems belong to the great year of Coleridge's poetic production, his twenty-fifth year. In poetic quality, above all in that most poetic of all qualities, a keen sense of, and delight in beauty, the infection of which lays hold upon the reader, they are quite out of proportion to all his other compositions.

The form in both is that of the ballad, with some of its terminology, and some also of its quaint conceits. They connect themselves with that revival of ballad literature, of which Percy's *Relics*,[43] and, in another way, Macpherson's *Ossian*[44] are monuments, and which afterwards so powerfully affected Scott—

> Young-eyed poesy
> All deftly masked as hoar antiquity.

The Ancient Mariner, as also, in its measure, *Christabel*, is a "romantic" poem, impressing us by bold invention, and appealing to that taste for the supernatural, that longing for *le frisson*, a shudder, to which the "romantic" school in Germany, and its derivations in England and France, directly ministered. In Coleridge, personally, this taste had been encouraged by his odd and out-of-the-way reading in the old-fashioned literature of the marvellous—books like Purchas's *Pilgrims*,[46] early voyages like Hakluyt's,[47] old naturalists and visionary moralists, like Thomas Burnet,[48] from whom he quotes the motto of *The Ancient Mariner*, "*Facile credo, plures esse naturas invisibiles quam visibiles in rerum universitate, etc.*"[49] Fancies of the strange things which may very well happen, even in broad daylight, to men shut up alone in ships far off on the sea, seem to have occurred to the human mind in all ages with a peculiar readiness, and often have about them, from the story of the stealing of Dionysus[50] downwards, the fascination of a certain dreamy grace, which distinguishes them from other kinds of marvellous inventions. This sort of fascination *The Ancient Mariner* brings to its highest degree: it is the delicacy, the dreamy grace, in his presentation of the marvellous, which makes Coleridge's work so remarkable. The too palpable intruders from a spiritual world in almost all ghost literature, in Scott and Shakespeare even, have a kind of crudity or coarseness. Coleridge's power is in the very fineness with which, as by some really ghostly finger, he brings home to our inmost sense his inventions, daring as they are—the skeleton ship, the polar spirit, the inspiriting of the dead corpses of the ship's crew. *The Rhyme of the Ancient Mariner* has the plausibility, the perfect adaptation to reason and the general aspect of life, which belongs to the marvellous, when actually presented as part of a credible experience in our dreams. Doubtless, the mere experience of the opium-eater,[51] the habit he must almost necessarily fall into of noting the more elusive phenomena of dreams, had something to do with that: in its essence, however, it is connected with a more purely intellectual circumstance in the development of Coleridge's poetic gift. Some one once asked William Blake, to whom Coleridge has many resemblances, when either is at his best (that whole episode of the re-inspiriting of the ship's crew in *The Ancient Mariner* being comparable to Blake's well-known design of the "Morning Stars singing together") whether he had ever seen a ghost, and was surprised when the famous seer, who ought, one might think, to have seen so many, answered frankly, "Only once!"[52] His "spirits," at once more delicate, and so much more real, than any ghost—the burden, as they were the privilege, of his *temperament*—like it, were an integral element in his everyday life. And the difference of mood expressed in that question and its answer, is indicative of a change of temper in regard to the supernatural which has passed over the whole modern mind, and of which the true measure is the influence of the writings of Swedenborg. What that change is we may see if we compare the vision by which Swedenborg was "called," as he thought, to his work, with the ghost which called Hamlet, or the spells of Marlowe's *Faust* with those of Goethe's.[53] The modern mind, so minutely self-scrutinising, if it is to be affected at all by a sense of the supernatural, needs to be more finely touched than was possible in the older, romantic presentment of it. The spectral object, so crude, so impossible, has become plausible, as

> The blot upon the brain,
> That *will* show itself without;[54]

and is understood to be but a condition of one's own mind, for which, according to the scepticism, latent at least, in so much of our modern philosophy, the so-called real things themselves are but *spectra* after all.

It is this finer, more delicately marvellous supernaturalism, fruit of his more delicate psychology, that Coleridge infuses into romantic adventure, itself also then a new or revived thing in English literature; and with a fineness of weird effect in *The Ancient Mariner*, unknown in those older, more simple, romantic legends and ballads. It is a flower of medieval

or later German romance, growing up in the peculiarly compounded atmosphere of modern psychological speculation,
and putting forth in it wholly new qualities. The quaint prose
commentary, which runs side by side with the verse of *The
Ancient Mariner*, illustrates this—a composition of quite a
different shade of beauty and merit from that of the verse
which it accompanies, connecting this, the chief poem of
Coleridge, with his philosophy, and emphasising therein that
psychological interest of which I have spoken, its curious
soul-lore.

Completeness, the perfectly rounded wholeness and unity
of the impression it leaves on the mind of a reader who fairly
gives himself to it—that, too, is one of the characteristics of
a really excellent work, in the poetic as in every other kind of
art; and by this completeness, *The Ancient Mariner* certainly
gains upon *Christabel*—a completeness, entire as that of
Wordsworth's *Leech-gatherer*, or Keats's *Saint Agnes' Eve*,
each typical in its way of such wholeness or entirety of effect
on a careful reader. It is Coleridge's one great complete work,
the one really finished thing, in a life of many beginnings.
Christabel remained a fragment. In *The Ancient Mariner* this
unity is secured in part by the skill with which the incidents
of the marriage-feast are made to break in dreamily from
time to time upon the main story. And then, how pleasantly,
how reassuringly, the whole nightmare story itself is made
to end, among the clear fresh sounds and lights of the bay,
where it began, with

> The moon-light steeped in silentness,
> The steady weather-cock.

So different from *The Rhyme of the Ancient Mariner* in
regard to this completeness of effect, *Christabel* illustrates the
same complexion of motives, a like intellectual situation.
Here, too, the work is of a kind peculiar to one who touches
the characteristic motives of the old romantic ballad, with a
spirit made subtle and fine by modern reflection; as we feel,
I think, in such passages as—

> But though my slumber had gone by,
> This dream it would not pass away—
> It seems to live upon mine eye;—

and—

> For she, belike, hath drunken deep
> Of all the blessedness of sleep;

and again—

> With such perplexity of mind
> As dreams too lively leave behind.[55]

And that gift of handling the finer passages of human feeling, at once with power and delicacy, which was another result of his finer psychology, of his exquisitely refined habit of self-reflection, is illustrated by a passage on Friendship in the *Second Part*—

> Alas! they had been friends in youth;
> But whispering tongues can poison truth;
> And constancy lives in realms above;
> And life is thorny; and youth is vain;
> And to be wroth with one we love,
> Doth work like madness in the brain.
> And thus it chanced, as I divine,
> With Roland and Sir Leoline.
> Each spake words of high disdain
> And insult to his heart's best brother:
> They parted—ne'er to meet again!
> But never either found another
> To free the hollow heart from paining—
> They stood aloof the scars remaining,
> Like cliffs which had been rent asunder;
> A dreary sea now flows between;
> But neither heat, nor frost, nor thunder,
> Shall wholly do away, I ween,
> The marks of that which once hath been.

I suppose these lines leave almost every reader with a quickened sense of the beauty and compass of human feeling; and it is the sense of such richness and beauty which, in spite of his "dejection," in spite of that burden of his morbid lassitude, accompanies Coleridge himself through life. A warm poetic joy in everything beautiful, whether it be a moral sentiment, like the friendship of Roland and Leoline, or only the flakes of falling light from the water-snakes[56]—this joy, visiting him, now and again, after sickly dreams, in sleep or

waking, as a relief not to be forgotten, and with such a power
of felicitous expression that the infection of it passes irresistibly to the reader—such is the predominant element in the
matter of his poetry, as cadence is the predominant quality
of its form. "We bless thee for our creation!" he might have
said, in his later period of definite religious assent, "because
the world is so beautiful: the world of ideas—living spirits,
detached from the divine nature itself, to inform and lift the
heavy mass of material things; the world of man, above all
in his melodious and intelligible speech; the world of living
creatures and natural scenery, the world of dreams." What
he really did say, by way of *A Tombless Epitaph*, is true
enough of himself—

> Sickness, 'tis true,
> Whole years of weary days, besieged him close,
> Even to the gates and inlets of his life!
> But it is true, no less, that strenuous, firm,
> And with a natural gladness, he maintained
> The citadel unconquered, and in joy
> Was strong to follow the delightful Muse.
> For not a hidden path, that to the shades
> Of the beloved Parnassian forest leads,
> Lurked undiscovered by him; not a rill
> There issues from the fount of Hippocrene,
> But he had traced it upward to its source,
> Through open glade, dark glen, and secret dell,
> Knew the gay wild flowers on its banks, and culled
> Its med'cinable herbs. Yea, oft alone,
> Piercing the long-neglected holy cave,
> The haunt obscure of old Philosophy,
> He bade with lifted torch its starry walls
> Sparkle, as erst they sparkled to the flame
> Of odorous lamps tended by saint and sage.
> O framed for calmer times and nobler hearts!
> O studious Poet, eloquent for truth!
> Philosopher! contemning wealth and death,
> Yet docile, childlike, full of Life and Love.

The student of empirical science asks, Are absolute principles attainable? What are the limits of knowledge? The answer
he receives from science itself is not ambiguous. What the
moralist asks is, Shall we gain or lose by surrendering human
life to the relative spirit? Experience answers that the dominant tendency of life is to turn ascertained truth into a dead

letter, to make us all the phlegmatic servants of routine. The relative spirit, by its constant dwelling on the more fugitive conditions or circumstances of things, breaking through a thousand rough and brutal classifications, and giving elasticity to inflexible principles, begets an intellectual *finesse* of which the ethical result is a delicate and tender justice in the criticism of human life. Who would gain more than Coleridge by criticism in such a spirit? We know how his life has appeared when judged by absolute standards. We see him trying to "apprehend the absolute," to stereotype forms of faith and philosophy, to attain, as he says, "fixed principles" in politics, morals, and religion, to fix one mode of life as the essence of life, refusing to see the parts as parts only; and all the time his own pathetic history pleads for a more elastic moral philosophy than his, and cries out against every formula less living and flexible than life itself.

"From his childhood he hungered for eternity." There, after all, is the incontestable claim of Coleridge. The perfect flower of any elementary type of life must always be precious to humanity, and Coleridge is a true flower of the *ennuyé*,[57] of the type of René.[58] More than Childe Harold,[59] more than Werther,[60] more than René himself, Coleridge, by what he did, what he was, and what he failed to do, represents that inexhaustible discontent, languor, and home-sickness, that endless regret, the chords of which ring all through our modern literature. It is to the romantic element in literature that those qualities belong. One day, perhaps, we may come to forget the distant horizon, with full knowledge of the situation, to be content with "what is here and now"; and herein is the essence of classical feeling. But by us of the present moment, certainly—by us for whom the Greek spirit, with its engaging naturalness, simple, chastened, debonair, τρυφῆς, ἁβρότητος, χλιδῆς, χαρίτων, ἱμέρου, πόθου πατήρ,[61] is itself the Sangrail[62] of an endless pilgrimage, Coleridge, with his passion for the absolute, for something fixed where all is moving, his faintness, his broken memory, his intellectual disquiet, may still be ranked among the interpreters of one of the constituent elements of our life.

1865, 1880

NOTES

1. Plato, *Phædrus*, 247C: "For the colorless, formless, intangible really existing being, with which all true knowledge deals, keeps this region [above the heavens] and is visible only to the mind, which is pilot to the soul."
2. For this story of Crœsus, see Herodotus, *History* I, 30-33.
3. Madame de Staël (1766–1817), notorious French High Romantic woman-of-letters, and nearly as a formidable a conversationalist as Coleridge himself.
4. *bizarreries:* "strangenesses."
5. "Asiatic" temperament suggests Pater's later dialectic (in *Greek Studies*) between on the one side "the centrifugal, the Ionian, the Asiatic tendency" and on the other "the centripetal, the Dorian, the European." Coleridge is thus an instance of "restless versatility," and "Asiatic" here is a synonym for "extravagant."
6. Thomas De Quincey, "Literary Reminiscences," *Collected Writings*, ed. David Masson (1896) II 185.
7. Charles Lamb, "On the Death of Coleridge."
8. Goethe's novel, *Wilhelm Meister's Lehrjahre* (1795–1796).
9. "The Rime of the Ancient Mariner," 367-381.
10. Friedrich Schelling (1775–1854), German metaphysician.
11. Heine's position, that there can be no plagiarism in philosophy, can be argued as being applicable to literature in general, as all influence is necessarily misinterpretation or misprision. Pater's defense of Coleridge here is more relevant today than ever before.
12. Giordano Bruno (1548–1600), great Italian speculator burned by the Inquisition.
13. Plotinus (205–270), Alexandrian founder of the Neoplatonic philosophy.
14. Georges Cuvier (1769–1832), French natural scientist.
15. Things "behind the veil" echoes Fitzgerald's *Rubaiyat of Omar Khayyam,* and refers to spiritual things.
16. Immanuel Kant (1724–1804), greatest of German philosophers.
17. Evidently refers to a passage by Robert Southwell, which Coleridge copied out under that title.
18. In Shelley's *Peter Bell the Third*, V.
19. From "On Observing a Blossom on the First of February, 1796."
20. From "Dejection: An Ode," 22.
21. Coleridge was born in Devonshire on October 21, 1772.
22. From Wordsworth's fragment of *The Recluse*; this passage

was printed as part of the verse—"Prospectus" to *The Excursion,* 1815.

23. Wordsworth's "Lines . . . Tintern Abbey," 28.
24. Wordsworth's "Resolution and Independence," 36.
25. "Always in excessive yearning."
26. "Dejection: An Ode," 39-46.
27. See De Quincey's "Literary and Lake Reminiscences," *Collected Writings II* 292.
28. *Annus mirabilis:* "marvelous year."
29. *Henry V,* Act IV, Scene VI, 15-17.
30. "To William Wordsworth," 89-91; Pater knew this poem under the title, "To a Gentleman."
31. In the "Preface" to *Lyrical Ballads.*
32. "To William Wordsworth," 17-20.
33. "To William Wordsworth," 46-47.
34. Both passages are from "Dejection: An Ode," but the first is misquoted from l. 44: "On that green light that lingers in the west," while the second accurately quotes ll. 28-29.
35. J. M. W. Turner (1775–1851), major English painter of landscape, sea, and sky; the particular favorite of Ruskin.
36. "Lines Written in the Album at Elbingerode, in the Hartz Forest," 16-21.
37. The three passages are from "Christable," 16-19, 33-34, 48-52.
38. "Dejection: An Ode," 9-14.
39. "The Nightingale," 8-11.
40. "Fears in Solitude," 1-3, 7-11, and 200-202 (not quite accurately).
41. *Exordium:* "introduction."
42. "France: An Ode," 97-98.
43. Bishop Thomas Percy, *Reliques of Ancient English Poetry,* 3 vols., 1765.
44. James Macpherson published *Fragments of Ancient Poetry* . . . (1760), supposedly translated from the Old Gaelic manuscripts of a bard named "Ossian," but Macpherson had concocted the manuscripts himself.
45. From Coleridge's "Monody on the Death of Chatterton," 143-144.
46. Samuel Purchas, *Purchas his Pilgrimes* (4 vols., 1625).
47. Richard Hakluyt, *The Principall Navigations, Voyages and Discoveries of the English Nation* (1589-1600).
48. Thomas Burnet, *The Sacred Theory of the Earth* (1681).
49. "I easily believe that there are more invisible than visible beings, in this universe of things, etc."
50. The god Dionysus was stolen as a boy by pirates, but he triumphed over them by metamorphizing them all into dolphins. Ezra Pound's "Canto II" beautifully retells the story, following Golding's version of Ovid.

51. Coleridge became addicted to opium after taking it first for rheumatic pains.
52. This anecdote is very dubious, like so many others in Alexander Gilchrist's *Life of William Blake*.
53. This psychologizing of the supernatural is to be expected of Pater, unlike his greatest disciple, Yeats.
54. Tennyson, *Maud*, II, IV, 60-61.
55. All three passages are from "Christabel," 557-559, 375-376, 385-386.
56. "The Rime of the Ancient Mariner," 276.
57. *Ennuyé:* "discontented and still yearning."
58. Chateaubriand's *René* (1805).
59. Byron's *Childe Harold's Pilgrimage* (1812-1817).
60. Goethe's *The Sorrows of Young Werther* (1774).
61. From Plato's *Symposium* 197 D, trans. Paul Shorey: "of wantonness, daintiness, luxury, grace, desire, and longing the sire."
62. The Holy Grail of the Arthurian myths.

Charles Lamb

Those English critics who at the beginning of the present century introduced from Germany, together with some other subtleties of thought transplanted hither not without advantage, the distinction between the *Fancy* and the *Imagination*, made much also of the cognate distinction between *Wit* and *Humour*, between that unreal and transitory mirth, which is as the crackling of thorns under the pot, and the laughter which blends with tears and even with the sublimities of the imagination, and which, in its most exquisite motives, is one with pity—the laughter of the comedies of Shakespeare, hardly less expressive than his moods of seriousness or solemnity, of that deeply stirred soul of sympathy in him, as flowing from which both tears and laughter are alike genuine and contagious.

This distinction between wit and humour, Coleridge and other kindred critics applied, with much effect, in their studies of some of our older English writers. And as the distinction between imagination and fancy, made popular by

Wordsworth, found its best justification in certain essential differences of stuff in Wordsworth's own writings, so this other critical distinction, between wit and humour, finds a sort of visible interpretation and instance in the character and writings of Charles Lamb;—one who lived more consistently than most writers among subtle literary theories, and whose remains are still full of curious interest for the student of literature as a fine art.

The author of the *English Humourists of the Eighteenth Century*, coming to the humourists of the nineteenth, would have found, as is true preeminently of Thackeray himself, the springs of pity in them deepened by the deeper subjectivity, the intenser and closer living with itself, which is characteristic of the temper of the later generation; and therewith, the mirth also, from the amalgam of which with pity humour proceeds, has become, in Charles Dickens, for example, freer and more boisterous.

To this more high-pitched feeling, since predominant in our literature, the writings of Charles Lamb, whose life occupies the last quarter of the eighteenth century and the first quarter of the nineteenth, are a transition; and such union of grave, of terrible even, with gay, we may note in the circumstances of his life, as reflected thence into his work. We catch the aroma of a singular, homely sweetness about his first years, spent on Thames' side, amid the red bricks and terraced gardens, with their rich historical memories of old-fashioned legal London. Just above the poorer class, deprived, as he says, of the "sweet food of academic institution," he is fortunate enough to be reared in the classical languages at an ancient school, where he becomes the companion of Coleridge, as at a later period he was his enthusiastic disciple. So far, the years go by with less than the usual share of boyish difficulties; protected, one fancies, seeing what he was afterwards, by some attraction of temper in the quaint child, small and delicate, with a certain Jewish expression in his clear, brown complexion, eyes not precisely of the same colour, and a slow walk adding to the staidness of his figure; and whose infirmity of speech, increased by agitation, is partly engaging.

And the cheerfulness of all this, of the mere aspect of Lamb's quiet subsequent life also, might make the more superficial reader think of him as in himself something slight, and of his mirth as cheaply bought. Yet we know that beneath this blithe surface there was something of the fateful domestic horror, of the beautiful heroism and devotedness too, of old Greek tragedy. His sister Mary, ten years his senior, in a sudden paroxysm of madness, caused the death of her mother, and was brought to trial for what an overstrained justice might have construed as the greatest of crimes. She was released on the brother's pledging himself to watch over her; and to this sister, from the age of twenty-one, Charles Lamb sacrificed himself, "seeking thenceforth," says his earliest biographer, "no connexion which could interfere with her supremacy in his affections, or impair his ability to sustain and comfort her." The "feverish, romantic tie of love," he cast away in exchange for the "charities of home." Only, from time to time, the madness returned, affecting him too, once; and we see the brother and sister voluntarily yielding to restraint. In estimating the humour of *Elia*, we must no more forget the strong undercurrent of this great misfortune and pity, than one could forget it in his actual story. So he becomes the best critic, almost the discoverer, of Webster, a dramatist of genius so sombre, so heavily coloured, so *macabre*. *Rosamund Grey*, written in his twenty-third year, a story with something bitter and exaggerated, an almost insane fixedness of gloom perceptible in it, strikes clearly this note in his work.

For himself, and from his own point of view, the exercise of his gift, of his literary art, came to gild or sweeten a life of monotonous labour, and seemed, as far as regarded others, no very important thing; availing to give them a little pleasure, and inform them a little, chiefly in a retrospective manner, but in no way concerned with the turning of the tides of the great world. And yet this very modesty, this unambitious way of conceiving his work, has impressed upon it a certain exceptional enduringness. For of the remarkable English writers contemporary with Lamb, many were greatly preoccupied with ideas of practice—religious, moral, political—ideas which have since, in some sense or other, entered permanently into the general consciousness; and, these having no longer any stimulus for a generation provided with a different stock of ideas, the writings of those who spent so much of themselves in their propagation have lost, with posterity, something of what they gained by them in immediate influence. Coleridge, Wordsworth, Shelley even—sharing so largely in the unrest of their own age, and made person-

ally more interesting thereby, yet, of their actual work, surrender more to the mere course of time than some of those
who may have seemed to exercise themselves hardly at all in
great matters, to have been little serious, or a little indifferent,
regarding them.

Of this number of the disinterested servants of literature,
smaller in England than in France, Charles Lamb is one. In
the making of prose he realises the principle of art for its
own sake, as completely as Keats in the making of verse.
And, working ever close to the concrete, to the details, great
or small, of actual things, books, persons, and with no part
of them blurred to his vision by the intervention of mere
abstract theories, he has reached an enduring moral effect
also, in a sort of boundless sympathy. Unoccupied, as he
might seem, with great matters, he is in immediate contact
with what is real, especially in its caressing littleness, that
littleness in which there is much of the whole woeful heart
of things, and meets it more than half-way with a perfect
understanding of it. What sudden, unexpected touches of
pathos in him!—bearing witness how the sorrow of humanity,
the *Weltschmerz*, the constant aching of its wounds, is ever
present with him: but what a gift also for the enjoyment of
life in its subtleties, of enjoyment actually refined by the
need of some thoughtful economies and making the most of
things! Little arts of happiness he is ready to teach to others.
The quaint remarks of children which another would scarcely
have heard, he preserves—little flies in the priceless amber of
his Attic wit—and has his "Praise of chimney-sweepers" (as
William Blake has written, with so much natural pathos, the
Chimney-sweeper's Song)[1] valuing carefully their white teeth,
and fine enjoyment of white sheets in stolen sleep at Arundel
Castle, as he tells the story, anticipating something of the
mood of our deep humourists of the last generation. His simple mother-pity for those who suffer by accident, or unkind-
ness of nature, blindness for instance, or fateful disease of
mind like his sister's, has something primitive in its largeness;
and on behalf of ill-used animals he is early in composing a
Pity's Gift.

And if, in deeper or more superficial sense, the dead *do*
care at all for their name and fame, then how must the souls
of Shakespeare and Webster have been stirred, after so long
converse with things that stopped their ears, whether above
or below the soil, at his exquisite appreciations of them; the

souls of Titian and of Hogarth too; for, what has not been observed so generally as the excellence of his literary criticism, Charles Lamb is a fine critic of painting also. It was as loyal, self-forgetful work for others, for Shakespeare's self first, for instance, and then for Shakespeare's readers, that that too was done: he has the true scholar's way of forgetting himself in his subject. For though "defrauded," as we saw, in his young years, "of the sweet food of academic institution," he is yet essentially a scholar, and all his work mainly retrospective, as I said; his own sorrows, affections, perceptions, being alone real to him of the present. "I cannot make these present times," he says once, "present to *me*."

Above all, he becomes not merely an expositor, permanently valuable, but for Englishmen almost the discoverer of the old English drama. "The book is such as I am glad there should be," he modestly says of the *Specimens of English Dramatic Poets who lived about the time of Shakespeare*; to which, however, he adds in a series of notes the very quintessence of criticism, the choicest savour and perfume of Elizabethan poetry being sorted, and stored here, with a sort of delicate intellectual epicureanism, which has had the effect of winning for these, then almost forgotten, poets, one generation after another of enthusiastic students. Could he but have known how fresh a source of culture he was evoking there for other generations, through all those years in which, a little wistfully, he would harp on the limitation of his time by business, and sigh for a better fortune in regard to literary opportunities!

To feel strongly the charm of an old poet or moralist, the literary charm of Burton, for instance, or Quarles, or The Duchess of Newcastle;[2] and then to interpret that charm, to convey it to others—he seeming to himself but to hand on to others, in mere humble ministration, that of which for them he is really the creator—this is the way of his criticism; cast off in a stray letter often, or passing note, or lightest essay or conversation. It is in such a letter, for instance, that we come upon a singularly penetrative estimate of the genius and writings of Defoe.

Tracking, with an attention always alert, the whole process of their production to its starting-point in the deep places of the mind, he seems to realise the but half-conscious intuitions of Hogarth or Shakespeare, and develops the great ruling unities which have swayed their actual work; or "puts up," and takes, the one morsel of good stuff in an old, forgotten writer. Even in what he says casually there comes an aroma of old English; noticeable echoes, in chance turn and phrase, of the great masters of style, the old masters. Godwin, seeing in quotation a passage from *John Woodvil*, takes it for a choice fragment of an old dramatist, and goes to Lamb to assist him in finding the author.[3] His power of delicate imitation in prose and verse reaches the length of a fine mimicry even, as in those last essays of Elia on Popular Fallacies, with their gentle reproduction or caricature of Sir Thomas Browne, showing, the more completely, his mastery, by disinterested study, of those elements of the man which were the real source of style in that great, solemn master of old English, who, ready to say what he has to say with fearless homeliness, yet continually overawes one with touches of a strange utterance from worlds afar. For it is with the delicacies of fine literature especially, its gradations of expression, its fine judgment, its pure sense of words, of vocabulary—things, alas! dying out in the English literature of the present, together with the appreciation of them in our literature of the past —that his literary mission is chiefly concerned. And yet, delicate, refining, daintily epicurean, as he may seem, when he writes of giants, such as Hogarth or Shakespeare, though often but in a stray note, you catch the sense of veneration with which those great names in past literature and art brooded over his intelligence, his undiminished impressibility by the great effects in them. Reading, commenting on Shakespeare, he is like a man who walks alone with a grand stormy sky, and among unwonted tricks of light, when powerful spirits might seem to be abroad upon the air; and the grim humour of Hogarth, as he analyses it, rises into a kind of spectral grotesque; while he too knows the secret of fine, significant touches like theirs.

There are traits, customs, characteristics of houses and dress, surviving morsels of old life, such as Hogarth has transferred so vividly into *The Rake's Progress*, or *Marriage à la Mode*, concerning which we well understand how, common, uninteresting, or even worthless in themselves, they have come to please us at last as things picturesque, being set in relief against the modes of our different age. Customs, stiff to us, stiff dresses, stiff furniture—types of cast-off fashions, left by accident, and which no one ever meant to preserve— we contemplate with more than good-nature, as having in them the veritable accent of a time, not altogether to be replaced by its more solemn and self-conscious deposits; like those tricks of individuality which we find quite tolerable in persons, because they convey to us the secret of lifelike expression, and with regard to which we are all to some extent humourists. But it is part of the privilege of the genuine humourist to anticipate this pensive mood with regard to the ways and things of his own day; to look upon the tricks in manner of the life about him with that same refined, purged sort of vision, which will come naturally to those of a later generation, in observing whatever may have survived by chance of its mere external habit. Seeing things always by the light of an understanding more entire than is possible for ordinary minds, of the whole mechanism of humanity, and seeing also the manner, the outward mode or fashion, always in strict connexion with the spiritual condition which determined it, a humourist such as Charles Lamb anticipates the enchantment of distance; and the characteristics of places, ranks, habits of life, are transfigured for him, even now and in advance of time, by poetic light; justifying what some might condemn as mere sentimentality, in the effort to hand on unbroken the tradition of such fashion or accent. "The praise of beggars," "the cries of London," the traits of actors just grown "old," the spots in "town" where the country, its fresh green and fresh water, still lingered on, one after another, amidst the bustle; the quaint, dimmed, just played-out farces, he had relished so much, coming partly through them to understand the earlier English theatre as a thing once really alive; those fountains and sun-dials of old gardens, of which he entertains such dainty discourse:—he feels the poetry of these things, as the poetry of things old indeed, but surviving as an actual part of the life of the present, and as something quite different from the poetry of things flatly gone from us and antique, which come back to us, if at all, as entire strangers, like Scott's old Scotch-border personages, their oaths and armour. Such gift of appreciation depends, as I said, on the habitual apprehension of men's life as a whole —its organic wholeness, as extending even to the least things in it—of its outward manner in connexion with its inward temper; and it involves a fine perception of the congruities, the musical accordance between humanity and its environment of custom, society, personal intercourse; as if all this, with its meetings, partings, ceremonies, gesture, tones of speech, were some delicate instrument on which an expert performer is playing.

These are some of the characteristics of Elia, one essentially an essayist, and of the true family of Montaigne, "never judging," as he says, "system-wise of things, but fastening on particulars;" saying all things as it were on chance occasion only, and by way of pastime, yet succeeding thus, "glimpse-wise," in catching and recording more frequently than others "the gayest, happiest attitude of things;" a casual writer for dreamy readers, yet always giving the reader so much more than he seemed to propose. There is something of the follower of George Fox[4] about him, and the Quaker's belief in the inward light coming to one passive, to the mere wayfarer, who will be sure at all events to lose no light which falls by the way—glimpses, suggestions, delightful half-apprehensions, profound thoughts of old philosophers, hints of the innermost reason in things, the full knowledge of which is held in reserve; all the varied stuff, that is, of which genuine essays are made.

And with him, as with Montaigne, the desire of self-portraiture is, below all more superficial tendencies, the real motive in writing at all—a desire closely connected with that intimacy, that modern subjectivity, which may be called the *Montaignesque* element in literature. What he designs is to give you himself, to acquaint you with his likeness; but must do this, if at all, indirectly, being indeed always more or less reserved for himself and his friends; friendship counting for so much in his life, that he is jealous of anything that might jar or disturb it, even to the length of a sort of insincerity, to which he assigns its quaint "praise"; this lover of stage plays significantly welcoming a little touch of the artificiality of play to sweeten the intercourse of actual life.

And, in effect, a very delicate and expressive portrait of him does put itself together for the duly meditative reader. In indirect touches of his own work, scraps of faded old letters, what others remembered of his talk, the man's likeness emerges; what he laughed and wept at, his sudden elevations, and longings after absent friends, his fine casuistries of affection and devices to jog sometimes, as he says, the lazy happiness of perfect love, his solemn moments of higher discourse with the young, as they came across him on occasion, and went along a little way with him, the sudden, surprised apprehension of beauties in old literature, revealing anew the deep soul of poetry in things, and withal the pure spirit of fun, having its way again; laughter, that most short-lived of all things (some of Shakespeare's even being grown hollow) wearing well with him. Much of all this comes out through his letters, which may be regarded as a department of his essays. He is an old-fashioned letter-writer, the essence of the old fashion of letter-writing lying, as with true essay-writing, in the dexterous availing oneself of accident and circumstance in the prosecution of deeper lines of observation; although, just as with the record of his conversation, one loses something, in losing the actual tones of the stammerer, still graceful in his halting, as he halted also in composition, composing slowly and by fits, "like a Flemish painter," as he tells us, so "it is to be regretted," says the editor of his letters, "that in the printed letters the reader will lose the curious varieties of writing with which the originals abound, and which are scrupulously adapted to the subject."

Also, he was a true "collector," delighting in the personal finding of a thing, in the colour an old book or print gets for him by the little accidents which attest previous ownership. Wither's *Emblems*, "that old book and quaint," long-desired, when he finds it at last, he values none the less because a child had coloured the plates with his paints.[5] A lover of household warmth everywhere, of that tempered atmosphere which our various habitations get by men's living within them, he "sticks to his favourite books as he did to his friends," and loved the "town," with a jealous eye for all its characteristics, "old houses" coming to have souls for him. The yearning for mere warmth against him in another, makes him content, all through life, with pure brotherliness, "the most kindly and natural species of love," as he says, in place of the *passion* of love. Brother and sister, sitting thus side by side, have, of course, their anticipations how one of them must sit at last in the faint sun alone, and set us speculating, as we read, as to precisely what amount of melancholy really accompanied for him the approach of old age, so steadily foreseen; make us note also, with pleasure, his successive wakings up to cheerful realities, out of a too curious musing over what is gone and what remains, of life. In his subtle capacity for enjoying the more refined points of earth, of human relationship, he could throw the gleam of poetry or humour on what seemed common or threadbare; has a care for the sighs, and the weary, humdrum preoccupations of very weak people, down to their little pathetic "gentilities," even; while, in the purely human temper, he can write of death, almost like Shakespeare.

And that care, through all his enthusiasm of discovery, for what is accustomed, in literature, connected thus with his close clinging to home and the earth, was congruous also with that love for the accustomed in religion, which we may notice in him. He is one of the last votaries of that old-world sentiment, based on the feelings of hope and awe, which may be described as the religion of men of letters (as Sir Thomas Browne has his *Religion of the Physician*)[6] religion as understood by the soberer men of letters in the last century, Addison, Gray, and Johnson; by Jane Austen and Thackeray, later. A high way of feeling developed largely by constant intercourse with the great things of literature, and extended in its turn to those matters greater still, this religion lives, in the main retrospectively, in a system of received sentiments and beliefs; received, like those great things of literature and art, in the first instance, on the authority of a long tradition, in the course of which they have linked themselves in a thousand complex ways to the conditions of human life, and no more questioned now than the feeling one keeps by one of the greatness—say! of Shakespeare. For Charles Lamb, such form of religion becomes the solemn background on which the nearer and more exciting objects of his immediate experience relieve themselves, borrowing from it an expression of calm; its necessary atmosphere being indeed a profound quiet, that quiet which has in it a kind of sacramental efficacy, working, we might say, on the principle of the *opus operatum*, almost without any co-operation of one's own, towards the assertion of the higher self. And, in truth, to men of Lamb's delicately attuned temperament mere physical stillness has its full value; such natures seeming to long for it sometimes, as for no merely negative thing, with a sort of mystical sensuality.

The writings of Charles Lamb are an excellent illustration of the value of reserve in literature. Below his quiet, his quaintness, his humour, and what may seem the slightness, the occasional or accidental character of his work, there lies, as I said at starting, as in his life, a genuinely tragic element. The gloom, reflected at its darkest in those hard shadows of *Rosamund Grey*, is always there, though not always realised either for himself or his readers, and restrained always in utterance. It gives to those lighter matters on the surface of life and literature among which he for the most part moved, a wonderful force of expression, as if at any moment these slight words and fancies might pierce very far into the deeper soul of things. In his writing, as in his life, that quiet is not the low-flying of one from the first drowsy by choice, and needing the prick of some strong passion or wordly ambition, to simulate him into all the energy of which he is capable; but rather the reaction of nature, after an escape from fate, dark and insane as in old Greek tragedy, following upon which the sense of mere relief becomes a kind of passion, as with one who, having narrowly escaped earthquake or shipwreck, finds a thing for grateful tears in just sitting quiet at home, under the wall, till the end of days.

He felt the genius of places;[7] and I sometimes think he resembles the places he new and liked best, and where his lot fell—London, sixty-five years ago, with Covent Garden and the old theatres, and the Temple gardens still unspoiled, Thames gliding down, and beyond to north and south the fields at Enfield or Hampton, to which, "with their living trees," the thoughts wander "from the hard wood of the desk"—fields fresher, and coming nearer to town then, but in one of which the present writer remembers, on a brooding early summer's day, to have heard the cuckoo for the first time. Here, the surface of things is certainly humdrum, the streets dingy, the green places, where the child goes a-maying, tame enough. But nowhere are things more apt to respond to the brighter weather, nowhere is there so much difference between rain and sunshine, nowhere do the clouds roll together more grandly; those quaint suburban pastorals gathering a certain quality of grandeur from the background of the great city, with its weighty atmosphere, and portent of storm in the rapid light on dome and bleached stone steeples.

1878

NOTES

1. Presumably Pater means "The Chimney Sweeper" of *Songs of Innocence,* and not of *Songs of Experience.*

2. Robert Burton (1577–1640), author of the *Anatomy of Melancholy;* Francis Quarles (1592–1644), best known for his *Emblems;* Margaret, Duchess of Newcastle (1624–1674), wrote poems, plays, and essays.
3. William Godwin (1756–1836), author of *Enquiry concerning Political Justice* and the novel, *Adventures of Caleb Williams;* remembered also as the husband of Mary Wollstonecraft, and subsequently as Shelley's father-in-law; *John Woodvil or Pride's Cure* is one of Lamb's failed tragic dramas.
4. George Fox (1624–1691) was one of the Quaker founders; his *Journal* (1694) is a marvelous book.
5. George Wither (1558-1667), primarily a satirical poet, was one of the many seventeenth-century writers revived by Lamb.
6. Sir Thomas Browne (1605-1682), whose *Religio Medici* (1643) influenced both Lamb and Pater.
7. "Genius of places": one feels, in this final paragraph, a kind of fusion betwen Lamb and Pater, as though Pater would have been glad to substitute this gentle precursor for his actual literary father, the ferocious Ruskin.

"Measure for Measure"

In *Measure for Measure*, as in some other of his plays, Shakespeare has remodelled an earlier and somewhat rough composition to "finer issues," suffering much to remain as it had come from the less skilful hand, and not raising the whole of his work to an equal degree of intensity. Hence perhaps some of that depth and weightiness which make this play so impressive, as with the true seal of experience, like a fragment of life itself, rough and disjointed indeed, but forced to yield in places its profounder meaning. In *Measure for Measure*, in contrast with the flawless execution of *Romeo and Juliet*, Shakespeare has spent his art in just enough modification of the scheme of the older play to make it exponent of this purpose, adapting its terrible essential incidents, so that Coleridge found it the only painful work among Shakespeare's dramas, and leaving for the reader of to-day more than the usual number of difficult expressions; but infusing a lavish colour and a profound significance into it, so that under his touch certain select portions of it rise far above the level of all but his own best poetry, and working out of it a morality so characteristic that the play might well pass for the central expression of his moral judgments. It remains a comedy, as indeed is congruous with the bland, half-humorous equity which informs the whole composition, sinking from the heights of sorrow and terror into the rough scheme of the earlier piece; yet it is hardly less full of what is really tragic in man's existence than if Claudio had indeed "stooped to death." Even the humorous concluding scenes have traits of special grace, retaining in less emphatic passages a stray line or word of power, as it seems, so that we watch to the end for the traces where the nobler hand has glanced along, leaving its vestiges, as if accidentally or wastefully, in the rising of the style.

The interest of *Measure for Measure*, therefore, is partly that of an old story told over again. We measure with curiosity that variety of resources which has enabled Shakespeare to refashion the original material with a higher motive; adding to the intricacy of the piece, yet so modifying its structure as to give the whole almost the unity of a single scene; lending, by the light of a philosophy which dwells much on what is complex and subtle in our nature, a true human propriety to its strange and unexpected turns of feeling and character, to incidents so difficult as the fall of Angelo, and the subsequent reconciliation of Isabella, so that she pleads successfully for his life. It was from Whetstone, a contemporary English writer, that Shakespeare derived the outline of Cinthio's "rare history" of *Promos and Cassandra*, one of that numerous class of Italian stories, like Boccaccio's *Tancred of Salerno*, in which the mere energy of southern passion has everything its own way, and which, though they may repel many a northern reader by a certain crudity in their colouring, seem to have been full of fascination for the Elizabethan age. This story, as it appears in Whetstone's endless comedy, is almost as rough as the roughest episode of actual criminal life. But the play seems never to have been acted, and some time after its publication Whetstone himself turned the thing into a tale, included in his *Heptameron of Civil Discourses*, where it still figures as a genuine piece, with touches of undesigned poetry, a quaint field-flower here and there of diction or sentiment, the whole strung up to an effective brevity, and with the fragrance of that admirable age of literature all about it. Here, then, there is something of the original Italian colour: in this narrative Shakespeare may well have caught the first glimpse of a composition with nobler proportions; and some artless sketch from his own hand, perhaps, putting together his first impressions, insinuated itself between Whetstone's work and the play as we actually read it. Out of these insignificant sources Shakespeare's play rises, full of solemn expression, and with a profoundly designed beauty, the new body of a higher, though sometimes remote and difficult poetry, escaping from the imperfect relics of the old story, yet not wholly transformed, and even as it stands but the preparation only, we might think, of a still more imposing design. For once we have in it a real example of that sort of writing which is sometimes described as *suggestive*, and which by the help of certain subtly calculated hints only, brings into distinct shape the reader's own half-developed imaginings. Often the quality is attributed to writing merely vague and unrealised, but in *Measure for Measure*, quite certainly, Shakespeare has directed the attention of sympathetic readers along certain channels of meditation beyond the immediate scope of his work.

Measure for Measure, therefore, by the quality of these higher designs, woven by his strange magic on a texture of poorer quality, is hardly less indicative than *Hamlet* even, of Shakespeare's reason, of his power of moral interpretation. It deals, not like *Hamlet* with the problems which beset one of exceptional temperament, but with mere human nature. It brings before us a group of persons, attractive, full of desire, vessels of the genial, seed-bearing powers of nature, a gaudy existence flowering out over the old court and city of Vienna, a spectacle of the fulness and pride of life which to some may seem to touch the verge of wantonness. Behind this group of people, behind their various action, Shakespeare inspires in us the sense of a strong tyranny of nature and circumstance. Then what shall there be on this side of it— on our side, the spectators' side, of this painted screen, with its puppets who are really glad or sorry all the time? what philosophy of life, what sort of equity?

Stimulated to read more carefully by Shakespeare's own profounder touches, the reader will note the vivid reality, the subtle interchange of light and shade, the strongly contrasted

characters of this group of persons, passing across the stage
so quickly. The slightest of them is at least not ill-natured:
the meanest of them can put forth a plea for existence—
Truly, sir, I am a poor fellow that would live!—they are
never sure of themselves, even in the strong tower of a cold
unimpressible nature: they are capable of many friendships
and of a true dignity in danger, giving each other a sympathetic, if transitory, regret—one sorry that another "should
be foolishly lost at a game of tick-tack." Words which seem
to exhaust man's deepest sentiment concerning death and life
are put on the lips of a gilded, witless youth; and the saintly
Isabella feels fire creep along her, kindling her tongue to
eloquence at the suggestion of shame. In places the shadow
deepens: death intrudes itself on the scene, as among other
things "a great disguiser," blanching the features of youth
and spoiling its goodly hair, touching the fine Claudio even
with its disgraceful associations. As in Orcagna's fresco at
Pisa, it comes capriciously, giving many and long reprieves
to Barnardine, who has been waiting for it nine years in
prison, taking another thence by fever, another by mistake of
judgment, embracing others in the midst of their music and
song. The little mirror of existence, which reflects to each
for a moment the stage on which he plays, is broken at last
by a capricious accident; while all alike, in their yearning for
untasted enjoyment, are really discounting their days, grasp-
ing so hastily and accepting so inexactly the precious pieces.
The Duke's quaint but excellent moralising at the beginning
of the third act does but express, like the chorus of a Greek
play, the spirit of the passing incidents. To him in Shakespeare's play, to a few here and there in the actual world,
this strange practical paradox of our life, so unwise in its
eager haste, reveals itself in all its clearness.

The Duke disguised as a friar, with his curious moralising
on life and death, and Isabella in her first mood of renunciation, a thing "ensky'd and sainted," come with the quiet of
the cloister as a relief to this lust and pride of life: like
some grey monastic picture hung on the wall of a gaudy
room, their presence cools the heated air of the piece. For a
moment we are within the placid conventual walls, whither
they fancy at first that the Duke has come as a man crossed
in love, with Friar Thomas and Friar Peter, calling each
other by their homely, English names, or at the nunnery
among the novices, with their little limited privileges, where

If you speak you must not show your face,
Or if you show your face you must not speak.

Not less precious for this relief in the general structure of
the piece, than for its own peculiar graces is the episode of
Mariana, a creature wholly of Shakespeare's invention, told,
by way of interlude, in subdued prose. The moated grange,
with its dejected mistress, its long, listless, discontented days,
where we hear only the voice of a boy broken off suddenly
in the midst of one of the lovelist songs of Shakespeare, or
of Shakespeare's school,* is the pleasantest of many glimpses
we get here of pleasant places—the field without the town,
Angelo's garden-house, the consecrated fountain. Indirectly
it has suggested two of the most perfect compositions among
the poetry of our own generation.[1] Again it is a picture
within a picture, but with fainter lines and a greyer atmosphere: we have here the same passions, the same wrongs,
the same continuance of affection, the same crying out
upon death, as in the nearer and larger piece, though softened, and reduced to the mood of a more dreamy scene.

Of Angelo we may feel at first sight inclined to say only
guarda e passa! or to ask whether he is indeed psychologically
possible.[2] In the old story, he figures as an embodiment of
pure and unmodified evil, like "Hyliogabalus of Rome or
Denis of Sicyll." But the embodiment of pure evil is no
proper subject of art, and Shakespeare, in the spirit of a
philosophy which dwells much on the complications of outward circumstance with men's inclinations, turns into a
subtle study in casuistry this incident of the austere judge
fallen suddenly into utmost corruption by a momentary contact with supreme purity. But the main interest in *Measure
for Measure* is not, as in *Promos and Cassandra*, in the relation of Isabella and Angelo, but rather in the relation of
Claudio and Isabella.

Greek tragedy in some of its noblest products has taken
for its theme the love of a sister, a sentiment unimpassioned
indeed, purifying by the very spectacle of its passionlessness,
but capable of a fierce and almost animal strength if
informed for a moment by pity and regret. At first Isabella
comes upon the scene as a tranquillising influence in it. But
Shakespeare, in the development of the action, brings quite

---

* Fletcher, in the *Bloody Brother*, gives the rest of it. (Pater's own note.)

different and unexpected qualities out of her. It is his characteristic poetry to expose this cold, chastened personality,
respected even by the worldly Lucio as "something ensky'd
and sainted, and almost an immortal spirit," to two sharp,
shameful trials, and wring out of her a fiery, revealing eloquence. Thrown into the terrible dilemma of the piece, called
upon to sacrifice that cloistral whiteness to sisterly affection,
become in a moment the ground of strong, contending passions, she develops a new character and shows herself suddenly of kindred with those strangely conceived women,
like Webster's Vittoria, who unite to a seductive sweetness
something of a dangerous and tigerlike changefulness of
feeling. The swift, vindictive anger leaps, like a white flame,
into this white spirit, and, stripped in a moment of all convention, she stands before us clear, detached, columnar,
among the tender frailties of the piece. Cassandra, the original of Isabella in Whetstone's tale, with the purpose of the
Roman Lucretia in her mind, yields gracefully enough to
the conditions of her brother's safety; and to the lighter
reader of Shakespeare there may seem something harshly
conceived, or psychologically impossible even, in the sudden-
ness of the change wrought in her, as Claudio welcomes for
a moment the chance of life through her compliance with
Angelo's will, and he may have a sense here of flagging skill,
as in words less finely handled than in the preceding scene.
The play, though still not without traces of nobler handiwork, sinks down, as we know, at last into almost homely
comedy, and it might be supposed that just here the grander
manner deserted it. But the skill with which Isabella plays
upon Claudio's well-recognised sense of honour, and endeavours by means of that to insure him beforehand from the
acceptance of life on baser terms, indicates no coming laxity
of hand just in this place. It was rather than there rose in
Shakespeare's conception, as there may for the reader, as
there certainly would in any good acting of the part, something of that terror, the seeking for which is one of the notes
of romanticism in Shakespeare and his circle. The stream of
ardent natural affection, poured as sudden hatred upon the
youth condemned to die, adds an additional note of expression to the horror of the prison where so much of the scene
takes place. It is not here only that Shakespeare has conceived of such extreme anger and pity as putting a sort of
genius into simple women, so that their "lips drop eloquence,"

and their intuitions interpret that which is often too hard or fine for manlier reason; and it is Isabella with her grand imaginative diction, and that poetry laid upon the "prone and speechless dialect" there is in mere youth itself, who gives utterance to the equity, the finer judgments of the piece on men and things.

From behind this group with its subtle lights and shades, its poetry, its impressive contrasts, Shakespeare, as I said, conveys to us a strong sense of the tyranny of nature and circumstance over human action. The most powerful expressions of this side of experience might be found here. The bloodless, impassible temperament does but wait for its opportunity, for the almost accidental coherence of time with place, and place with wishing, to annul its long and patient discipline, and become in a moment the very opposite of that which under ordinary conditions it seemed to be, even to itself. The mere resolute self-assertion of the blood brings to others special temptations, temptations which, as defects or over-growths, lie in the very qualities which make them otherwise imposing or attractive; the very advantage of men's gifts of intellect or sentiment being dependent on a balance in their use so delicate that men hardly maintain it always. Something also must be conceded to influences merely physical, to the complexion of the heavens, the skyey influences, shifting as the stars shift; as something also to the mere caprice of men exercised over each other in the dispensations of social or political order, to the chance which makes the life or death of Claudio dependent on Angelo's will.

The many veins of thought which render the poetry of this play so weighty and impressive unite in the image of Claudio, a flowerlike young man, whom, prompted by a few hints from Shakespeare, the imagination easily clothes with all the bravery of youth, as he crosses the stage before us on his way to death, coming so hastily to the end of his pilgrimage. Set in the horrible blackness of the prison, with its various forms of unsightly death, this flower seems the braver. Fallen by "prompture of the blood," the victim of a suddenly revived law against the common fault of youth like his, he finds his life forfeited as if by the chance of a lottery. With that instinctive clinging to life, which breaks through the subtlest casuistries of monk or sage apologising for an early death, he welcomes for a moment the chance of life through his sister's shame, though he revolts hardly less from the notion of perpetual imprisonment so repulsive to the buoyant energy of youth. Familiarised, by the words alike of friends and the indifferent, to the thought of death, he becomes gentle and subdued indeed, yet more perhaps through pride than real resignation, and would go down to darkness at last hard and unblinded. Called upon suddenly to encounter his fate, looking with keen and resolute profile straight before him, he gives utterance to some of the central truths of human feeling, the sincere, concentrated expression of the recoiling flesh. Thoughts as profound and poetical as Hamlet's arise in him; and but for the accidental arrest of sentence he would descend into the dust, a mere gilded, idle flower of youth indeed, but with what are perhaps the most eloquent of all Shakespeare's words upon his lips.[3]

As Shakespeare in *Measure for Measure* has refashioned, after a nobler pattern, materials already at hand, so that the relics of other men's poetry are incorporated into his perfect dramatic composition which had for its function the inculcat-work, so traces of the old "morality," that early form of dramatic composition which had for its function the inculcat-ing of some moral theme, survive in it also, and give it a peculiar ethical interest. This ethical interest, though it can escape no attentive reader, yet, in accordance with that artis-tic law which demands the predominance of form everywhere over the mere matter or subject handled, is not to be wholly separated from the special circumstances, necessities, embar-rassments, of these particular dramatic persons. The old "moralities" exemplified most often some rough-and-ready lesson. Here the very intricacy and subtlety of the moral world itself, the difficulty of seizing the true relations of so complex a material, the difficulty of just judgment, of judg-ment that shall not be unjust, are the lessons conveyed. Even in Whetstone's old story this peculiar vein of moralising comes to the surface: even there, we notice the tendency to dwell on mixed motives, the contending issues of action, the presence of virtues and vices alike in unexpected places, on "the hard choice of two evils," on the "imprisoning" of men's "real intents." *Measure for Measure* is full of expres-sions drawn from a profound experience of these casuistries, and that ethical interest becomes predominant in it: it is no longer *Promos and Cassandra*, but *Measure for Measure*, its new name expressly suggesting the subject of *poetical justice*.

The action of the play, like the action of life itself for the keener observer, develops in us the conception of this poetical justice, and the yearning to realise it, the true justice of which Angelo knows nothing, because it lies for the most part beyond the limits of any acknowledged law. The idea of justice involves the idea of rights. But at bottom rights are equivalent to that which really is, to facts; and the recognition of his rights therefore, the justice he requires of our hands, or our thoughts, is the recognition of that which the person, in his inmost nature, really is; and as sympathy alone can discover that which really is in matters of feeling and thought, true justice is in its essence a finer knowledge through love.

> 'Tis very pregnant:
> The jewel that we find we stoop and take it,
> Because we see it; but what we do not see
> We tread upon, and never think of it.

It is for this finer justice, a justice based on a more delicate appreciation of the true conditions of men and things, a true respect of persons in our estimate of actions, that the people in *Measure for Measure* cry out as they pass before us; and as the poetry of this play is full of the peculiarities of Shakespeare's poetry, so in its ethics it is an epitome of Shakespeare's moral judgments. They are the moral judgments of an observer, of one who sits as a spectator, and knows how the threads in the design before him hold together under the surface: they are the judgments of the humourist also, who follows with a half-amused but always pitiful sympathy, the various ways of human disposition, and sees less distance than ordinary men between what are called respectively great and little things. It is not always that poetry can be the exponent of morality; but it is this aspect of morals which it represents most naturally, for this true justice is dependent on just those finer appreciations which poetry cultivates in us the power of making, those peculiar valuations of action and its effect which poetry actually requires.

1874

NOTES

1. Both by Tennyson: "Mariana," and "Mariana in the South."
2. Yet Angelo is hardly a figure either to be on our guard against, or to be passed by. Pater does not understand Angelo.
3. Presumably Act III, Scene I, 116-130.

Aesthetic Poetry[1]

The "æsthetic" poetry is neither a mere reproduction of Greek or mediæval poetry, nor only an idealisation of modern life and sentiment. The atmosphere on which its effect depends belongs to no simple form of poetry, no actual form of life. Greek poetry, mediæval or modern poetry, projects, above the realities of its time, a world in which the forms of things are transfigured. Of that transfigured world this new poetry takes possession, and sublimates beyond it another still fainter and more spectral, which is literally an artificial or "earthly paradise."[2] It is a finer ideal, extracted from what in relation to any actual world is already an ideal. Like some strange second flowering after date, it renews on a more delicate type the poetry of a past age, but must not be confounded with it. The secret of the enjoyment of it is that inversion of homesickness known to some, that incurable thirst for the sense of escape, which no actual form of life satisfies, no poetry even, if it be merely simple and spontaneous.[3]

The writings of the "romantic school," of which the æsthetic poetry is an afterthought, mark a transition not so much from the pagan to the mediæval ideal, as from a lower to a higher degree of passion in literature. The end of the eighteenth century, swept by vast disturbing currents, experienced an excitement of spirit of which one note was a reaction against an outworn classicism severed not more from nature than from the genuine motives of ancient art;

and a return to true Hellenism was as much a part of this reaction as the sudden preoccupation with things mediæval. The mediæval tendency is in Goethe's *Goetz von Berlichingen*, the Hellenic in his *Iphigenie*. At first this mediævalism was superficial, or at least external. Adventure, romance in the frankest sense, grotesque individualism—that is one element in mediæval poetry, and with it alone Scott and Goethe dealt. Beyond them were the two other elements of the mediæval spirit: its mystic religion at its apex in Dante and Saint Louis, and its mystic passion, passing here and there into the great romantic loves of rebellious flesh, of Lancelot and Abelard. That stricter, imaginative mediævalism which re-creates the mind of the Middle Age, so that the form, the presentment grows outward from within, came later with Victor Hugo in France, with Heine in Germany.

In the *Defence of Guenevere: and Other Poems*, published by Mr. William Morris now many years ago,[4] the first typical specimen of æsthetic poetry, we have a refinement upon this later, profounder mediævalism. The poem which gives its name to the volume is a thing tormented and awry with passion, like the body of Guenevere defending herself from the charge of adultery, and the accent falls in strange, unwonted places with the effect of a great cry. In truth these Arthurian legends, in their origin prior to Christianity, yield all their sweetness only in a Christian atmosphere. What is characteristic in them is the strange suggestion of a deliberate choice between Christ and a rival lover. That religion, monastic religion at any rate, has its sensuous side, a dangerously sensuous side, has been often seen: it is the experience of Rousseau as well as of the Christian mystics. The Christianity of the Middle Age made way among a people whose loss was in the life of the senses, partly by its æsthetic beauty, a thing so profoundly felt by the Latin hymn-writers, who for one moral or spiritual sentiment have a hundred sensuous images. And so in those imaginative loves, in their highest expression, the Provençal poetry, it is a rival religion with a new rival *cultus* that we see.[5] Coloured through and through with Christian sentiment, they are rebels against it. The rejection of one worship for another is never lost sight of. The jealousy of that other lover, for whom these words and images and refined ways of sentiment were first devised, is the secret here of a borrowed, perhaps factitious colour and heat. It is the mood of the cloister taking a new direction, and winning so a later space of life it never anticipated.

Hereon, as before in the cloister, so now in the *château*, the reign of reverie set in. The devotion of the cloister knew that mood thoroughly, and had sounded all its stops. For the object of this devotion was absent or veiled, not limited to one supreme plastic form like Zeus at Olympia or Athena in the Acropolis, but distracted, as in a fever dream, into a thousand symbols and reflections. But then, the Church, that new Sibyl, had a thousand secrets to make the absent near. Into this kingdom of reverie, and with it into a paradise of ambitious refinements, the earthly love enters, and becomes a prolonged somnambulism. Of religion it learns the art of directing towards an unseen object sentiments whose natural direction is towards objects of sense. Hence a love defined by the absence of the beloved, choosing to be without hope, protesting against all lower uses of love, barren, extravagant, antinomian. It is the love which is incompatible with marriage, for the chevalier who never comes, of the serf for the *châtelaine*, of the rose for the nightingale, of Rudel for the Lady of Tripoli.[6] Another element of extravagance came in with the feudal spirit: Provençal love is full of the very forms of vassalage. To be the servant of love, to have offended, to taste the subtle luxury of chastisement, of reconciliation—the religious spirit, too, knows that, and meets just there, as in Rousseau, the delicacies of the earthly love. Here, under this strange complex of conditions, as in some medicated air, exotic flowers of sentiment expand, among people of a remote and unaccustomed beauty, somnambulistic, frail, androgynous, the light almost shining through them. Surely, such loves were too fragile and adventurous to last more than for a moment.

That monastic religion of the Middle Age was, in fact, in many of its bearings, like a beautiful disease or disorder of the senses: and a religion which is a disorder of the senses must always be subject to illusions. Reverie, illusion, delirium: they are the three stages of a fatal descent both in the religion and the loves of the Middle Age. Nowhere has the impression of this delirium been conveyed as by Victor Hugo in *Notre Dame de Paris*. The strangest creations of sleep seem here, by some appalling licence, to cross the limit of the dawn. The English poet too has learned the secret. He has diffused through *King Arthur's Tomb* the maddening white glare of the sun, and tyranny of the moon, not tender and far-off, but close down—the sorcerer's moon, large and feverish. The colouring is intricate and delirious, as of "scarlet lilies." The influence of summer is like a poison in one's blood, with a sudden bewildered sickening of life and all things.[7] In *Galahad: a Mystery*, the frost of Christmas night on the chapel stones acts as a strong narcotic: a sudden shrill ringing pierces through the numbness: a voice proclaims that the Grail has gone forth through the great forest. It is in the *Blue Closet* that this delirium reaches its height with a singular beauty, reserved perhaps for the enjoyment of the few.

A passion of which the outlets are sealed, begets a tension of nerve, in which the sensible world comes to one with a reinforced brilliancy and relief—all redness is turned into blood, all water into tears. Hence a wild, convulsed sensuousness in the poetry of the Middle Age, in which the things of nature begin to play a strange delirious part. Of the things of nature the mediæval mind had a deep sense; but its sense of them was not objective, no real escape to the world without us. The aspects and motions of nature only reinforced its prevailing mood, and were in conspiracy with one's own brain against one. A single sentiment invaded the world: everything was infused with a motive drawn from the soul. The amorous poetry of Provence, making the starling and the swallow its messengers, illustrates the whole attitude of nature in this electric atmosphere, bent as by miracle or magic to the service of human passion.

The most popular and gracious form of Provençal poetry was the *nocturn*, sung by the lover at night at the door or under the window of his mistress. These songs were of different kinds, according to the hour at which they were intended to be sung. Some were to be sung at midnight— songs inviting to sleep, the *serena*, or *serenade*; others at break of day—waking songs, the *aube* or *aubade*.* This waking-song is put sometimes into the mouth of a comrade of the lover, who plays sentinel during the night, to watch for and announce the dawn: sometimes into the mouth of one of the lovers, who are about to separate. A modification of it is familiar to us all in *Romeo and Juliet*, where the lovers

---

* Fauriel's *Histoire de la Poésie Provençale*, tome ii. ch. xviii. (Pater's own note.)

debate whether the song they hear is of the nightingale or
the lark; the aubade, with the two other great forms of love-
poetry then floating in the world, the sonnet and the epitha-
lamium, being here refined, heightened, and inwoven into
the structure of the play. Those, in whom what Rousseau
calls *les frayeurs nocturnes*[8] are constitutional, know what
splendour they give to the things of the morning; and how
there comes something of relief from physical pain with
the first white film in the sky. The Middle Age knew those
terrors in all their forms; and these songs of the morning
win hence a strange tenderness and effect. The crown of the
English poet's book is one of these appreciations of the
dawn:—

> "Pray but one prayer for me 'twixt thy closed lips,
>   Think but one thought of me up in the stars.
> The summer-night waneth, the morning light slips,
>   Faint and gray 'twixt the leaves of the aspen,
>   betwixt the cloud-bars,
> That are patiently waiting there for the dawn:
>   Patient and colourless, though Heaven's gold
> Waits to float through them along with the sun.
> Far out in the meadows, above the young corn,
>   The heavy elms wait, and restless and cold
> The uneasy wind rises; the roses are dun;
> Through the long twilight they pray for the dawn,
> Round the lone house in the midst of the corn.
>   Speak but one word to me over the corn,
>   Over the tender, bow'd locks of the corn."[9]

It is the very soul of the bridegroom which goes forth to the
bride: inanimate things are longing with him: all the sweetness of the imaginative loves of the Middle Age, with a
superadded spirituality of touch all its own, is in that!

The *Defence of Guenevere* was published in 1858; the
Life and Death of Jason in 1867; to be followed by *The
Earthly Paradise*; and the change of manner wrought in the
interval, entire, almost a revolt, is characteristic of the
æsthetic poetry. Here there is no delirium or illusion, no
experiences of mere soul while the body and the bodily
sense sleep, or wake with convulsed intensity at the prompting of imaginative love; but rather the great primary passions under broad daylight as of the pagan Veronese.[10]
This simplification interests us, not merely for the sake of an

individual poet—full of charm as he is—but chiefly because it explains through him a transition which, under many forms, is one law of the life of the human spirit, and of which what we call the Renaissance is only a supreme instance. Just so the monk in his cloister, through the "open vision," open only to the spirit, divined, aspired to, and at last apprehended, a better daylight, but earthly, open only to the senses. Complex and subtle interests, which the mind spins for itself, may occupy art and poetry or our own spirits for a time; but sooner or later they come back with a sharp rebound to the simple elementary passions—anger, desire, regret, pity, and fear: and what corresponds to them in the sensuous world—bare, abstract fire, water, air, tears, sleep, silence, and what De Quincey has called the "glory of motion."

This reaction from dreamlight to daylight gives, as always happens, a strange power in dealing with morning and the things of the morning. Not less is this Hellenist of the Middle Age master of dreams, of sleep and the desire of sleep—sleep in which no one walks, restorer of childhood to men—dreams, not like Galahad's or Guenevere's, but full of happy, childish wonder as in the earlier world. It is a world in which the centaur and the ram with the fleece of gold are conceivable. The song sung always claims to be sung for the first time. There are hints at a language common to birds and beasts and men. Everywhere there is an impression of surprise, as of people first waking from the golden age, at fire, snow, wine, the touch of water as one swims, the salt taste of the sea. And this simplicity at first hand is a strange contrast to the sought-out simplicity of Wordsworth. Desire here is towards the body of nature for its own sake, not because a soul is divined through it.

And yet it is one of the charming anachronisms of a poet, who, while he handles an ancient subject, never becomes an antiquarian, but animates his subject by keeping it always close to himself, that between whiles we have a sense of English scenery as from an eye well practised under Wordsworth's influence, as from "the casement half opened on summernights," with the song of the brown bird among the willows, the

"Noise of bells, such as in moonlit lanes
Rings from the grey team on the market night."

Nowhere but in England is there such a "paradise of birds," the fern-owl, the water-hen, the thrush in a hundred sweet variations, the gerfalcon, the kestrel, the starling, the pea-fowl; birds heard from the field by the townsman down in the streets at dawn; doves everywhere, pink-footed, grey-winged, flitting about the temple, troubled by the temple incense, trapped in the snow. The sea-touches are not less sharp and firm, surest of effect in places where river and sea, salt and fresh waves, conflict.

In handling a subject of Greek legend, anything in the way of an actual revival must always be impossible. Such vain antiquarianism is a waste of the poet's power. The composite experience of all the ages is part of each one of us; to deduct from that experience, to obliterate any part of it, to come face to face with the people of a past age, as if the Middle Age, the Renaissance, the eighteenth century had not been, is as impossible as to become a little child, or enter again into the womb and be born. But though it is not possible to repress a single phase of that humanity, which, because we live and move and have our being in the life of humanity, makes us what we are, it is possible to isolate such a phase, to throw it into relief, to be divided against ourselves in zeal for it; as we may hark back to some choice space of our own individual life. We cannot truly conceive the age: we can conceive the element it has contributed to our culture: we can treat the subjects of the age bringing that into relief. Such an attitude towards Greece, aspiring to but never actually reaching its way of conceiving life, is what is possible for art.

The modern poet or artist who treats in this way a classical story comes very near, if not to the Hellenism of Homer, yet to the Hellenism of Chaucer, the Hellenism of the Middle Age, or rather of that exquisite first period of the Renaissance within it. Afterwards the Renaissance takes its side, becomes, perhaps, exaggerated or facile. But the choice life of the human spirit is always under mixed lights, and in mixed situations, when it is not too sure of itself, is still expectant, girt up to leap forward to the promise. Such a situation there was in that earliest return from the over-wrought spiritualities of the Middle Age to the earlier, more ancient life of the senses; and for us the most attractive form of classical story is the monk's conception of it, when he escapes from the sombre atmosphere of his cloister to natural light. The fruits of this mood, which, divining more than it understands, infuses into the scenery and figures of Christian history some subtle reminiscence of older gods, or into the story of Cupid and Psyche that passionate stress of spirit which the world owes to Christianity, constitute a peculiar vein of interest in the art of the fifteenth century.

And so, before we leave *Jason* and *The Earthly Paradise*, a word must be said about their mediævalisms, delicate inconsistencies, which, coming in a poem of Greek subject, bring into this white dawn thoughts of the delirious night just over and make one's sense of relief deeper. The opening of the fourth book of *Jason* describes the embarkation of the Argonauts: as in a dream, the scene shifts and we go down from Iolchos to the sea through a pageant of the Middle Age in some French or Italian town. The gilded vanes on the spires, the bells ringing in the towers, the trellis of roses at the window, the close planted with apple-trees, the grotesque undercroft with its close-set pillars, change by a single touch the air of these Greek cities and we are at Glastonbury by the tomb of Arthur. The nymph in furred raiment who seduces Hylas[11] is conceived frankly in the spirit of Teutonic romance; her song is of a garden enclosed, such as that with which the old church glass-stainer surrounds the mystic bride of the song of songs. Medea herself has a hundred touches of the mediæval sorceress, the sorceress of the Streckelberg or the Blocksberg: her mystic changes are Christabel's.[12] It is precisely this effect, this grace of Hellenism relieved against the sorrow of the Middle Age, which forms the chief motives of *The Earthly Paradise:* with an exquisite dexterity the two threads of sentiment are here interwoven and contrasted. A band of adventurers sets out from Norway, most northerly of northern lands, where the plague is raging—the bell continually ringing as they carry the Sacrament to the sick. Even in Mr. Morris's earliest poems snatches of the sweet French tongue had always come with something of Hellenic blitheness and grace. And now it is below the very coast of France, through the fleet of Edward the Third, among the gaily painted mediæval sails, that we pass to a reserved fragment of Greece, which by some divine good fortune lingers on in the western sea into the Middle Age. There the stories of *The Earthly Paradise* are told, Greek story and romantic alternating; and for the crew of the *Rose Garland*, coming across the sins of the earlier world with the sign of the cross, and drinking Rhine-wine in Greece, the two worlds of sentiment are confronted.

One characteristic of the pagan spirit the æsthetic poetry has, which is on its surface—the continual suggestion, pensive or passionate, of the shortness of life. This is contrasted with the bloom of the world, and gives new seduction to it—the sense of death and the desire of beauty: the desire of beauty quickened by the sense of death. But that complexion of sentiment is at its height in another "æsthetic" poet of whom I have to speak next, Dante Gabriel Rossetti.

NOTES

1. That is, Pre-Raphaelite poetry; by "aesthetic criticism," Pater seems to have meant genuine literary criticism; "aesthetic poetry" seems to mean, for him, the genuine poetry of his own generation.
2. Though he has *The Earthly Paradise* cycle of poems by Morris in mind, Pater emphasizes primarily the artificiality (in the good sense, of *artifice*) of the lower or earthly paradise. "Sublimates" here is being used in something very close to Nietzsche's sense, rather than Plato's or a Christian sense.
3. There is a partial rejection of Wordsworth here, in favor of the element in Keats ("Ode on Melancholy," "Eve of St. Mark") that Rossetti and Morris followed.
4. *The Defence of Guenevere* appeared in 1858.
5. Pater seriously proposes the *cultus* of Romantic love as a religion here, one that overtly opposes itself to Christianity.
6. Browning wrote a remarkable poem on this frustrated relationship.
7. These sentences, as Pater came to realize, read like a parody of Pater; that is, they read like Oscar Wilde or rather Wilde's Lord Henry Wotton in *Dorian Gray*.
8. *Les frayeurs nocturnes:* "nocturnal terrors."
9. The poem is "Summer Dawn," one of Morris's best.
10. Veronese: Paolo Cagliari, called Paul Veronese (1528–1588), great Venetian painter.
11. Hylas, page to Heracles and one of the Argonauts, drowned when pulled into a spring by its amorous nymphs.
12. Pater must mean the vampire-lady Geraldine, in Coleridge's *Christabel*.

Dante Gabriel Rossetti

It was characteristic of a poet who had ever something about him of mystic isolation, and will still appeal perhaps, though with a name it may seem now established in English literature, to a special and limited audience, that some of his poems had won a kind of exquisite fame before they were in the full sense published. *The Blessed Damozel*, although actually printed twice before the year 1870,[1] was eagerly circulated in manuscript; and the volume which it now opens came at last to satisfy a long-standing curiosity as to the poet, whose pictures also had become an object of the same peculiar kind of interest. For those poems were the work of a painter, understood to belong to, and to be indeed the leader, of a new school then rising into note;[2] and the reader of to-day may observe already, in *The Blessed Damozel*, written at the age of eighteen, a prefiguration of the chief characteristics of that school, as he will recognise in it also, in proportion as he really knows Rossetti, many of the characteristics which are most markedly personal and his own. Common to that school and to him, and in both alike of primary significance, was the quality of sincerity, already felt as one of the charms of that earliest poem—a perfect sincerity, taking effect in the deliberate use of the most direct and unconventional expression, for the conveyance of a poetic sense which recognised no conventional standard of what poetry was called upon to be. At a time when poetic originality in England might seem to have had its utmost play, here was certainly one new poet more, with a structure and music of verse, a vocabulary, an accent, unmistakably novel, yet felt to be no mere tricks of manner adopted with a view to forcing attention—an accent which might rather count as the very seal of reality on one man's own proper speech; as that speech itself was the wholly natural expression of certain wonderful things he really felt and saw. Here was one, who had a matter to present to his readers, to himself at least, in the first instance, so valuable,

so real and definite, that his primary aim, as regards form
or expression in his verse, would be but its exact equivalence to those *data*[3] within. That he had this gift of transparency in language—the control of a style which did but
obediently shift and shape itself to the mental motion, as a
well-trained hand can follow on the tracing-paper the outline of an original drawing below it, was proved afterwards
by a volume of typically perfect translations from the delightful but difficult "early Italian poets":[4] such transparency
being indeed the secret of all genuine style, of all such style
as can truly belong to one man and not to another. His own
meaning was always personal and even recondite, in a certain sense learned and casuistical, sometimes complex or
obscure; but the term was always, one could see, deliberately
chosen from many competitors, as the just transcript of
that peculiar phase of soul which he alone knew, precisely
as he knew it.

One of the peculiarities of *The Blessed Damozel* was a
definiteness of sensible imagery, which seemed almost grotesque to some, and was strange, above all, in a theme so
profoundly visionary. The gold bar of heaven from which
she leaned, her hair yellow like ripe corn, are but examples
of a general treatment, as naively detailed as the pictures of
those early painters contempoary with Dante,[5] who has
shown a similar care for minute and definite imagery in his
verse; there, too, in the very midst of profoundly mystic
vision. Such definition of outline is indeed one among many
points in which Rossetti resembles the great Italian poet, of
whom, led to him at first by family circumstances, he was
ever a lover—a "servant and singer," faithful as Dante,
"of Florence and of Beatrice"[6]—with some close inward conformities of genius also, independent of any mere circumstances of education. It was said by a critic of the last
century, not wisely though agreeably to the practice of his
time, that poetry rejoices in abstractions. For Rossetti, as for
Dante, without question on his part, the first condition of
the poetic way of seeing and presenting things is particularisation. "Tell me now," he writes, for Villon's[7]

> Dictes-moy où, n'en quel pays,
> Est Flora, la belle Romaine—
>
> Tell me now, in what hidden way is
> Lady Flora the lovely Roman:

—"way," in which one might actually chance to meet her; the unmistakably poetic effect of the couplet in English being dependent on the definiteness of that single word (though actually lighted on in the search after a difficult double rhyme) for which every one else would have written, like Villon himself, a more general one, just equivalent to place or region.

And this delight in concrete definition is allied with another of his conformities to Dante, the really imaginative vividness, namely, of his personifications—his hold upon them, or rather their hold upon him, with the force of a Frankenstein,[8] when once they have taken life from him. Not Death only and Sleep, for instance, and the winged spirit of Love, but certain particular aspects of them, a whole "populace" of special hours and places, "the hour" even "which might have been, yet might not be," are living creatures, with hands and eyes and articulate voices.[9]

> Stands it not by the door—
> Love's Hour—till she and I shall meet;
> With bodiless form and unapparent feet
> That cast no shadow yet before,
> Though round its head the dawn begins to pour
> The breath that makes day sweet?—
>
> Nay, why
> Name the dead hours? I mind them well:
> Their ghosts in many darkened doorways dwell
> With desolate eyes to know them by.

Poetry as a *mania*—one of Plato's two higher forms of "divine" mania—has, in all its species, a mere insanity incidental to it, the "defect of its quality," into which it may lapse in its moment of weakness;[10] and the insanity which follows a vivid poetic anthropomorphism like that of Rossetti may be noted here and there in his work, in a forced and almost grotesque materialising of abstractions, as Dante also became at times a mere subject of the scholastic realism of the Middle Age.

In *Love's Nocturn* and *The Stream's Secret*, congruously perhaps with a certain feverishness of soul in the moods they present, there is at times a near approach (may it be said?) to such insanity of realism—

> Pity and love shall burn
> In her pressed cheek and cherishing hands;

> And from the living spirit of love that stands
>   Between her lips to soothe and yearn,
> Each separate breath shall clasp me round in turn
>   And loose my spirit's bands.[11]

But even if we concede this; even if we allow, in the very plan of those two compositions, something of the literary conceit—what exquisite, what novel flowers of poetry, we must admit them to be, as they stand! In the one, what a delight in all the natural beauty of water, all its details for the eye of a painter; in the other, how subtle and fine the imaginative hold upon all the secret ways of sleep and dreams! In both of them, with much the same attitude and tone, Love—sick and doubtful Love—would fain inquire of what lies below the surface of sleep, and below the water; stream or dream being forced to speak by Love's powerful "control"; and the poet would have it foretell the fortune, issue, and event of his wasting passion. Such artifices, indeed, were not unknown in the old Provençal poetry[12] of which Dante had learned something. Only, in Rossetti at least, they are redeemed by a serious purpose, by that sincerity of his, which allies itself readily to a serious beauty, a sort of grandeur of literary workmanship, to a great style. One seems to hear there a really new kind of poetic utterance, with effects which have nothing else like them; as there is nothing else, for instance, like the narrative of Jacob's Dream in *Genesis*,[13] or Blake's design of the Singing of the Morning Stars,[14] or Addison's Nineteenth Psalm.[15]

With him indeed, as in some revival of the old mythopœic age, common things—dawn, noon, night—are full of human or personal expression, full of sentiment. The lovely little sceneries scattered up and down his poems, glimpses of a landscape, not indeed of broad open-air effects, but rather that of a painter concentrated upon the picturesque effect of one or two selected objects at a time—the "hollow brimmed with mist," or the "ruined weir," as he sees it from one of the windows, or reflected in one of the mirrors of his "house of life" (the vignettes for instance seen by Rose Mary in the magic beryl)[16] attest, by their very freshness and simplicity, to a pictorial or descriptive power in dealing with the inanimate world, which is certainly also one half of the charm, in that other, more remote and mystic, use of it. For with Rossetti this sense of lifeless nature, after all, is translated to a higher service, in which it does but incorporate itself with some phase of strong emotion. Every one understands how this may happen at critical moments of life; what a weirdly expressive soul may have crept, even in full noonday, into "the white-flower'd elder-thicket," when Godiva saw it "gleam through the Gothic archways in the wall," at the end of her terrible ride.[17] To Rossetti it is so always, because to him life is a crisis at every moment. A sustained impressibility towards the mysterious conditions of man's everyday life, towards the very mystery itself in it, gives a singular gravity to all his work: those matters never became trite to him. But throughout, it is the ideal intensity of love—of love based upon a perfect yet peculiar type of physical or material beauty—which is enthroned in the midst of those mysterious powers; Youth and Death, Destiny and Fortune, Fame, Poetic Fame, Memory, Oblivion, and the like. Rossetti is one of those who, in the words of Mérimée, *se passionnent pour la passion*,[18] one of Love's lovers.

And yet, again as with Dante, to speak of his ideal type of beauty as material, is partly misleading. Spirit and matter, indeed, have been for the most part opposed, with a false contrast or antagonism by schoolmen, whose artificial creation those abstractions really are. In our actual concrete experience, the two trains of phenomena which the words *matter* and *spirit* do but roughly distinguish, play inextricably into each other. Practically, the church of the Middle Age by its æsthetic worship, its sacramentalism, its real faith in the resurrection of the flesh, had set itself against that Manichean[19] opposition of spirit and matter, and its results in men's way of taking life; and in this, Dante is the central representative of its spirit. To him, in the vehement and impassioned heat of his conceptions, the material and the spiritual are fused and blent: if the spiritual attains the definite visibility of a crystal, what is material loses its earthiness and impurity. And here again, by force of instinct, Rossetti is one with him. His chosen type of beauty is one,

> Whose speech Truth knows not from her thought,
> Nor Love her body from her soul.[20]

Like Dante, he knows no region of spirit which shall not be sensuous also, or material. The shadowy world, which he realises so powerfully, has still the ways and houses, the land

and water, the light and darkness, the fire and flowers, that had so much to do in the moulding of those bodily powers and aspects which counted for so large a part of the soul, here.

For Rossetti, then, the great affections of persons to each other, swayed and determined, in the case of his highly pictorial genius, mainly by that so-called material loveliness, formed the great undeniable reality in things, the solid resisting substance, in a world where all beside might be but shadow. The fortunes of those affections—of the great love so determined; its casuistries, its languor sometimes; above all, its sorrows; its fortunate or unfortunate collisions with those other great matters; how it looks, as the long day of life goes round, in the light and shadow of them: all this, conceived with an abundant imagination, and a deep, a philosophic, reflectiveness, is the matter of his verse, and especially of what he designed as his chief poetic work, "a work to be called *The House of Life*," towards which the majority of his sonnets and songs were contributions.

The dwelling-place in which one finds oneself by chance or destiny, yet can partly fashion for oneself; never properly one's own at all, if it be changed too lightly; in which every object has its associations—the dim mirrors, the portraits, the lamps, the books, the hair-tresses of the dead and visionary magic crystals in the secret drawers, the names and words scratched on the windows, windows open upon prospects the saddest or the sweetest; the house one must quit, yet taking perhaps, how much of its quietly active light and colour along with us!—grown now to be a kind of raiment to one's body, as the body, according to Swedenborg,[21] is but the raiment of the soul—under that image, the whole of Rossetti's work might count as a *House of Life*, of which he is but the "Interpreter." And it is a "haunted" house. A sense of power in love, defying distance, and those barriers which are so much more than physical distance, of unutterable desire penetrating into the world of sleep, however "lead-bound," was one of those anticipative notes obscurely struck in *The Blessed Damozel*, and, in his later work, makes him speak sometimes almost like a believer in mesmerism. Dream-land, as we said, with its "phantoms of the body," deftly coming and going on love's service, is to him, in no mere fancy or figure of speech, a real country, a veritable expansion of, or addition to, our waking life; and he did well perhaps to wait carefully upon sleep, for the lack of it became mortal disease with him. One may even recognise a sort of morbid and over-hasty making-ready for death itself, which increases on him; thoughts concerning it, its imageries, coming with a frequency and importunity, in excess, one might think, of even the very saddest, quite wholesome wisdom.

And indeed the publication of his second volume of *Ballads and Sonnets*[22] preceded his death by scarcely a twelvemonth. That volume bears witness to the reverse of any failure of power, or falling-off from his early standard of literary perfection, in every one of his then accustomed forms of poetry—the song, the sonnet, and the ballad. The newly printed sonnets, now completing *The House of Life*, certainly advanced beyond those earlier ones, in clearness; his dramatic power in the ballad, was here at its height; while one monumental, gnomic piece, *Soothsay*, testifies, more clearly even than the *Nineveh* of his first volume, to the reflective force, the dry reason, always at work behind his imaginative creations, which at no time dispensed with a genuine intellectual structure. For in matters of pure reflection also, Rossetti maintained the painter's sensuous clearness of conception; and this has something to do with the capacity, largely illustrated by his ballads, of telling some red-hearted story of impassioned action with effect.

Have there, in very deed, been ages, in which the external conditions of poetry such as Rossetti's were of more spontaneous growth than in our own? The archaic side of Rossetti's work, his preferences in regard to earlier poetry, connect him with those who have certainly thought so, who fancied they could have breathed more largely in the age of Chaucer, or of Ronsard,[23] in one of those ages, in the words of Stendhal—*ces siècles de passions où les âmes pouvaient se livrer franchement à la plus haute exaltation, quand les passions qui font la possibilité comme les sujets des beaux arts existaient.*[24] We may think, perhaps, that such old time as that has never really existed except in the fancy of poets; but it was to find it, that Rossetti turned so often from modern life to the chronicle of the past. Old Scotch history, perhaps beyond any other, is strong in the matter of heroic and vehement hatreds and love, the tragic Mary herself being but the perfect blossom of them; and it is from that history that Rossetti has taken the subjects of the two longer ballads of his second volume: of the three admirable ballads in it,

The King's Tragedy (in which Rossetti has dexterously
interwoven some relics of James's[25] own exquisite early
verse) reaching the highest level of dramatic success, and
marking perfection, perhaps, in this kind of poetry; which, in
the earlier volume, gave us, among other pieces, *Troy Town*,
Sister Helen, and *Eden Bower*.

Like those earlier pieces, the ballads of the second volume
bring with them the question of the poetic value of the
"refrain"—

> Eden bower's in flower:
> And O the bower and the hour![26]

—and the like. Two of those ballads—*Troy Town* and *Eden
Bower*, are terrible in theme; and the refrain serves, perhaps,
to relieve their bold aim at the sentiment of terror. In *Sister
Helen* again, the refrain has a real, and sustained purpose
(being here duly varied also) and performs the part of a
chorus, as the story proceeds. Yet even in these cases, whatever its effect may be in actual recitation, it may fairly be
questioned, whether, to the mere reader their actual effect is
not that of a positive interruption and drawback, at least
in pieces so lengthy; and Rossetti himself, it would seem,
came to think so, for in the shortest of his later ballads, *The
White Ship*—that old true history of the generosity with
which a youth, worthless in life, flung himself upon death—
he was contented with a single utterance of the refrain, "given
out" like the keynote or tune of a chant.

In *The King's Tragedy*, Rossetti has worked upon motive,
broadly human (to adopt the phrase of popular criticism)
such as one and all may realise. Rossetti, indeed, with all his
self-concentration upon his own peculiar aim, by no means
ignored those general interests which are external to poetry
as he conceived it; as he has shown here and there, in this
poetic, as also in pictorial, work. It was but that, in a life to
be shorter even than the average, he found enough to occupy
him in the fulfilment of a task, plainly "given him to do."
Perhaps, if one had to name a single composition of his to
readers desiring to make acquaintance with him for the first
time, one would select: *The King's Tragedy*—that poem so
moving, so popularly dramatic, and lifelike. Notwithstanding
this, his work, it must be conceded, certainly through no
narrowness or egotism, but in the faithfulness of a true work-

man to a vocation so emphatic, was mainly of the esoteric order. But poetry, at all times, exercises two distinct functions: it may reveal, it may unveil to every eye, the ideal aspects of common things, after Gray's way (though Gray too, it is well to remember, seemed in his own day, seemed even to Johnson, obscure)[27] or it may actually add to the number of motives poetic and uncommon in themselves, by the imaginative creation of things that are ideal from their very birth. Rossetti did something, something excellent, of the former kind; but his characteristic, his really revealing work, lay in the adding to poetry of fresh poetic material, of a new order of phenomena, in the creation of a new ideal.

1883

NOTES

1. "The Blessed Damozel," Rossetti's most famous lyric, was printed in the Pre-Raphaelite magazine, *The Germ,* in 1850, and in the *Oxford and Cambridge Magazine,* in 1856, before it appeared in his *Poems* of 1870.
2. The "new school," of painting and poetry, of the Pre-Raphaelites began as a Brotherhood of younger painters—Hunt, Millais, Rossetti—in 1848, when the group banded together against the imitators of Raphael, in a return to the style of Gozzoli (1421–1497) and other Pisan painters. In the mid-Fifties, at Oxford, William Morris and the painter Burne-Jones became disciples of Rossetti, and subsequently jointed him in London. Swinburne, George Meredith, and Christina Rossetti became associated with this literary and artistic grouping.
3. *Data:* "given things"
4. *The Early Italian Poets . . . together with Dante's Vita Nuova,* translated by D. G. Rossetti, London, 1861.
5. Raphael came later than Dante; like Rossetti, Pater makes Dante a kind of Pre-Raphaelite poet, but the "minute and definite imagery" of Dante has little in common with the naturalizing phantasmagoria of Rossetti and his followers.
6. See Rossetti's poem "Dante at Verona."
7. François Villon (1431–1463?), whose poem quoted here in its first two lines is accompanied by the matching lines of Rossetti's translation, "The Ballad of Dead Ladies."
8. The reference here, as is now customary, is to the actually nameless *dæmon* or "monster" in Mary Shelley's novel, and not to Victor Frankenstein, its creator.

9. See Rossetti's major poem, "The Stream's Secret," 169-174, 25-28.
10. See Plato's *Phaedrus* 244 B, 245 A.
11. Rossetti's "The Stream's Secret," 109-114.
12. Pater also linked Morris to Provençal tradition.
13. Genesis 28:12-16.
14. From Blake's Illustrations to the Book of Job, no. XIV: "When the morning Stars sang together . . ."
15. Joseph Addison (1672–1719), "The spacious firmament on high . . ."
16. See Rossetti's "Rose Mary" I, st. 43 and 28; for the scenes above, see "The House of Life: A Sonnet Sequence."
17. See Tennyson's poem "Godiva," 63-64.
18. Those who "rouse themselves into passion for the sake of the passion"; Prosper Mérimée (1803–1870), French story-teller, was one of Pater's particular favorites.
19. The Manichean heresy, founded ultimately upon a third-century A.D. Persian religion, proposed a radical dualism, in which the human body and the earth belonged to a god of darkness, and the realm of the spirit to a god of light.
20. Rossetti's "Love-Lily," final lines.
21. Emanuel Swedenborg (1688–1722), Swedish visionary writer.
22. Rossetti's second volume of verse, *Ballads and Sonnets*, was published in 1881, the year before his death.
23. Pierre de Ronsard (1524–1585), major French poet.
24. "Those ages of passion, when men's souls freely could release themselves to the highest point of exaltation, when the passions that are possible subjects for the fine arts were alive"; from Stendhal's *History of Painting in Italy*.
25. James I (1394–1437), King of Scotland.
26. In "Eden Bower," these two lines, in alternation, are the refrains.
27. In Dr. Samuel Johnson's "Life of Gray" in his *Lives of the Poets;* Pater underestimates Johnson's detestation of Gray.

Postscript[1] (Romanticism)

αἰνεῖ δὲ παλαιὸν, μὲν οἶνον, ἄνθεα δ' ὕμνων νεωτέρων[2]

The words, *classical* and *romantic*, although, like many other critical expressions, sometimes abused by those who have understood them too vaguely or too absolutely, yet define two real tendencies in the history of art and literature. Used in an exaggerated sense, to express a greater opposition between those tendencies than really exists, they have at times tended to divide people of taste into opposite camps. But in that *House Beautiful*,[3] which the creative minds of all generations—the artists and those who have treated life in the spirit of art—are always building together, for the refreshment of the human spirit, these oppositions cease; and the *Interpreter*[4] of the *House Beautiful*, the true æsthetic critic, uses these divisions, only so far as they enable him to enter into the peculiarities of the objects with which he has to do. The term *classical*, fixed, as it is, to a well-defined literature, and a well-defined group in art, is clear, indeed; but then it has often been used in a hard, and merely scholastic sense, by the praisers of what is old and accustomed, at the expense of what is new, by critics who would never have discovered for themselves the charm of any work, whether new or old, who value what is old, in art or literature, for its accessories, and chiefly for the conventional authority that has gathered about it—people who would never really have been made glad by any Venus fresh-risen from the sea, and who praise the Venus of old Greece and Rome, only because they fancy her grown now into something staid and tame.

And as the term, *classical*, has been used in a too absolute, and therefore in a misleading sense, so the term, *romantic*, has been used much too vaguely, in various accidental senses. The sense in which Scott is called a romantic writer is chiefly this; that, in opposition to the literary tradition of the last century, he loved strange adventure, and sought it in the Middle Age.[5] Much later, in a Yorkshire village, the spirit of romanticism bore a more really characteristic fruit in the work of a young girl, Emily Brontë, the romance of *Wuthering Heights*; the figures of Hareton Earnshaw, of Catherine Linton, and of Heathcliffe—tearing open Catherine's grave, removing one side of her coffin, that he may really lie beside her in death—figures so passionate, yet woven on a background of delicately beautiful, moorland scenery, being typical examples of that spirit.[6] In Germany, again, that spirit is shown less in Tieck,[7] its professional representative, than in Meinhold, the author of *Sidonia the Sorceress* and the *Amber-Witch*.[8] In Germany and France, within the last hundred years, the term has been used to describe a particular school of writers;[9] and, consequently, when Heine[10] criticises the

Romantic School in Germany—that movement which culmin-
ated in Goethe's *Goetz von Berlichingen*;[11] or when Théophile
Gautier criticises the romantic movement in France,[12] where,
indeed, it bore its most characteristic fruits, and its play is
hardly yet over where, by a certain audacity, or *bizarrerie*[13]
of motive, united with faultless literary execution, it still
shows itself an imaginative literature, they use the word, with
an exact sense of special artistic qualities, indeed; but use it,
nevertheless, with a limited application to the manifestation
of those qualities at a particular period. But the romantic
spirit is, in reality, an ever-present, an enduring principle, in
the artistic temperament; and the qualities of thought and
style which that, and other similar uses of the word *romantic*
really indicate, are indeed but symptoms of a very continuous
and widely working influence.

Though the words *classical* and *romantic*, then, have
acquired an almost technical meaning, in application to certain developments of German and French taste, yet this is but
one variation of an old opposition, which may be traced from
the very beginning of the formation of European art and
literature. From the first formation of anything like a standard
of taste in these things, the restless curiosity of their more
eager lovers necessarily made itself felt, in the craving for
new motives, new subjects of interest, new modifications of
style. Hence, the opposition between the classicists and the
romanticists—between the adherents, in the culture of
beauty, of the principles of liberty, and authority, respectively
—of strength, and order or what the Greeks called
κοσμιότης.[14]

Sainte-Beauve,[15] in the third volume of the *Causeries du
Lundi*, has discussed the question, *What is meant by a classic?* It was a question he was well fitted to answer, having
himself lived through many phases of taste, and having been
in earlier life an enthusiastic member of the romantic school:
he was also a great master of that sort of "philosophy of
literature," which delights in tracing traditions in it, and the
way in which various phases of thought and sentiment maintain themselves, through successive modifications, from epoch
to epoch. His aim, then, is to give the word *classic* a wider
and, as he says, a more generous sense than it commonly
bears, to make it expressly *grandiose et flottant*;[16] and, in
doing this, he develops, in a masterly manner, those qualities
of measure, purity, temperance, of which it is the especial

function of classical art and literature, whatever meaning, narrower or wider, we attach to the term, to take care.

The charm, therefore, of what is classical, in art or literature, is that of the well-known tale, to which we can, nevertheless, listen over and over again, because it is told so well. To the absolute beauty of its artistic form, is added the accidental, tranquil, charm of familiarity. There are times, indeed, at which these charms fail to work on our spirits at all, because they fail to excite us. "*Romanticism*," says Stendhal,[17] "is the art of presenting to people the literary works which, in the actual state of their habits and beliefs, are capable of giving them the greatest possible pleasure; *classicism*, on the contrary, of presenting them with that which gave the greatest possible pleasure to their grandfathers." But then, beneath all changes of habits and beliefs, our love of that mere abstract proportion—of music—which what is classical in literature possesses, still maintains itself in the best of us, and what pleased our grandparents may at least tranquillise us. The "classic" comes to us out of the cool and quiet of other times, as the measure of what a long experience has shown will at least never displease us. And in the classical literature of Greece and Rome, as in the classics of the last century, the essentially classical element is that quality of order in beauty, which they possess, indeed, in a pre-eminent degree, and which impresses some minds to the exclusion of everything else in them.

It is the addition of strangeness to beauty, that constitutes the romantic character in art: and the desire of beauty being a fixed element in every artistic organisation, it is the addition of curiosity to this desire of beauty, that constitutes the romantic temper.[18] Curiosity and the desire of beauty, have each their place in art, as in all true criticism. When one's curiosity is deficient, when one is not eager enough for new impressions, and new pleasures, one is liable to value mere academical proprieties too highly, to be satisfied with worn-out or conventional types, with the insipid ornament of Racine,[19] or the prettiness of that later Greek sculpture, which passed so long for true Hellenic work;[20] to miss those places where the handiwork of nature, or of the artist, has been most cunning; to find the most stimulating products of art a mere irritation. And when one's curiosity is in excess, when it overbalances the desire of beauty, then one is liable to value in works of art what is inartistic in them; to be satisfied with what is exaggerated in art, with productions like some of those of the romantic school in Germany; not to distinguish, jealously enough, between what is admirably done, and what is done not quite so well, in the writings, for instance, of Jean Paul.[21] And if I had to give instances of these defects, then I should say, that Pope, in common with the age of literature to which he belonged, had too little curiosity, so that there is always a certain insipidity in the effect of his work, exquisite as it is; and coming down to our own time, that Balzac[22] had an excess of curiosity—curiosity not duly tempered with the desire of beauty.

But, however falsely those two tendencies may be opposed by critics, or exaggerated by artists themselves, they are tendencies really at work at all times in art, moulding it, with the balance sometimes a little on one side, sometimes a little on the other, generating, respectively, as the balance inclines on this side or that, two principles, two traditions, in art, and in literature so far as it partakes of the spirit of art. If there is a great overbalance of curiosity, then, we have the grotesque in art: if the union of strangeness and beauty, under very difficult and complex conditions, be a successful one, if the union be entire, then the resultant beauty is very exquisite, very attractive. With a passionate care for beauty, the romantic spirit refuses to have it, unless the condition of strangeness be first fulfilled. Its desire is for a beauty born of unlikely elements, by a profound alchemy, by a difficult initiation, by the charm which wrings it even out of terrible things; and a trace of distortion, of the grotesque, may perhaps linger, as an additional element of expression, about its ultimate grace. Its eager, excited spirit will have strength, the grotesque, first of all—the trees shrieking as you tear off the leaves;[23] for Jean Valjean,[24] the long years of convict life; for Redgauntlet,[25] the quicksands of Solway Moss; then, incorporate with this strangeness, and intensified by restraint, as much sweetness, as much beauty, as is compatible with that. *Énergique, frais, et dispos*—these, according to Sainte-Beuve, are the characteristics of a genuine classic—*les ouvrages anciens ne sont pas classiques parce qu'ils sont vieux, mais parce qu'ils sont énergiques, frais, et dispos.*[26] Energy, freshness, intelligent and masterly disposition:—these are characteristics of Victor Hugo when his alchemy is complete, in certain figures, like Marius and Cosette,[27] in certain scenes, like that in the opening of *Les Travailleurs de la Mer*,[28] where Déruchette

writes the name of *Gilliatt* in the snow, on Christmas morning; but always there is a certain note of strangeness discernible there, as well.

The essential elements, then, of the romantic spirit are
curiosity and the love of beauty; and it is only as an illustration of these qualities, that it seeks the Middle Age, because
in the overcharged atmosphere of the Middle Age, there are
unworked sources of romantic effect, of a strange beauty, to
be won, by strong imagination, out of things unlikely or
remote.

Few, probably, now read Madame de Staël's *De l'Allemagne*,[29] though it has its interest, the interest which never
quite fades out of work really touched with the enthusiasm
of the spiritual adventurer, the pioneer in culture. It was
published in 1810, to introduce to French readers a new
school of writers—the romantic school, from beyond the
Rhine; and it was followed, twenty-three years later, by
Heine's *Romantische Schule*, as at once a supplement and a
correction. Both these books, then, connect romanticism with
Germany, with the names especially of Goethe and Tieck; and,
to many English readers, the idea of romanticism is still
inseparably connected with Germany—that Germany which,
in its quaint old towns, under the spire of Strasburg or the
towers of Heidelberg, was always listening in rapt inaction to
the melodious, fascinating voices of the Middle Age, and
which, now that it has got Strasburg back again, has, I suppose, almost ceased to exist.[30] But neither Germany, with its
Goethe and Tieck, nor England, with its Byron and Scott, is
nearly so representative of the romantic temper as France,
with Murger,[31] and Gautier, and Victor Hugo. It is in French
literature that its most characteristic expression is to be
found; and that, as most closely derivative, historically, from
such peculiar conditions, as ever reinforce it to the utmost.

For, although temperament has much to do with the generation of the romantic spirit, and although this spirit, with
its curiosity, its thirst for a curious beauty, may be always
traceable in excellent art (traceable even in Sophocles) yet
still, in a limited sense, it may be said to be a product of
special epochs. Outbreaks of this spirit, that is, come naturally with particular periods—times, when, in men's
approaches towards art and poetry, curiosity may be noticed
to take the lead, when men come to art and poetry, with a
deep thirst for intellectual excitement, after a long *ennui*, or

in reaction against the strain of outward, practical things: in
the later Middle Age, for instance; so that medieval poetry,
centering in Dante, is often opposed to Greek and Roman
poetry, as romantic poetry to the classical. What the romanticism of Dante is, may be estimated, if we compare the
lines in which Virgil describes the hazelwood, from whose
broken twigs flows the blood of Polydorus, not without the
expression of a real shudder at the ghastly incident, with the
whole canto of the *Inferno*,[32] into which Dante has expanded
them, beautifying and softening it, meanwhile, by a sentiment
of profound pity. And it is especially in that period of intellectual disturbance, immediately preceding Dante, amid
which the romance languages define themselves at last, that
this temper is manifested. Here, in the literature of Provence,
the very name of *romanticism* is stamped with its true sig-
nification: here we have indeed a romantic world, grotesque
even, in the strength of its passions, almost insane in its
curious expression of them, drawing all things into its sphere,
making the birds, nay! lifeless things, its voices and messengers, yet so penetrated with the desire for beauty and sweetness, that it begets a wholly new species of poetry, in which
the *Renaissance* may be said to begin.[33] The last century was
pre-eminently a classical age, an age in which, for art and
literature, the element of a comely order was in the ascend-
ant; which, passing away, left a hard battle to be fought
between the classical and the romantic schools. Yet, it is in
the heart of this century, of Goldsmith and Stothard, of
Watteau and the *Siècle de Louis XIV.*—in one of its central,
if not most characteristic figures, in Rousseau—that the modern or French romanticism really originates.[34] But, what in
the eighteenth century is but an exceptional phenomenon,
breaking through its fair reserve and discretion only at rare
intervals, is the habitual guise of the nineteenth, breaking
through it perpetually, with a feverishness, an incomprehen-
sible straining and excitement, which all experience to some
degree, but yearning also, in the genuine children of the
romantic school to be *énergique, frais, et dispos*—for those
qualities of energy, freshness, comely order; and often, in
Murger, in Gautier, in Victor Hugo, for instance, with singular felicity attaining them.

It is in the terrible tragedy of Rousseau, in fact, that French
romanticism, with much else, begins: reading his *Confessions*
we seem actually to assist at the birth of this new, strong

spirit in the French mind. The wildness which has shocked so many, and the fascination which has influenced almost every one, in the squalid, yet eloquent figure, we see and hear so clearly in that book, wandering under the apple-blossoms and among the vines of Neuchâtel or Vevey[85] actually give it the quality of a very successful romantic invention. His strangeness or distortion, his profound subjectivity, his passionateness—the *cor laceratum*[36]—Rousseau makes all men in love with these. *Je ne suis fait comme aucun de ceux que j'ai sus. Mais si je ne vaux pas mieux, au moins je suis autre.*—"I am not made like any one else I have ever known: yet, if I am not better, at least I am different." These words, from the first page of the *Confessions*, anticipate all the Werthers, Renés, Obermanns, of the last hundred years.[87] For Rousseau did but anticipate a trouble in the spirit of the whole world; and thirty years afterwards, what in him was a peculiarity, became part of the general consciousness. A storm was coming: Rousseau, with others, felt it in the air, and they helped to bring it down: they introduced a disturbing element into French literature, then so trim and formal, like our own literature of the age of Queen Anne.

In 1815, the storm had come and gone, but had left, in the spirit of "young France," the *ennui* of an immense disillusion. In the last chapter of Edgar Quinet's *Révolution Française*,[88] a work itself full of irony, of disillusion, he distinguishes two books, Senancour's *Obermann* and Chateaubriand's *Génie du Christianisme*,[89] as characteristic of the first decade of the present century. In those two books we detect already the disease and the cure—in *Obermann* the irony, refined into a plaintive philosophy of "indifference"—in Chateaubriand's *Génie du Christianisme*, the refuge from a tarnished actual present, a present of disillusion, into a world of strength and beauty in the Middle Age, as at an earlier period—in *René* and *Atala*[40]—into the free play of them in savage life. It is to minds in this spiritual situation, weary of the present, but yearning for the spectacle of beauty and strength, that the works of French romanticism appeal. They set a positive value on the intense, the exceptional; and a certain distortion is sometimes noticeable in them, as in conceptions like Victor Hugo's *Quasimodo*, or *Gwynplaine*,[41] something of a terrible grotesque, of the *macabre*, as the French themselves call it; though always combined with perfect literary execution, as in Gautier's *La Morte Amoureuse*,[42] or the scene of the "maimed" burial-rites of the player, dead of the frost, in his *Capitaine Fracasse*—true "flowers of the yew." It becomes grim humour in Victor Hugo's combat of Gilliatt with the devil-fish,[43] or the incident, with all its ghastly comedy drawn out at length, of the great gun detached from its fastenings on shipboard, in *Quatre-Vingt-Trieze*[44] (perhaps the most terrible of all the accidents that can happen by sea) and in the entire episode, in that book, of the *Convention*.[45] Not less surely does it reach a genuine pathos; for the habit of noting and distinguishing one's own most intimate passages of sentiment makes one sympathetic, begetting, as it must, the power of entering, by all sorts of finer ways, into the intimate recesses of other minds; so that pity is another quality of romanticism, both Victor Hugo and Gautier being great lovers of animals, and charming writers about them, and Murger being unrivalled in the pathos of his *Scènes de la Vie de Jeunesse*.[46] Penetrating so finely into all situations which appeal to pity, above all, into the special or exceptional phases of such feeling, the romantic humour is not afraid of the quaintness or singularity of its circumstances or expression, pity, indeed, being of the essence of humour; so that Victor Hugo does but turn his romanticism into practice, in his hunger and thirst after practical *Justice!*—a justice which shall no longer wrong children, or animals, for instance, by ignoring in a stupid, mere breadth of view, minute facts about them. Yet the romanticists are antinomian,[47] too, sometimes, because the love of energy and beauty, of distinction in passion, tended naturally to become a little *bizarre*, plunging into the Middle Age, into the secrets of old Italian story. *Are we in the Inferno?*—we are tempted to ask, wondering at something malign in so much beauty. For over all a care for the refreshment of the human spirit by fine art manifests itself, a predominant sense of literary charm, so that, in their search for the secret of exquisite expression, the romantic school went back to the forgotten world of early French poetry, and literature itself became the most delicate of the arts—like "goldsmith's work," says Sainte-Beuve, of Bertrand's *Gaspard de la Nuit*[48]—and that peculiarly French gift, the gift of exquisite speech, *argute loqui*,[49] attained in them a perfection which it had never seen before.

Stendhal, a writer whom I have already quoted, and of whom English readers might well know much more than they do, stands between the earlier and later growths of the romantic spirit. His novels are rich in romantic quality; and his other writings—partly criticism, partly personal reminiscences—are a very curious and interesting illustration of the needs out of which romanticism arose. In his book on *Racine and Shakespeare*, Stendhal argues that all good art was romantic in its day; and this is perhaps true in Stendhal's sense. That little treatise, full of "dry light"[50] and fertile ideas, was published in the year 1823, and its object is to defend an entire independence and liberty in the choice and treatment of subject, both in art and literature, against those who upheld the exclusive authority of precedent. In pleading the cause of romanticism, therefore, it is the novelty, both of form and of motive, in writings like the *Hernani* of Victor Hugo[51] (which soon followed it, raising a storm of criticism) that he is chiefly concerned to justify. To be interesting and really stimulating, to keep us from yawning even, art and literature must follow the subtle movements of that nimbly-shifting *Time-Spirit*, or *Zeit-Geist*, understood by French not less than by German criticism, which is always modifying men's taste, as it modifies their manners and their pleasures. This, he contends, is what all great workmen had always understood. Dante, Shakespeare, Molière, had exercised an absolute independence in their choice of subject and treatment. To turn always with that ever-changing spirit, yet to retain the flavour of what was admirably done in past generations, in the classics, as we say—is the problem of true romanticism. "Dante," he observes, "was pre-eminently the romantic poet. He adored Virgil, yet he wrote the *Divine Comedy*, with the episode of Ugolino,[52] which is as unlike the *Æneid* as can possibly be. And those who thus obey the fundamental principle of romanticism, one by one become classical, and are joined to that ever-increasing common league, formed by men of all countries, to approach nearer and nearer to perfection."

Romanticism, then, although it has its epochs, is in its essential characteristics rather a spirit which shows itself at all times, in various degrees, in individual workmen and their work, and the amount of which criticism has to estimate in them taken one by one, than the peculiarity of a time or a school. Depending on the varying proportion of curiosity and the desire of beauty, natural tendencies of the artistic spirit at all times, it must always be partly a matter of individual temperament. The eighteenth century in England has been regarded as almost exclusively a classical period; yet William Blake, a type of so much which breaks through what are conventionally thought the influences of that century, is still a noticeable phenomenon in it, and the reaction in favour of naturalism in poetry begins in that century, early. There are, thus, the born romanticists and the born classicists. There are the born classicists who start with *form*, to whose minds the comeliness of the old, immemorial, well-recognised types in art and literature, have revealed themselves impressively; who will entertain no matter which will not go easily and flexibly into them; whose work aspires only to be a variation upon, or study from, the older masters. " 'Tis art's decline, my son!"[53] they are always saying, to the progressive element in their own generation; to those who care for that which in fifty years' time every one will be caring for. On the other hand, there are the born romanticists, who start with an original, untried *matter*, still in fusion; who conceive this vividly, and hold by it as the essence of their work; who, by the very vividness and heat of their conception, purge away, sooner or later, all that is not organically appropriate to it, till the whole effect adjusts itself in clear, orderly, proportionate form; which form, after a very little time, becomes classical in its turn.

The romantic or classical character of a picture, a poem, a literary work, depends, then, on the balance of certain qualities in it; and in this sense, a very real distinction may be drawn between good classical and good romantic work. But all critical terms are relative; and there is at least a valuable suggestion in that theory of Stendhal's, that all good art was romantic in its day. In the beauties of Homer and Pheidias, quiet as they now seem, there must have been, for those who confronted them for the first time, excitement and surprise, the sudden, unforeseen satisfaction of the desire of beauty. Yet the *Odyssey*, with its marvellous adventure, is more romantic than the *Iliad*, which nevertheless contains, among many other romantic episodes, that of the immortal horses of Achilles, who weep at the death of Patroclus. Æschylus is more romantic than Sophocles, whose *Philoctetes*, were it written now, might figure, for the strangeness of its motive and the perfectness of its execution, as typically romantic;[54] while, of Euripides, it may be said, that his method in writing his plays is to sacrifice readily almost everything else, so that he may attain the fulness of a single romantic effect. These two tendencies, indeed, might be applied as a measure or standard, all through Greek and Roman art and poetry, with very illuminating results; and for an analyst of the romantic principle in art, no exercise would be more profitable, than to walk through the collection of classical antiquities at the Louvre, or the British Museum, or to examine some representative collection of Greek coins, and note how the element of curiosity, of the love of strangeness, insinuates itself into classical design, and record the effects of the romantic spirit there, the traces of struggle, of the grotesque even, though over-balanced here by sweetness; as in the sculpture of Chartres and Rheims,[55] the real sweetness of mind in the sculptor is often overbalanced by the grotesque, by the rudeness of his strength.

Classicism, then, means for Stendhal, for that younger enthusiastic band of French writers whose unconscious method he formulated into principles, the reign of what is pedantic, conventional, and narrowly academical in art; for him, all good art is romantic. To Sainte-Beuve, who understands the term in a more liberal sense, it is the characteristic of certain epochs, of certain spirits in every epoch, not given to the exercise of original imagination, but rather to the working out of refinements of manner on some authorised matter; and who bring to their perfection, in this way, the elements of sanity, of order and beauty in manner. In general criticism, again, it means the spirit of Greece and Rome, of some phases in literature and art that may seem of equal authority with Greece and Rome, the age of Louis the Fourteenth, the age of Johnson;[56] though this is at best an uncritical use of the term, because in Greek and Roman work there are typical examples of the romantic spirit. But explain the terms as we may, in application to particular epochs, there are these two elements always recognisable; united in perfect art—in Sophocles, in Dante, in the highest work of Goethe, though not always absolutely balanced there; and these two elements may be not inappropriately termed the classical and romantic tendencies.

Material for the artist, motives of inspiration, are not yet exhausted: our curious, complex, aspiring age still abounds in subjects for æsthetic manipulation by the literary as well as by other forms of art. For the literary art, at all events, the problem just now is, to induce order upon the contorted, proportionless accumulation of our knowledge and experience, our science and history, our hopes and disillusion, and, in effecting this, to do consciously what has been done hitherto for the most part too unconsciously, to write our English language as the Latins wrote theirs, as the French write, as scholars should write. Appealing, as he may, to precedent in this matter, the scholar will still remember that if "the style is the man" it is also the age: that the nineteenth century too will be found to have had its style, justified by necessity—a style very different, alike from the baldness of an impossible "Queen Anne" revival, and an incorrect, incondite[57] exuberance, after the mode of Elizabeth:[58] that we can only return to either at the price of an improverishment of form or matter, or both, although, an intellectually rich age such as ours being necessarily an eclectic one, we may well cultivate some of the excellences of literary types so different as those: that in literature as in other matters it is well to unite as many diverse elements as may be: that the individual writer or artist, certainly, is to be estimated by the number of graces he combines, and his power of interpenetrating them in a given work. To discriminate schools, of art, of literature, is, of course, part of the obvious business of literary criticism: but, in the work of literary production, it is easy to be overmuch occupied concerning them. For, in truth, the legitimate contention is, not of one age or school of literary art against another, but of all successive schools alike, against the stupidity which is dead to the substance, and the vulgarity which is dead to form.

1876

NOTES

1. "Romanticism" was the original title, in 1876; in 1889, this became the "Postscript" to *Appreciations*, suggesting a critical Credo. Lionel Trilling usefully contrasts this essay with Arnold's "The Study of Poetry," and I suspect "Romanticism" was an implicit reply to Arnold's essay, opposing the criterion of "energy" to Arnold's moral strictures.
2. From Pindar's *Olympian Odes IX* 48-49: "When you praise the wine that is old, you should praise also the flowers of songs that are new."

3. Where Christian, in Bunyan's *Pilgrim's Progress,* is granted a vision of the Delectable Mountains.

4. Bunyan's "Interpreter" aids Christian in understanding his journey.

5. A sensible exclusion on Pater's part; he grants the romance-element in Scott, but refuses to identify this with Romanticism.

6. *Wuthering Heights* was published in 1847.

7. Johann Ludwig Tieck (1773–1853), German Romantic novelist.

8. Wilhelm Meinhold (1797–1851), one of Pater's rare failures in taste; Meinhold had a certain gift for historical reconstruction, which fascinated Pater.

9. Pater rightly criticizes French and German historians of literature for failing to see Romanticism as a recurrent and universal phenomenon, rather than a phenomenon of a particular time-bound school of writers.

10. Heinrich Heine (1797–1856), major German poet, published a book about Romanticism in 1836.

11. Goethe's *Goetz von Berlichingen* (1773), an idealizing prose-drama.

12. Théophile Gautier's *History of Romanticism* came out in 1874, two years after the poet's death.

13. *Bizarrerie:* "extravagance."

14. "Orderly behavior."

15. Charles-Augustin Sainte-Beuve (1804–1869), major French literary critic. His *Causeries du Lundi* (Monday Conversations) ran in Parisian newspapers from 1849 to 1869. Increasingly, his criticism became anti-Romantic.

16. *Grandiose et flottant:* "grand and comprehensive (not rigid)."

17. From Stendhal's (Henri Beyle's, 1783–1842) *Racine and Shakespeare* (1823–1825), two essays in defense of Romanticism.

18. This definition, though much disparaged in our time, remains the best brief definition Romanticism has received.

19. An extraordinary misjudgment of Racine, but not just Pater's in nineteenth-century England, where Racine was in disfavor.

20. Pater, though not a thorough classical scholar, showed remarkable insight into the different phases of Greek art and culture.

21. Jean Paul Friedrich Richter (1763–1825), German novelist and aesthetician, wrote under the name "Jean Paul."

22. Balzac was one of Pater's failures in contemporary insight; a world in which every janitor was a genius is hardly a Paterian one.

23. Virgil, *Aeneid* III 19–72.

24. Hero of Hugo's *Les Misérables.*

25. Chief character in Scott's *Redgauntlet*.
26. "Ancient works are classics not because they are old, but because they are energetic, fresh, and well-organized." Sainte-Beuve took this observation from Goethe.
27. Marius and Cosette are young people in love with one another in Hugo's *Les Misérables*.
28. *Toilers of the Sea*.
29. A famous chapter of Madame de Staël's *De l'Allemagne* (1810), on Germany and its cultural contributions, contains a contrast between Classical and Romantic poetry. Heine's *Romantic School* is a better book, as Pater implies.
30. Strasbourg, chief city of Alsace-Lorraine, became French in 1681, and reverted to Germany after the French defeat in 1870. Pater's irony here is reinforced by subsequent history, as Strasbourg became French again in 1919, German again in 1940, and French again in 1945, presumably for good.
31. Henri Murger (1822–1851) was a novelist hardly in Gautier's class, let alone Hugo's.
32. *Inferno*, Canto XIII.
33. Primarily, Pater refers here to the love poetry of the troubadours of southern France in the twelfth century, but the sentence is an epitome of his entire vision of cultural history.
34. Evidently Pater regards all these as Pre-Romantic: Oliver Goldsmith (1730–1774), Anglo-Irish poet, novelist, playwright, and essayist; Thomas Stothard (1755–1834), English painter particularly hated by Blake; Jean-Antoine Watteau (1684–1721), great French painter; and Voltaire's *Age of Louis XIV* (1751). It is a curiously assorted list.
35. Towns in northwest Switzerland that evoke Rousseau.
36. *Cor laceratum:* "a lacerated or torn heart."
37. The young men of ravaged sensibility, in Goethe's *Sorrows of Young Werther* (1774), Chateaubriand's *René* (1802), and Senancour's *Obermann* (1804).
38. Published in two volumes, 1865.
39. *The Genius of Christianity* (1802) in five volumes, including *René*.
40. *Atala* (1801), included a year later in *The Genius of Christianity*. Atala, daughter of an American Indian chief, turns Christian and later dies in the conflict between her new faith and her older passion.
41. Quasimodo is the hunchback of *The Hunchback of Notre Dame;* Gwynplaine is a deformed boy in *The Man Who Laughs*.
42. Gautier's supernatural stories (1857).
43. In *Toilers of the Sea*.
44. An incident in *Ninety-three*.
45. The Convention, meeting in 1793, promulgated the Terror.
46. A volume of short stories (1851) dealing with social pathos.

47. "Antinomian" generally means opposed to all conceptions of morality; Pater gives it a more Romantic meaning, closer to Blake's dialectic in *The Marriage of Heaven and Hell*.
48. A fantastic book of prose-poems (1842), written by Louis Bertrand (1807-1841) about 1830.
49. *Argate loqui:* "to speak impressively."
50. "Dry light" alludes to a supposed saying of Heracleitus (reported by Plutarch) that "The most perfect soul is a dry light."
51. One of the triumphs of French Romanticism, in 1830; Hugo's play provoked fierce demonstrations at its first two performances, where the Romantic partisans out-shouted their opponents.
52. *Inferno, Canto* XXXIII.
53. From Browning's great dramatic monologue, "Fra Lippo Lippi," 233.
54. Philoctetes, a Greek warrior, was abandoned by his fellows on the way to Troy, after a serpent's wound caused him to exude a horrible stench. Unable to capture Troy without the bow and arrows of Heracles, now possessed by Philoctetes, his comrades return to beg the wounded hero's aid.
55. Meaning the sculpture in their cathedrals.
56. Louis XIV (1643–1715); Dr. Samuel Johnson (1709–1784).
57. "Incondite": crude.
58. Though Pater makes a negative judgment upon neo-Elizabethanism here, it was a legitimate and necessary element in English Romanticism.

from *Plato and Platonism*

The Genius of Plato

All true criticism of philosophic doctrine, as of every other product of human mind, must begin with an historic estimate of the conditions, antecedent and contemporary, which helped to make it precisely what it was. But a complete criticism does not end there. In the evolution of abstract doctrine as we find it written in the history of philosophy, if there is always, on one side, the fatal, irresistible, mechanic play of circumstance—the circumstances of a particular age, which may be analysed and explained; there is always also, as if acting from the opposite side, the comparatively inexplicable force of a personality, resistant to, while it is moulded by, them. It might even be said that the trial-task of criticism, in regard to literature and art no less than to philosophy, begins exactly where the estimate of general conditions, of the conditions common to all the products of this or that particular age—of the "environment"—leaves off, and we touch what is unique in the individual genius which contrived after all, by force of will, to have its own masterful way with that environment. If in reading Plato, for instance, the philosophic student has to re-construct for himself, as far as possible, the general character of an *age*, he must also, so far as he may, reproduce the portrait of a *person*. The Sophists, the Sophistical world, around him; his master, Socrates; the Pre-Socratic philosophies; the mechanic influence, that is to say, of past and present:—of course we can know nothing at all of the Platonic doctrine except so far as we see it in well-ascertained contact with all that; but there is also Plato himself in it.

—A personality, we may notice at the outset, of a certain complication. The great masters of philosophy have been for the most part its noticeably single-minded servants. As if in emulation of Aristotle's simplicity of character, his absorbing intellectualism—impressive certainly, heroic enough, in its way—they have served science, science *in vacuo*, as if nothing beside, faith, imagination, love, the bodily sense, could detach them from it for an hour. It is not merely that we know little of their lives (there was so little to tell!) but that we know nothing at all of their *temperaments*; of which, that one leading abstract or scientific force in them was in fact strictly exclusive. Little more than intellectual abstractions themselves, in them philosophy was wholly faithful to its colours, or its colourlessness; rendering not grey only, as Hegel said of it, but all colours alike, in grey.

With Plato it was otherwise. In him, the passion for truth did but bend, or take the bent of, certain ineradicable predispositions of his nature, in themselves perhaps somewhat opposed to that. It is however in the blending of diverse elements in the mental constitution of Plato that the peculiar Platonic quality resides. Platonism is in one sense an emphatic witness to the unseen, the transcendental, the non-experienced, the beauty, for instance, which is not for the bodily eye. Yet the author of this philosophy of the unseen was,—Who can doubt it who has read but a page of him? this, in fact, is what has led and kept to his pages many who have little or no turn for the sort of questions Plato actually discusses:—The author of this philosophy of the unseen was one, for whom, as was said of a very different French writer, "the *visible* world really existed." Austere as he seems, and on well-considered principle really is, his temperance or austerity, æsthetically so winning, is attained only by the chastisement, the control, of a variously interested, a richly sensuous nature. Yes, the visible world, so pre-eminently worth eye-sight at Athens just then, really existed for him: exists still—there's the point!—is active still everywhere, when he seems to have turned away from it to invisible things.

To the somewhat sad-coloured school of Socrates, and its discipline towards apathy or contempt in such matters, he had brought capacities of bodily sense with the making in them of an *Odyssey*; or (shall we say?) of a poet after the order of Sappho or Catullus; as indeed also a practical intelligence, a popular management of his own powers, a skill in philosophic yet mundane Greek prose, which might have constituted him the most successful of Sophists. You cannot help seeing that his mind is a storehouse of all the liveliest imageries of men and things. Nothing, if it really arrests eye or ear at all, is too trivial to note. Passing through the crowd of human beings, he notes the sounds alike of their solemn hymns and of their pettiest handicraft. A conventional philosopher might speak of "dumb matter," for instance; but Plato has lingered too long in braziers' workshops to lapse into so stupid an epithet. And if the persistent hold of sensible things upon him thus reveals itself in trifles, it is manifest no less in the way in which he can tell a long story,—no one more effectively! and again, in his graphic presentment of whole scenes from actual life, like that with which *The Republic* opens. His Socrates, like other people, is curious to witness a new religious function: how they will do it. As in modern times, it would be a pleasant occasion also for meeting the acquaintance one likes best—Ξυνεσόμεθα πολλοῖς τῶν νέων αὐτόθι. "We shall meet a number of our youth there: we shall have a dialogue: there will be a torchlight procession in honour of the goddess, an equestrian procession: a novel feature!—What? Torches in their hands, passed on as they race? Aye, and an illumination, through the entire night. It will be worth seeing!"—that old midnight hour, as Carlyle says of another vivid scene, "shining yet on us, ruddy-bright through the centuries." Put alongside of that, and, for life-like charm, side by side with Murillo's Beggar-boys[1] (you catch them, if you look at his canvas on the sudden, actually moving their mouths, to laugh and speak and munch their crusts, all at once) the scene in the *Lysis* of the dice-players. There the boys are! in full dress, to take part in a religious ceremony. It is scarcely over; but they are already busy with the knuckle-bones, some just outside the door, others in a corner. Though Plato never tells one without due motive, yet he loves a story for its own sake, can make one of fact or fancy at a moment's notice, or re-tell other people's better: how those dear skinny grasshoppers of Attica, for instance, had once been human creatures, who, when the Muses first came on earth, were so absorbed by their music that they forgot even to eat and drink, till they died of it.[2] And then the story of Gyges in *The Republic*, and the ring that can make its wearer invisible:—it goes as easily, as the ring itself round the finger.[3] Like all masters of literature, Plato has of course varied excellences; but perhaps none of them has won for him a larger number of friendly readers than this impress of visible reality. For him, truly (as he supposed the highest sort of knowledge must of necessity be) all knowledge was like knowing a *person*. The Dialogue itself, being, as it is, the special creation of his literary art, becomes in his hands, and by his masterly conduct of it, like a single living person; so comprehensive a sense does he bring to bear upon it of the slowly-developing physiognomy of the thing—its organic structure, its symmetry and expression—combining all the various, disparate subjects of *The Republic*, for example, into a manageable whole, so entirely that, looking back, one fancies this long dialogue of at least three hundred pages might have occupied, perhaps an afternoon.

And those who take part in it! If Plato did not create the "Socrates" of his Dialogues, he has created other characters hardly less life-like.[4] The young Charmides, the incarnation of natural, as the aged Cephalus of acquired, temperance;[5] his Sophoclean amenity as he sits there pontifically at the altar, in the court of his peaceful house; the large company, of varied character and of every age, which moves in those Dialogues, though still oftenest the young in all their youthful liveliness:—who that knows them at all can doubt Plato's hold on persons, that of persons on him? Sometimes, even when they are not formally introduced into his work, characters that had interested, impressed, or touched him, inform and colour it, as if with their personal influence, showing through what purports to be the wholly abstract analysis of some wholly abstract moral situation. Thus, the form of the dying Socrates himself is visible pathetically in the description of the suffering righteous man, actually put into his own mouth in the second book of *The Republic*; as the winning brilliancy of the lost spirit of Alcibiades infuses those pages of the sixth, which discuss the nature of one by birth and endowments an aristocrat, amid the dangers to which it is exposed in the Athens of that day—the qualities which must make him, if not the saviour, the destroyer, of a society which cannot remain unaffected by his showy presence. *Corruptio optimi pessima!*[6] Yet even here, when Plato is dealing with the inmost elements of personality, his eye is still on its object, on *character* as seen in *characteristics*, through those details, which make character a sensible fact, the changes of colour in the face as of tone in the voice, the gestures, the really physiognomic value, or the mere tricks, of gesture and glance and speech. What is visibly expressive in, or upon, persons; those flashes of temper which check yet give renewed interest to the course of a conversation; the delicate touches of intercourse, which convey to the very senses all the subtleties of the heart or of the intelligence:—it is always more than worth his while to make note of these.

We see, for instance, the sharp little pygmy bit of a soul that catches sight of any little thing so keenly, and makes a very proper lawyer.[7] We see, as well as hear, the "rhapsodist," whose sensitive performance of his part is nothing less than an "interpretation" of it, artist and critic at once:[8] the personal vanities of the various speakers in his Dialogues, as though Plato had observed, or overheard them, alone; and the inevitable prominence of youth wherever it is present at all, nothwithstanding the real sweetness of manner and modesty of soul he records of it so affectionately. It is this he loves best to linger by; to feel himself in contact with a condition of life, which translates all it is, so immediately, into delightful colour, and movement, and sound. The eighth and ninth books of *The Republic* are a grave contribution, as you know, to abstract moral and political theory, a generalisation of weighty changes of character in men and states.[9] But his observations on the concrete traits of individuals, young or old, which enliven us on the way; the difference in sameness of sons and fathers, for instance; the influence of servants on their masters; how the minute ambiguities of rank, as a family becomes impoverished, tell on manners, on temper; all the play of moral colour in the reflex of mere circumstance on what men really are:—the characterisation of all this has with Plato a touch of the peculiar fineness of Thackeray, one might say. Plato enjoys it for its own sake, and would have been an excellent writer of fiction.

There is plenty of humour in him also of course, and something of irony—salt, to keep the exceeding richness and sweetness of his discourse from cloying the palate. The affectations of sophists, or professors, their staginess or their inelegance, the harsh laugh, the swaggering ways, of Thrasymachus,[10] whose determination to make the general company share in a private conversation, is significant of his whole character, he notes with a finely-pointed pencil, with something of the fineness of malice,—*malin*, as the French say. Once Thrasymachus had been actually seen to blush. It is with a very different sort of fineness Plato notes the blushes of the young; of Hippocrates, for instance, in the *Protagoras*. The great Sophist was said to be in Athens, at the house of Callicles, and the diligent young scholar is up betimes, eager to hear him. He rouses Socrates before daylight. As they linger in the court, the lad speaks of his own intellectual aspirations; blushes at his confidence. It was just then that the morning sun blushed with his first beam, as if to reveal the lad's blushing face.—Καὶ ὃς εἶπεν ἐρυθριάσας, ἤδη γὰρ ὑπέφαινέ τι ἡμέρας ὥστε καταφανῆ αὐτὸν γενέσθαι. He who noted that so precisely had, surely, the delicacy of the artist, a fastidious eye for the subtleties of colour as soul made visibly expressive. "Poor creature as I am," says the Platonic Socrates, in the *Lysis*, concerning another youthful blush, "Poor creature as I am, I have one talent: I can recognise, at first sight, the lover and the beloved."

So it is with the audible world also. The exquisite monotony of the voice of the great sophist, for example, "once set in motion, goes ringing on like a brazen pot, which if you strike it continues to sound till some one lays his hand upon it." And if the delicacy of eye and ear, so also the keenness and constancy of his observation, are manifest in those elaborately wrought images for which the careful reader lies in wait: the mutiny of the sailors in the ship— ship of the state,[11] or of one's own soul: the echoes and beams and shadows of that half-illuminated cavern, the human mind:[12] the caged birds in the *Theœtetus*, which are like the flighty, half-contained notions of an imperfectly educated understanding. *Real* notions are to be ingrained by persistent thoroughness of the "dialectic" method,[13] as if by conscientious dyers. He makes us stay to watch such dyers busy with their purple stuff, as he had done;[14] adding as it were ethic colour to what he sees with the eye, and painting while he goes, as if on the margin of his high philosophical discourse, himself scarcely aware; as the monkish scribe set bird or flower, with so much truth of earth, in the blank spaces of his heavenly meditation.

Now Plato is one for whom the visible world thus "really exists" because he is by nature and before all things, from first to last, unalterably a lover. In that, precisely, lies the secret of the susceptible and diligent eye, the so sensitive ear. The central interest of his own youth—of his profoundly impressible youth—as happens always with natures of real capacity, gives law and pattern to all that succeeds it. Τὰ ἐρωτικά, as he says, the experience, the discipline, of love, had been that for Plato; and, as love must of necessity deal above all with visible persons, this discipline involved an exquisite culture of the senses. It is "as lovers use," that he is ever on the watch for those dainty messages, those finer intimations, to eye and ear. If in the later development of his philosophy the highest sort of knowledge comes to seem like the knowledge of a person, the relation of the reason to truth like the commerce of one person with another, the peculiarities of personal relationship thus moulding his conception of the properly invisible world of ideas, this is partly because, for a lover, the entire visible world, its hues and outline, its attractiveness, its power and bloom, must have associated themselves pre-eminently with the power and bloom of visible living persons. With these, as they made themselves known by word and glance and touch, through the medium of the senses, lay the forces, which, in that inexplicable tyranny of one person over another, shaped the soul.

Just there, then, is the secret of Plato's intimate concern with, his power over, the sensible world, the apprehensions of the sensuous faculty: he is a lover, a great lover, somewhat after the manner of Dante. For him, as for Dante, in the impassioned glow of his conceptions, the material and the spiritual are blent and fused together. While, in that fire and heat, what is spiritual attains the definite visibility of a crystal, what is material, on the other hand, will lose its earthiness and impurity.[15] It is of the amorous temper, therefore, you must think in connexion with Plato's youth— of this, amid all the strength of the genius in which it is so large a constituent,—indulging, developing, refining, the sensuous capacities, the powers of eye and ear, of the fancy also which can re-fashion, of the speech which can best respond to and reproduce, their liveliest presentments. That is why when Plato speaks of visible things it is as if you saw them. He who in the *Symposium* describes so vividly the pathway, the ladder, of love, its joyful ascent towards a more perfect beauty than we have ever yet actually seen, by way of a parallel to the gradual elevation of mind towards perfect knowledge, knew all that, we may be sure—τὰ ἐρωτικά —all the ways of lovers, in the literal sense. He speaks of them retrospectively indeed, but knows well what he is talking about. Plato himself had not been always a mere Platonic lover; was rather, naturally, as he makes Socrates say of himself, ἥττων τῶν καλῶν—subject to the influence of fair persons. A certain penitential colour amid that glow of fancy and expression, hints that the final harmony of his nature had been but gradually beaten out, and invests the temperance, actually so conspicuous in his own nature, with the charms of a patiently elaborated effect of art.

For we must remind ourselves just here, that, quite naturally also, instinctively, and apart from the austere influences which claimed and kept his allegiance later, Plato, with a kind of unimpassioned passion, was a lover in particular of temperance; of temperance too, as it may be *seen*, as a visible thing—seen in Charmides, say! in that subdued and grey-eyed loveliness, "clad in sober grey"; or in those youthful athletes which, in ancient marble, reproduce him and the like of him with sound, firm outlines, such as temperance secures.¹⁶ Still, that some more luxurious sense of physical beauty had at one time greatly disturbed him, divided him against himself, we may judge from his own words in a famous passage of the *Phœdrus* concerning the management, the so difficult management, of those winged steeds of the body, which is the chariot of the soul.¹⁷

Puzzled, in some degree, Plato seems to remain, not merely in regard to the higher love and the lower, Aphrodite Urania and Aphrodite Pandemus, as he distinguishes them in the *Symposium*; nor merely with the difficulty of arbitrating between some inward beauty, and that which is outward; with the odd mixture everywhere, save in its still unapprehended but eternal essence, of the beautiful with what is otherwise; but he is yet more harassed by the experience (it is in this shape that the world-old puzzle of the existence of evil comes to him) that even to the truest eyesight, to the best trained faculty of soul, the beautiful would never come to seem strictly concentric with the good. That seems to have taxed his understanding as gravely as it had tried his will, and he was glad when in the mere natural course of years he was become at all events less ardent a lover. 'Tis he is the authority for what Sophocles had said on the happy decay

of the passions as age advanced: it was "like being set free
from service to a band of madmen." His own distinguishing
note is tranquil afterthought upon his conflict, with a kind of
envy of the almost disembodied old age of Cephalus, who
quotes that saying of Sophocles amid his placid sacrificial
doings. Connect with this quiet scene, and contrast with the
luxuriant power of the *Phœdrus* and the *Symposium*, what,
for a certain touch of later mysticism in it, we might call
Plato's evening prayer, in the ninth book of *The Republic.*—

> When any one, being healthfully and temperately disposed
> towards himself, turns to sleep, having stirred the reasonable
> part of him with a feast of fair thoughts and high problems,
> being come to full consciousness, himself with himself; and
> has, on the other hand, committed the element of desire
> neither to appetite, nor to surfeiting, to the end that this may
> slumber well, and, by its pain or pleasure, cause no trouble to
> that part which is best in him, but may suffer it, alone by
> itself, in its pure essence, to behold and aspire towards some
> object, and apprehend what it knows not—some event, of the
> past, it may be, or something that now is, or will be hereafter;
> and in like manner has soothed hostile impulse, so that, falling
> to no angry thoughts against any, he goes not to rest with a
> troubled spirit, but with those two parts at peace within, and
> with that third part, wherein reason is engendered, on the
> move:—you know, I think, that in sleep of this sort he lays
> special hold on truth, and then least of all is there lawlessness
> in the visions of his dreams.   *Republic*, 571.

For Plato, being then about twenty-eight years old, had
listened to the "Apology" of Socrates; had heard from them
all that others had heard or seen of his last hours; himself
perhaps actually witnessed those last hours. "Justice itself"—
the "absolute" Justice—had then become almost a visible
object, and had greatly solemnised him. The rich young man,
rich also in intellectual gifts, who might have become (we
see this in the adroit management of his written work) the
most brilliant and effective of Sophists; who might have
developed dialogues into plays, tragedy, perhaps comedy, as
he cared; whose sensuous or graphic capacity might have
made him the poet of an *Odyssey*, a Sappho, or a Catullus,
or, say! just such a poet as, just because he was so attractive, would have been disfranchised in the Perfect City;[18]
was become the creature of an immense seriousness, of a
fully adult sense, unusual in Greek perhaps even more than in

Roman writers, "of the weightiness of the matters concerning which he has to discourse, and of the frailty of man." He inherits, alien as they might be to certain powerful influences in his own temper, alike the sympathies and the antipathies of that strange, delightful teacher, who had given him (most precious of gifts!) an inexhaustible interest in himself.[19] It is in this way he inherits a preference for those trying severities of thought which are characteristic of the Eleatic school;[20] an antagonism to the successful Sophists of the day, in whom the old sceptical "philosophy of motion" seemed to be renewed as a theory of morals;[21] and henceforth, in short, this master of visible things, this so ardent lover, will be a lover of the invisible, with—Yes! there it is constantly, in the Platonic dialogues, not to be explained away—with a certain asceticism, amid all the varied opulence, of sense, of speech and fancy, natural to Plato's genius.[22]

The lover, who is become a lover of the invisible, but still a lover, and therefore, literally, a seer, of it, carrying an elaborate cultivation of the bodily senses, of eye and ear, their natural force and acquired fineness—gifts akin properly to τὰ ἐρωτικά, as he says, to the discipline of sensuous love—into the world of intellectual abstractions; seeing and hearing there too, associating for ever all the imagery of things seen with the conditions of what primarily exists only for the mind, filling that "hollow land" with delightful colour and form, as if now at last the mind were veritably dealing with living people there, living people who play upon us through the affinities, the repulsion and attraction, of *persons* towards one another, all the magnetism, as we call it, of actual human friendship or love:—There, is the *formula* of Plato's genius, the essential condition of the specially Platonic temper, of Platonism. And his style, because it really is Plato's style, conforms to, and in its turn promotes in others, that mental situation.[23] He breaks as it were visible colour into the very texture of his work: his vocabulary, the very stuff he manipulates, has its delightful æsthetic qualities; almost every word, one might say, its figurative value. And yet no one perhaps has with equal power literally sounded the unseen depths of thought, and, with what may be truly called "substantial" word and phrase, given locality there to the mere adumbrations, the dim hints and surmise, of the speculative mind. For him, all gifts of sense and intelligence converge in one supreme faculty of theoretic vision, θεωρία, the imaginative reason.

To trace that thread of physical colour, entwined throughout, and multiplied sometimes into large tapestried figures, is the business, the enjoyment, of the student of the Dialogues, as he reads them. For this or that special literary quality indeed we may go safely by preference to this or that particular Diagloue; to the *Gorgias*,[24] for instance, for the readiest Attic wit, and a manly practical sense in the handling of philosophy; to the *Charmides*,[25] for something like the effect of sculpture in modelling a person; to the *Timœus*,[26] for certain brilliant chromatic effects. Yet who that reads the *Theœtetus*,[27] or the *Phœdrus*,[28] or the seventh book of *The Republic*,[29] can doubt Plato's gift in precisely the opposite direction; that gift of sounding by words the depths of thought, a plastic power literally, moulding to term and phrase what might have seemed in its very nature too impalpable and abstruse to lend itself, in any case, to language? He gives names to the invisible acts, processes, creations, of abstract mind, as masterly, as efficiently, as Adam himself to the visible living creations of old. As Plato speaks of them, we might say, those abstractions too become visible living creatures. We read the speculative poetry of Wordsworth, or Tennyson; and we may observe that a great metaphysical force has come into language which is by no means purely technical or scholastic; what a help such language is to the understanding, to a real hold over the things, the thoughts, the mental processes, those words denote; a vocabulary to which thought freely commits itself, trained, stimulated, raised, thereby, towards a high level of abstract conception, surely to the increase of our general intellectual powers. That, of course, is largely due to Plato's successor, to Aristotle's life-long labour of analysis and definition, and to his successors the Schoolmen, with their systematic culture of a precise instrument for the registration, by the analytic intellect, of its own subtlest movements. But then, Aristotle, himself the first of the Schoolmen, had succeeded Plato, and did but formulate, as a terminology "of art," as technical language, what for Plato is still vernacular, original personal, the product in him of an instinctive imaginative power—a sort of *visual* power, but causing others also to see what is matter of original intuition for him.

From first to last our faculty of thinking is limited by our command of speech. Now it is straight from Plato's lips, as if in natural conversation, that the language came, in which the mind has ever since been discoursing with itself concerning itself, in that inward dialogue, which is the "active principle" of the dialectic method as an instrument for the attainment of truth. For, the essential, or dynamic, dialogue, is ever that dialogue of the mind with itself, which any converse with Socrates or Plato does but promote. The very words of Plato, then, challenge us straightway to larger and finer apprehension of the processess of our own minds; are themselves a discovery in the sphere of mind. It was he made us freemen of those solitary places, so trying yet so attractive: so remote and high, they seem, yet are naturally so close to us: he peopled them with intelligible forms. Nay more! By his peculiar gift of verbal articulation he divined the mere hollow spaces which a knowledge, then merely potential, and an experience still to come, would one day occupy. And so, those who cannot admit his actual speculative results, precisely *his* report on the invisible theoretic world, have been to the point sometimes, in their objection, that by sheer effectiveness of abstract language, he gave an illusive air of reality or substance to the mere nonentities of metaphysic hypothesis—of a mind trying to feed itself on its own emptiness.

Just there—in the situation of one, shaped, by combining nature and circumstance, into a seer who has a sort of sensuous love of the unseen—is the paradox of Plato's genius, and therefore, always, of Platonism, of the Platonic temper. His aptitude for things visible, with the gift of words, empowers him to express, as if for the eyes, what except to the eye of the mind is strictly invisible, what an acquired asceticism induces him to rank above, and sometimes, in terms of harshest dualism, oppose to, the sensible world. Plato is to be interpreted not merely by his antecedents, by the influence upon him of those who preceded him, but by his successors, by the temper, the intellectual alliances, of those who directly or indirectly have been sympathetic with him. Now it is noticeable that, at first sight somewhat incongruously, a certain number of Manicheans have always been of his company; people who held that matter was evil. Pointing significantly to an unmistakable vein of Manichean, or Puritan sentiment actually there in the Platonic Dialogues, these rude companions or successors of his, carry us back to his great predecessor, to Socrates, whose personal influence had so strongly enforced on Plato the severities, moral and intellectual, alike of Parmenides and of the Pythagoreans. The cold breath of a harshly abstract, a too incorporeal philosophy, had blown, like an east wind, on that last depressing day in the prison-cell of Socrates; and the venerable commonplaces then put forth, in which an overstrained pagan sensuality seems to be reacting, to be taking vengeance, on itself, turned now sick and suicidal, will lose none of their weight with Plato:—That "all who rightly touch philosophy, study nothing else than to *die*, and to be *dead*,"—that "the soul reasons best, when, as much as possible, it comes to be alone with itself, bidding good-bye to the body, and, to the utmost of its power, rejecting communion with it, with the very touch of it, aiming at what *is*." It was, in short, as if for the soul to have come into a human body at all, had been the seed of disease in it, the beginning of its own proper death.

As for any adornments or provision for this body, the master had declared that a true philosopher as such would make as little of them as possible. To those young hearers, the words of Socrates may well have seemed to anticipate, not the visible world he had then delineated in glowing colour as if for the bodily eye, but only the chilling influence of the hemlock; and it was because Plato was only half convinced of the Manichean or Puritan element in his master's doctrine, or rather was in contact with it on one side only of his complex and genial nature, that Platonism became possible, as a temper for which, in strictness, the opposition of matter to spirit has no ultimate or real existence. Not to be "pure" from the body, but to identify it, in its utmost fairness, with the fair soul, by a gymnastic "fused in music,"[30] became, from first to last, the aim of education as he conceived it. That the body is but "a hindrance to the attainment of philosophy, if one takes it along with one as a companion in one's search" (a notion which Christianity, at least in its later though wholly legitimate developments, will correct) can hardly have been the last thought of Plato himself on quitting it. He opens his door indeed to those austere monitors. They correct the sensuous richness of his genius, but could not suppress it. The sensuous lover becomes a lover of the invisible, but still a lover, after his earlier pattern, carrying into the world of intellectual vision, of θεωρία, all the associations of the actual world of sight. Some of its invisible realities he can all but see with the bodily eye: the absolute Temperance, in the person of the youthful Charmides; the absolute Righteousness, in the person of the dying Socrates. Yes, truly! all true knowledge will be like the knowledge of a person, of living persons, and truth, for Plato, in spite of his Socratic asceticism, to the last, something to *look* at. The eyes which had noted physical things, so finely, vividly, continuously, would be still at work; and, Plato thus qualifying the Manichean or Puritan element in Socrates by his own capacity for the world of sense, Platonism has contributed largely, has been an immense encouragement towards, the redemption of matter, of the world of sense, by art, by all right education, by the creeds and worship of the Christian Church—towards the vindication of the dignity of the body.[81]

It was doubtless because Plato was an excellent scholar that he did not begin to teach others till he was more than forty years old—one of the great scholars of the world, with Virgil and Milton:[82] by which is implied that, possessed of the inborn genius, of those natural powers, which sometimes bring with them a certain defiance of rule, of the intellectual habits of others, he acquires, by way of habit and rule, all that can be taught and learned; and what is thus derived from others by docility and discipline, what is *rangé*,[83] comes to have in him, and in his work, an equivalent weight with what is unique, impulsive, underivable. Raphael—Raphael, as you see him in the Blenheim *Madonna*, is a supreme example of such scholarship in the sphere of art. Born of a romantically ancient family, understood to be the descendant of Solon himself, Plato had been in early youth a writer of verse. That he turned to a more vigorous, though pedestrian[34] mode of writing, was perhaps an effect of his corrective intercourse with Socrates, through some of the most important years of his life,—from twenty to twenty-eight.

He belonged to what was just then the discontented class, and might well have taken refuge from active political life in political ideals, or in a kind of self-imposed exile. A traveller, adventurous for that age, he certainly became. After the *Lehr-jahre*, the *Wander-jahre!*—all round the Mediterranean coasts as far west as Sicily. Think of what all that must have meant just then, for eyes which could see. If those journeys had begun in angry flight from home,[35] it was for purposes of self-improvement they were continued: the delightful fruit of them is evident in what he writes; and finding him in friendly intercourse with Dionysius the elder, with Dio, and Dionysius the younger, at the polished court of Syracuse,[36] we may understand that they were a search also for "the philosophic king,"[37] perhaps for the opportune moment of realising "the ideal state." In that case, his quarrels with those capricious tyrants show that he was disappointed. For the future he sought no more to pass beyond the charmed theoretic circle, "speaking wisdom," as was said of Pythagoras, only "among the perfect." He turns finally to Athens; and there, in the quiet precincts of the *Acadêmus,* which has left a somewhat dubious name to places where people come to be taught or to teach, founds, not a state, nor even a brotherhood, but only the first college, with something of a common life, of communism on that small scale, with Aristotle for one of its scholars, with its chapel, its gardens, its library with the authentic text of his *Dialogues* upon the shelves: we may just discern the sort of place through the scantiest notices. His reign was after all to be in his writings. Plato himself does nothing in them to retard the effacement which mere time brings to persons and their abodes; and there had been that, moreover, in his own temper, which promotes self-effacement. Yet as he left it, the place remained for centuries, according to his will, to its original use. What he taught through the remaining forty years of his life,[88] the method of that teaching, whether it was less or more esoteric than the teaching of the extant *Dialogues,* is but matter of surmise. Writers, who in their day might still have said much we should have liked to hear, give us little but old, quasi-supernatural stories, told as if they had been new ones, about him. The year of his birth fell, according to some, in the very year of the death of Pericles (a significant date!) but is not precisely ascertainable: nor is the year of his death, nor its manner. *Scribens est mortuus,* says Cicero:—after the manner of a true scholar, "he died pen in hand."

NOTES

1. In the Munich Gallery, Pater had seen three paintings of destitute children by the Spanish painter Bartolomé Esteban Murillo (1617–1682). He refers here to at least two of them, "The Dice Players" and "The Melon Eaters."
2. The story of the grasshoppers is told by Socrates in Plato's *Phaedrus*.
3. For the story of Gyges and the ring, see *The Republic*, at the start of Book II.
4. We do not know the precise relation between Plato's "Socrates" and the historical Socrates.
5. For Charmides, see the dialogue bearing his name; for Cephalus, see particularly *The Republic*, Book I, 329.
6. *Corruptio optima pessima!:* "Nothing is worst than the corruption of the best."
7. See Plato's *Theaetetus* 172.
8. In the *Ion*, though Pater (deliberately?) refuses to see Plato's irony here.
9. They concern falsity both in governments and in moral character.
10. In Plato's *Euthydemus*.
11. See Plato's *The Statesman*, 302.
12. In *The Republic*, start of Book VII.
13. The "dialectic" of Socrates as opposed to the "rhetoric" of the Sophists.
14. See *The Republic*, IV, 429.
15. An equivocal sentence, but Pater liked to think of himself as a "crystal man," rather like his descendant in Wallace Stevens's "Asides on the Oboe," a very Paterian poem, as is so much of Stevens.
16. See the essay from *Greek Studies*, "The Age of Athletic Prizemen."
17. *Phaedrus*, 254.
18. Plato's quarrel with poetry was immensely complex; the reference here is to *Republic*, III, 398. Se Eric Havelock's *Preface to Plato* for a controversial modern commentary.
19. This is highly Paterian, and closer to Pater's Marius than to Plato.
20. The Eleatic school followed Parmenides of Elea (end of sixth century B.C.), whose doctrine is discussed by Pater in Chapter 2 of *Plato and Platonism*.
21. The "philosophy of motion," the skepticism of Heraclitus, is discussed in *Plato and Platonism's* first chapter.
22. Again an assimilation of Plato to Pater, with the more complex sublimation of Plato converted to the *askesis* of Pater.

23. A similar assimilation, informed by Pater's essay on "Style."
24. The *Gorgias*, a dialogue in which Socrates is peculiarly forceful and evangelistic.
25. Though poorly argued, the *Charmides* appealed to Pater because it sketched "the great beauty of the day," young Charmides, who is charmed by the not very beautiful Socrates, a "Caliban of Letters" like Pater himself.
26. What it was about the *Timaeus* that aesthetically moved Pater, I find difficult to see; the "brilliant chromatic effects" are presumably due to the grotesque but powerful mythopoeic force of the dialogue.
27. The *Theaetetus* is another curious choice for Pater to have made, though he may have interpreted this dialogue as being more skeptical than it is.
28. The *Phaedrus*, an old favorite of literary people, is both a treatise upon love, and a critique of the limits of literature, and in both regards crucial for Pater.
29. Opening with the great conceptual image of the cave of the mind, *Republic* VII goes on to an apotheosis of dialectic, in one of Plato's finest literary progressions.
30. A gymnastic "fused in music" means a physical discipline assimilated to the highest spiritual discipline, and helps suggest Pater's underlying meaning in "The School of Giorgione" when he experiences the vision of all the arts moving toward an apocalypse of music.
31. This appears to be a better description of the Renaissance Neoplatonism than of Platonism itself.
32. This is "scholar" in a high, honorific sense, similar to its use in "Style." Emerson is a good analogue, and Stevens, in using "scholar" and "poet" as synonyms, seems to follow an amalgam of Pater and Emerson.
33. *rangé:* "ordered, tidy, steady."
34. "Pedestrian" is used here rather literally, meaning "one who goes on foot" as opposed to riding the Pegasus of verse.
35. "Angry flight from home" is rather strong for Plato's self-exile.
36. All these were rulers of Syracuse, whom Plato hoped to influence toward founding a truly philosophic state.
37. Pater's ideal here was Marcus Aurelius, for whom see Chapter XVII of *Marius the Epicurean*.
38. Plato was eighty when he died, in 347 B.C.

from *Greek Studies*

Hippolytus Veiled

A STUDY FROM EURIPIDES[1]

Centuries of zealous archæology notwithstanding, many phases of the so varied Greek genius are recorded for the modern student in a kind of shorthand only, or not at all. Even for Pausanias,[2] visiting Greece before its direct part in affairs was quite played out, much had perished or grown dim—of its art, of the truth of its outward history, above all of its religion as a credible or practicable thing. And yet Pausanias visits Greece under conditions as favourable for observation as those under which later travellers, Addison or Eustace,[3] proceed to Italy. For him the impress of life in those old Greek cities is not less vivid and entire than that of medieval Italy to ourselves; at Siena, for instance, with its ancient palaces still in occupation, its public edifices as serviceable as if the old republic had but just now vacated them, the tradition of their primitive worship still unbroken in its churches. Had the opportunities in which Pausanias was fortunate been ours, how many haunts of the antique Greek life unnoticed by him we should have peeped into, minutely systematic in our painstaking! how many a view would broaden out where he notes hardly anything at all on his map of Greece![4]

One of the most curious phases of Greek civilisation which has thus perished for us, and regarding which, as we may fancy, we should have made better use of that old traveller's facilities, is the early Attic deme-life[5]—its picturesque, intensely localised variety, in the hollow or on the spur of mountain or sea-shore; and with it many a relic of primitive religion, many an early growth of art parallel to what Vasari records of artistic beginnings in the smaller cities of Italy. Colonus and Acharnæ, surviving still so vividly by the magic of Sophocles, of Aristophanes, are but isolated examples of a wide-spread manner of life, in which, amid many provincial peculiarities, the first, yet perhaps the most costly and telling steps were made in all the various departments of Greek culture. Even in the days of Pausanias, Piræus was still traceable as a distinct township, once the possible rival of Athens, with its little old covered market by the seaside, and the symbolical picture of the place, its Genius, visible on the wall. And that is but the type of what there had been to know of threescore and more village communities, each having its own altars, its special worship and place of civic assembly, its trade and crafts, its name drawn from physical peculiarity or famous incident, its body of heroic tradition. Lingering on while Athens, the great deme, gradually absorbed into itself more and more of their achievements, and passing away almost completely as political factors in the Peloponnesian war,[6] they were still felt, we can hardly doubt, in the actual physiognomy of Greece. That variety in unity, which its singular geographical formation secured to Greece as a whole, was at its utmost in these minute reflexions of the national character, with all the relish of local difference—new art, new poetry, fresh ventures in political combination, in the conception of life, springing as if straight from the soil, like the thorn-blossom of early spring in magic lines over all that rocky land. On the other hand, it was just here that ancient habits clung most tenaciously—that old-fashioned, homely, delightful existence, to which the refugee, pent up in Athens in the years of the Peloponnesian war, looked back so fondly. If the impression of Greece generally is but enchanced by the littleness of the physical scene of events intellectually so great—such a system of grand lines, restrained within so narrow a compass, as in one of its fine coins—still more would this be true of those centres of country life. Here, certainly, was that assertion of seemingly small interests, which brings into free play, and gives his utmost value to, the individual; making his warfare, equally with his more peaceful rivalries, deme against deme, the mountain against the plain, the seashore, (as in our own old Border life,[7] but played out here by wonderfully gifted people) tangible as a personal history, to the doubling of its fascination for those whose business is with the survey of the dramatic side of life.

As with civil matters, so it was also, we may fairly suppose, with religion; the deme-life was a manifestation of religious custom and sentiment, in all their primitive local variety. As Athens, gradually drawing into itself the various elements of provincial culture, developed, with authority, the central religious position, the demes-men did but add the worship of Athene Polias, the goddess of the capital, to their own preexistent ritual uses. Of local and central religion alike, time and circumstance had obliterated much when Pausanias came. A devout spirit, with religion for his chief interest, eager for the trace of a divine footstep, anxious even in the days of Lucian[8] to deal seriously with what had counted for so much to serious men, he has, indeed, to lament that "Pan is dead": —"They come no longer!"—"These things happen no longer!" But the Greek—his very name also, *Hellen*, was the title of a priesthood—had been religious abundantly, sanctifying every detail of his actual life with the religious idea; and as Pausanias goes on his way he finds many a remnant of that earlier estate of religion, when, as he fancied, it had been nearer the gods, as it was certainly nearer the earth. It is marked, even in decay, with varieties of place; and is not only continuous but *in situ*.[9] At Phigaleia he makes his offerings to Demeter, agreeably to the paternal rites of the inhabitants, wax, fruit, undressed wool "still full of the *sordes* of the sheep."[10] A dream from heaven cuts short his notice of the mysteries of Eleusis.[11] He sees the stone, "big enough for a little man," on which Silenus was used to sit and rest; at Athens, the tombs of the Amazons, of the purple-haired Nisus, of Deucalion;—"it is a manifest token that he had dwelt there."[12] The worshippers of Poseidon, even at his temple among the hills, might still feel the earth fluctuating beneath their feet. And in care for divine things, he tells us, the Athenians outdid all other Greeks.[13] Even in the days of Nero it revealed itself oddly; and it is natural to suppose that of this temper the demes, as the proper home of conservatism, were exceptionally expressive. Scattered in those remote, romantic villages, among their olives or seaweeds, lay the heroic graves, the relics, the sacred images, often rude enough amid the delicate tribute of later art; this too oftentimes finding in such retirement its best inspirations, as in some Attic Fiesole.[14] Like a network over the

land of gracious poetic tradition, as also of undisturbed ceremonial usage surviving late for those who cared to seek it, the
local religions had been never wholly superseded by the
worship of the great national temples. They were, in truth,
the most characteristic developments of a faith essentially
earth-born or indigenous.

And how often must the student of fine art, again, wish
he had the same sort of knowledge about its earlier growth
in Greece, that he actually possesses in the case of Italian
art! Given any development at all in this matter, there must
have been phases of art, which, if immature, were also veritable expressions of power to come, intermediate discoveries
of beauty, such as are by no means a mere anticipation,
and of service only as explaining historically larger subsequent achievements, but of permanent attractiveness in
themselves, being often, indeed, the true maturity of certain
amiable artistic qualities. And in regard to Greek art at its
best—the Parthenon—no less than to the art of the Renaissance at its best—the Sistine Chapel—the more instructive
light would be derived rather from what precedes than what
follows such central success, from the determination to
apprehend the fulfilment of past effort rather than the eve of
decline, in the critical, central moment which partakes of
both. Of such early promise, early achievement, we have in
the case of Greek art little to compare with what is extant
of the youth of the arts in Italy. Overbeck's[15] careful
gleanings of its history form indeed a sorry relic as contrasted with Vasari's intimations of the beginnings of the
Renaissance. Fired by certain fragments of its earlier days,
of a beauty, in truth, absolute, and vainly longing for more,
the student of Greek sculpture indulges the thought of an
ideal of youthful energy therein, yet withal of youthful self-
restraint; and again, as with survivals of old religion, the
privileged home, he fancies, of that ideal must have been in
those venerable Attic townships, as to a large extent it
passed away with them.

The budding of new art, the survival of old religion, at
isolated centres of provincial life, where varieties of human
chartacter also were keen, abundant, asserted in correspond-
ingly effective incident—this is what irresistible fancy superin-
duces on historic details, themselves meagre enough. The
sentiment of antiquity is indeed a characteristic of all culti-
vated people, even in what may seem the freshest ages, and

not exclusively a humour of our later world. In the earliest notices about them, as we know, the people of Attica appear already impressed by the immense antiquity of their occupation of its soil, of which they claim to be the very first flower. Some at least of those old demesmen we may well fancy sentimentally reluctant to change their habits, fearful of losing too much of themselves in the larger stream of life, clinging to what is antiquated as the work of centralisation goes on, needful as that work was, with the great "Eastern difficulty" already ever in the distance. The fear of Asia, barbaric, splendid, hardly known, yet haunting the curious imagination of those who had borrowed thence the art in which they were rapidly excelling it, developing, as we now see, in the interest of Greek humanity, crafts begotten of tyrannic and illiberal luxury, was finally to suppress the rivalries of those primitive centres of activity, when the "invincible armada" of the common foe came into sight.[16]

At a later period civil strife was to destroy their last traces. The old hoplite,[17] from Rhamnus or Acharnæ, pent up in beleaguered Athens during that first summer of the Peloponnesian war, occupying with his household a turret of the wall, as Thucydides describes—one of many picturesque touches in that severe historian—could well remember the ancient provincial life which this conflict with Sparta was bringing to an end. He could recall his boyish, half-scared curiosity concerning those Persian ships, coming first as merchantmen, or with pirates on occasion, in the half-savage, wicked splendours of their decoration, the monstrous figureheads, their glittering freightage. Men would hardly have trusted their women or children with that suspicious crew, hovering through the dusk. There were soothsayers, indeed, who had long foretold what happened soon after, giving shape to vague, supernatural terrors. And then he had crept from his hiding-place with other lads to go view the enemies' slain at Marathon,[18] beside those belated Spartans, this new war with whom seemed to be reviving the fierce local feuds of his younger days. *Paraloi* and *Diacrioi* had ever been rivals.[19] Very distant it all seemed now, with all the stories he could tell; for in those crumbling little towns, as heroic life had lingered on into the actual, so, at an earlier date, the supernatural into the heroic. Like mist at dawn, the last traces of its divine visitors had then vanished from the land, where, however, they had already begotten "our best and oldest families."

It was Theseus,[20] uncompromising young master of the situation, in fearless application of "the modern spirit" of his day to every phase of life where it was applicable, who, at the expense of Attica, had given Athens a people, reluctant enough, in truth, as Plutarch suggests, to desert "their homes and religious usages and many good and gracious kings of their own" for this elect youth, who thus figures, passably, as a kind of mythic shorthand for civilisation, making roads and the like, facilitating travel, suppressing various forms of violence, but many innocent things as well. So it must needs be in a world where, even hand in hand with a god-assisted hero, Justice goes blindfold. He slays the bull of Marathon and many another local tyrant, but also exterminates that delightful creature, the Centaur. The Amazon, whom Plato will reinstate as the type of improved womanhood, has no better luck than Phæa, the sow-pig of Crommyon, foul old landed-proprietress.[21] They exerted, however, the prerogative of poetic protest, and survive thereby. Centaur and Amazon, as we see them in the fine art of Greece, represent the regret of Athenians themselves for something that could never be brought to life again, and have their pathos. Those young heroes contending with Amazons on the frieze of the Mausoleum[22] had best make haste with their bloody work, if young people's eyes can tell a true story. A type still of progress triumphant through injustice, set on improving things off the face of the earth, Theseus took occasion to attack the Amazons[23] in their mountain home, not long after their ruinous conflict with Hercules, and hit them when they were down. That greater bully had laboured off on the world's highway, carrying with him the official girdle of Antiope, their queen, gift of Ares, and therewith, it would seem, the mystic secret of their strength. At sight of this new foe, at any rate, she came to a strange submission. The savage virgin had turned to very woman, and was presently a willing slave, returning on the gaily appointed ship in all haste to Athens, where in supposed wedlock she bore King Theseus a son.

With their annual visit—visit to the Gargareans!—for the purpose of maintaining their species, parting with their boys early, these husbandless women could hardly be supposed a very happy, certainly not a very joyous people. They figure rather as a sorry measure of the luck of the female sex in taking a hard natural law into their own hands, and by abnegation of all tender companionship making shift with bare independence, as a kind of second-best—the best practicable by them in the imperfect actual condition of things. But the heart-strings would ache still where the breast had been cut away. The sisters of Antiope had come, not immediately, but in careful array of battle, to bring back the captive. All along the weary roads from the Caucasus to Attica, their traces had remained in the great graves of those who died by the way. Against the little remnant, carrying on the fight to the very midst of Athens, Antiope herself had turned, all other thoughts transformed now into wild idolatry of her hero. Superstitious, or in real regret, the Athenians never forgot their tombs. As for Antiope, the conscience of her perfidy remained with her, adding the pang of remorse to her own desertion, when King Theseus, with his accustomed bad faith to women, set her, too, aside in turn. Phædra, the true wife, was there, peeping suspiciously at her arrival; and even as Antiope yielded to her lord's embraces the thought had come that a male child might be the instrument of her anger, and one day judge her cause.

In one of these doomed, decaying villages, then, King Theseus placed the woman and her babe, hidden, yet secure, within the Attic border, as men veil their mistakes or crimes. They might pass away, they and their story, together with the memory of other antiquated creatures of such places, who had had connubial dealings with the stars. The white, paved waggon-track, a by-path of the sacred way to Eleusis, zigzagged through sloping olive-yards, from the plain of silvered blue, with Athens building in the distance, and passed the door of the rude stone house, furnished scantily, which no one had ventured to inhabit of late years till they came there. On the ledges of the grey cliffs above, the laurel groves, stem and foliage of motionless bronze, had spread their tents. Travellers bound northwards were glad to repose themselves there, and take directions, or provision for their journey onwards, from the highland people, who came down hither to sell their honey, their cheese, and woollen stuff, in the tiny market-place. At dawn the great stars seemed to halt a while, burning as if for sacrifice to some pure deity, on those distant, obscurely named heights, like broken swords, the rim of the world. A little later you could just see the newly opened quarries, like streaks of snow on their russet-brown bosoms. Thither in spring-time all eyes turned from Athens devoutly, intent till the first shaft of lightning gave signal for the departure of the sacred ship to Delos.[24] Racing over those rocky surfaces, the virgin air descended hither with the secret of profound sleep, as the child lay in its cubicle hewn in the stone, the white fleeces heaped warmly round him. In the wild Amazon's soul, to her surprise, and at first against her will, the maternal sense had quickened from the moment of his conception, and (that burst of angry tears with which she had received him into the world once dried up), kindling more eagerly at every token of manly growth, had at length driven out every other feeling. And this animal sentiment, educating the human hand and heart in her, had become a moral one, when, King Theseus leaving her in anger, visibly unkind, the child had crept to her side, and tracing with small fingers the wrinkled lines of her woebegone brow, carved there as if by a thousand years of sorrow, had sown between himself and her the seed of an undying sympathy.

She was thus already on the watch for a host of minute recognitions on his part, of the self-sacrifice involved in her devotion to a career of which she must needs drain out the sorrow, careful that he might taste only the joy. So far, amid their spare living, the child, as if looking up to the warm broad wing of her love above him, seemed replete with comfort. Yet in his moments of childish sickness, the first passing shadows upon the deep joy of her motherhood, she teaches him betimes to soothe or cheat pain—little bodily pains only, hitherto. She ventures sadly to assure him of the harsh necessities of life: "Courage, child! Every one must take his share of suffering. Shift not thy body so vehemently. Pain, taken quietly, is easier to bear."

Carefully inverting the habits of her own rude childhood, she learned to spin the wools, white and grey, to clothe and cover him pleasantly. The spectacle of his unsuspicious happiness, though at present a matter of purely physical conditions, awoke a strange sense of poetry, a kind of artistic sense in her, watching, as her own long-deferred recreation in life, his delight in the little delicacies she prepared to his liking—broiled kids' flesh, the red wine, the mushrooms sought through the early dew—his hunger and thirst so daintily satisfied, as he sat at table, like the first-born of King

Theseus, with two wax-lights and a fire at dawn or nightfall dancing to the prattle and laughter, a bright child, never stupidly weary. At times his very happiness would seem to her like a menace of misfortune to come. Was there not with herself the curse of that unsisterly action? and not far from him, the terrible danger of the father's, the step-mother's jealousy, the mockery of those half-brothers to come? Ah! how perilous for happiness the sensibilities which make him so exquisitely happy now! Before they started on their dreadful visit to the Minotaur,[25] says Plutarch, the women told their sons many tales and other things to en-courage them; and, even as she had furnished the child betimes with rules for the solace of bodily pain, so now she would have brought her own sad experience into service in precepts for the ejection of its festering power out of any other trouble that might visit him. Already those little dis-appointments which are as the shadow beside all conscious enjoyment, were no petty things to her, but had for her their pathos, as children's troubles will have, in spite of the longer chance before them. They were as the first steps in a long story of deferred hopes, or anticipations of death itself and the end of them.

The gift of Ares gone, the mystic girdle she would fain have transferred to the child, that bloody god of storm and battle, hereditary patron of her house, faded from her thoughts together with the memory of her past life—the more completely, because another familiar though some-what forbidding deity, accepting certainly a cruel and for-bidding worship, was already in possession, and reigning in the new home when she came thither. Only, thanks to some kindly local influence (by grace, say, of its delicate air), Artemis, this other god she had known in the Scythian wilds,[26] had put aside her fierce ways, as she paused awhile on her heavenly course among these ancient abodes of men, gliding softly, mainly through their dreams, with abundance of salutary touches. Full, in truth, of grateful memory of some timely service at human hands! In these highland vil-lages the tradition of celestial visitants clung fondly, of god or hero, belated or misled on long journeys, yet pleased to be among the sons of men, as their way led them up the steep, narrow, crooked street, condescending to rest a little, as one, under some sudden stress not clearly ascertained, had done here, in this very house, thereafter for ever sacred. The place and its inhabitants, of course, had been something bigger in the days. of those old mythic hospitalities, unless, indeed, divine persons took kindly the will for the deed— very different, surely, from the present condition of things, for there was little here to detain a delicate traveller, even in the abode of Antiope and her son, though it had been the residence of a king.

Hard by stood the chapel of the goddess, who had thus adorned the place with her memories. The priests, indeed, were already departed to Athens, carrying with them the ancient image, the vehicle of her actual presence, as the surest means of enriching the capital at the expense of the country, where she must now make poor shift of the occasional worshipper on his way through these mountain passes. But safely roofed beneath the sturdy tiles of grey Hymettus marble,[27] upon the walls of the little square recess enclosing the deserted pedestal, a series of crowded imageries, in the devout spirit of earlier days, were eloquent concerning her. Here from scene to scene, touched with silver among the wild and human creatures in dun bronze, with the moon's disk around her head, shrouded closely, the goddess of the chase still glided mystically through all the varied incidents of her story, in all the detail of a written book.

A book for the delighted reading of a scholar, willing to ponder at leisure, to make his way surely, and understand. Very different, certainly, from the cruel-featured little idol his mother had brought in her bundle—the old Scythian Artemis, hanging there on the wall, side by side with the forgotten Ares, blood-red,—the goddess reveals herself to the lad, poring through the dusk by taper-light, as at once a virgin, necessarily therefore the creature of solitude, yet also as the assiduous nurse of children, and patroness of the young. Her friendly intervention at the act of birth everywhere, her claim upon the nursling, among tame and wild creatures equally, among men as among gods, nay! among the stars (upon the very star of dawn), gave her a breadth of influence seemingly coextensive with the sum of things. Yes! his great mother was in touch with everything. Yet throughout he can but note her perpetual chastity, with pleasurable though half-suspicious wonder at the mystery, he knows not what, involved therein, as though he awoke suddenly in some distant, unexplored region of her person and activity. Why the lighted torch always, and that long straight vesture rolled round so formally? Was it only against the cold of these northern heights?

To her, nevertheless, her maternity, her solitude, to this virgin mother, who, with no husband, no lover, no fruit of her own, is so tender to the children of others, in a full heart he devotes himself—his immaculate body and soul. Dedicating himself thus, he has the sense also that he becomes more entirely than ever the chevalier of his mortal mother, of her sad cause. The devout, diligent hands clear away carefully the dust, the faded relics of her former worship; a worship renewed once more as the sacred spring, set free from emcumbrance, in answer to his willing ministries murmurs again under the dim vault in its marble basin, work of primitive Titanic fingers—flows out through its rocky channel, filling the whole township with chaste thoughts of her.

Through much labour at length he comes to the veritable story of her birth, like a gift direct from the goddess herself to this loyal soul. There were those in later times who, like Æschylus, knew Artemis as the daughter not of Leto but of Demeter, according to the version of her history now conveyed to the young Hippolytus,[28] together with some deepened insight into her character. The goddess of Eleusis, on a journey, in the old days when, as Plato says, men lived nearer the gods, finding herself with child by some starry inmate of those high places, had lain down in the rock-hewn cubicle of the inner chamber, and, certainly in sorrow, brought forth a daughter. Here was the secret at once of the genial, all-embracing maternity of this new strange Artemis, and of those more dubious tokens, the lighted torch, the winding-sheet, the arrow of death on the string—of sudden death, truly, which may be thought after all the kindest, as prevenient of all disgraceful sickness or waste in the unsullied limbs. For the late birth into the world of this so shadowy daughter was somehow identified with the sudden passing into Hades of her first-born, Persephone.[29] As he scans those scenes anew, an awful surmise comes to him; his divine patroness moves there as death, surely. Still, however, gratefully putting away suspicion, he seized even in these ambiguous imageries their happier suggestions, satisfied in thinking of his new mother as but the giver of sound sleep, of the benign night, whence—mystery of mysteries!—good things are born softly, from which he awakes betimes for his health-

ful service to her. Either way, sister of Apollo or sister of
Persephone, to him she should be a power of sanity, sweet as
the flowers he offered her gathered at dawn, setting daily
their purple and white frost against her ancient marbles.
There was more certainly than the first breath of day in them.
Was there here something of her person, her sensible presence, by way of direct response to him in his early devotion,
astir for her sake before the very birds, nesting here so freely,
the quail above all, in some privileged connexion with her
story still unfathomed by the learned youth? Amid them he
too found a voice, and sang articulately the praises of the
great goddess.

Those more dubious traits, nevertheless, so lightly disposed
of by Hippolytus (Hecate[30] thus counting for him as Artemis
goddess of health), became to his mother, in the light of her
sad experience, the sum of the whole matter. While he drew
only peaceful inducements to sleep from that two-sided figure, she reads there a volume of sinister intentions, and
liked little this seemingly dead goddess, who could but move
among the living banefully, stealing with her night-shade into
the day where she had no proper right. The gods had ever
had much to do with the shaping of her fortunes and the
fortunes of her kindred; and the mortal mother felt nothing
less than jealousy from the hour when the lad had first
delightedly called her to share his discoveries, and learn the
true story (if it were not rather the malicious counterfeit) of
the new divine mother to whom he has thus absolutely
entrusted himself. Was not this absolute chastity itself a kind
of death? She, too, in secret makes her gruesome midnight offering with averted eyes. She dreams one night he is
in danger; creeps to his cubicle to see; the face is covered, as
he lies, against the cold. She traces the motionless outline,
raises the coverlet; with the nice black head deep in the fleecy
pillow he is sleeping quietly, he dreams of that other mother
gliding in upon the moonbeam, and awaking turns sympathetically upon the living woman, is subdued in a moment to the
expression of her troubled spirit, and understands.

And when the child departed from her for the first time,
springing from his white bed before the dawn, to accompany
the elders on their annual visit to the Eleusinian goddess, the
after-sense of his wonderful happiness, tranquillising her in
spite of herself by its genial power over the actual moment,
stirred nevertheless a new sort of anxiety for the future. Her

work in life henceforward was defined as a ministry to so precious a gift, in full consciousness of its risk; it became her religion, the centre of her pieties. She missed painfully his continual singing hovering about the place, like the earth itself made audible in all its humanities. Half-selfish for a moment, she prays that he may remain for ever a child, to her solace; welcomes now the promise of his chastity (though chastity were itself a kind of death) as the pledge of his abiding always with her. And these thoughts were but infixed more deeply by the sudden stroke of joy at his return home in ceremonial trim and grown more manly, with much increase of self-confidence in that brief absence among his fellows.

For, from the first, the unwelcome child, the outcast, had been successful, with that special good fortune which sometimes attends the outcast. His happiness, his invincible happiness, had been found engaging, perhaps by the gods, certainly by men; and when King Theseus came to take note how things went in that rough life he had assigned them, he felt a half liking for the boy, and bade him come down to Athens and see the sights, partly by way of proof to his already somewhat exacting wife of the difference between the old love and the new as measured by the present condition of their respective offspring. The fine nature, fastidious by instinct, but bred with frugality enough to find the charm of continual surprise in that delicate new Athens, draws, as he goes, the full savour of its novelties; the marbles, the space and finish, the busy gaiety of its streets, the elegance of life there, contrasting with while it adds some mysterious endearment to the thought of his own rude home. Without envy, in hope only one day to share, to win them by kindness, he gazes on the motley garden-plots, the soft bedding, the showy toys, the delicate keep of the children of Phædra, who turn curiously to their half-brother, venture to touch his long strange gown of homespun grey, like the soft coat of some wild creature who might let one stroke it. Close to their dainty existence for a while, he regards it as from afar; looks forward all day to the lights, the prattle, the laughter, the white bread, like sweet cake to him, of their ordinary evening meal; returns again and again, in spite of himself, to watch, to admire, feeling a power within him to merit the like; finds his way back at last, still light of heart, to his own poor fare, able to do without what he would enjoy so much. As, grateful

for his scanty part in things—for the make-believe of a feast
in the little white loaves she too has managed to come by,
sipping the thin white wine, he touches her dearly, the
mother is shocked with a sense of something unearthly in his
contentment, while he comes and goes, singing now more
abundantly than ever a new canticle to her divine rival. Were
things, after all, to go grudgingly with him? Sensible of that
curse on herself, with her suspicions of his kinsfolk, of this
dubious goddess to whom he has devoted himself, she anticipates with more foreboding than ever his path to be, with
or without a wife—her own solitude, or his—the painful
heats and cold. She fears even these late successes; it were
best to veil their heads. The strong as such had ever been
against her and hers. The father came again; noted the boy's
growth. Manliest of men, like Hercules in his cloak of lion's
skin, he has after all but scant liking, feels, through a certain
meanness of soul, scorn for the finer likeness of himself.
Might this creature of an already vanishing world, who for all
his hard rearing had a manifest distinction of character, one
day become his rival, full of loyalty as he was already to the
deserted mother?

To charming Athens, nevertheless, he crept back, as occasion served, to gaze peacefully on the delightful good fortune
of others, waiting for the opportunity to take his own turn
with the rest, driving down thither at last in a chariot gal-
lantly, when all the town was assembled to celebrate the
king's birthday. For the goddess, herself turning ever kinder,
and figuring more and more exclusively as the tender nurse of
all things, had transformed her young votary from a hunter
into a charioteer, a rearer and driver of horses, after the
fashion of his Amazon mothers before him. Thereupon, all the
lad's wholesome vanity had centered on the fancy of the world-
famous games then lately established, as, smiling down his
mother's terrors, and grateful to his celestial mother for many
a hair-breadth escape, he practised day by day, fed the animals, drove them out, amused though companionless, visited
them affectionately in the deserted stone stables of the ancient
king. A chariot and horses, as being the showiest outward
thing the world afforded, was like the pawn he moved to
represent the big demand he meant to make, honestly, generously, on the ample fortunes of life. There was something
of his old miraculous kindred, alien from this busy new
world he came to, about the boyish driver with the fame of a

scholar, in his grey fleecy cloak and hood of soft white woollen stuff, as he drove in that morning. Men seemed to have seen a star flashing, and crowded round to examine the little mountainbred beasts, in loud, friendly intercourse with the hero of the hour—even those usually somewhat unsympathetic half-brothers now full of enthusiasm for the outcast and his good fight for prosperity. Instinctively people admired his wonderful placidity, and would fain have shared its secret, as it were the carelessness of some fair flower upon his face. A victor in the day's race, he carried home as his prize a glittering new harness in place of the very old one he had come with. "My chariot and horses!" he says now, with his single touch of pride. Yet at home, savouring to the full his old solitary happiness, veiled again from time to time in that ancient life, he is still the student, still ponders the old writings which tell of his divine patroness. At Athens strange stories are told in turn of him, his nights upon the mountains, his dreamy sin, with that hypocritical virgin goddess, stories which set the jealous suspicions of Theseus at rest once more. For so "dream" not those who have the tangible, appraisable world in view. Even Queen Phædra looks with pleasure, as he comes, on the once despised illegitimate creature, at home now here too, singing always audaciously, so visibly happy, occupied, popular.

Encompassed by the luxuries of Athens, far from those peaceful mountain places, among people further still in spirit from their peaceful light and shade, he did not forget the kindly goddess, still sharing with his earthly mother the prizes, or what they would buy, for the adornment of their spare abode. The tombs of the fallen Amazons, the spot where they had breathed their last, he piously visited, informed himself of every circumstance of the event with devout care, and, thinking on them amid the dainties of the royal table, boldly brought them too their share of the offerings to the heroic dead. Aphrodite, indeed—Aphrodite, of whom he had scarcely so much as heard—was just then the best-served deity in Athens, with all its new wealth of colour and form, its gold and ivory, the acting, the music, the fantastic women, beneath the shadow of the great walls still rising steadily.[81] Hippolytus would have no part in her worship; instead did what was in him to revive the neglected service of his own goddess, stirring an old jealousy. For Aphrodite too had looked with delight upon the youth, already the centre of a hundred less dangerous human rivalries among the maidens of Greece, and was by no means indifferent to his indifference, his instinctive distaste; while the sterner, almost forgotten Artemis found once more her great moon-shaped cake, set about with starry tapers, at the appointed seasons.

They know him now from afar, by his emphatic, shooting, arrowy movements; and on the day of the great chariot races "he goes in and wins." To the surprise of all he compounded his handsome prize for the old wooden image taken from the chapel at home, lurking now in an obscure shrine in the meanest quarter of the town. Sober amid the noisy feasting which followed, unashamed, but travelling by night to hide it from their mockery, warm at his bosom, he reached the passes at twilight, and through the deep peace of the glens bore it to the old resting-place, now more worthy than ever of the presence of its mistress, his mother and all the people of the village coming forth to salute her, all doors set mystically open, as she advances.

Phædra too, his step-mother, a fiery soul with wild strange blood in her veins, forgetting her fears of this illegitimate rival of her children, seemed now to have seen him for the first time, loved at last the very touch of his fleecy cloak, and would fain have had him of her own religion. As though the once neglected child had been another, she tries to win him as a stranger in his manly perfection, growing more than an affectionate mother to her husband's son. But why thus intimate and congenial, she asks, always in the wrong quarter? Why not compass two ends at once? Why so squeamishly neglect the powerful, any power at all, in a city so full of religion? He might find the image of her sprightly goddess everywhere, to his liking, gold, silver, native or stranger, new or old, graceful, or indeed, if he preferred it so, in iron or stone.[82] By the way, she explains the delights of love, of marriage, the husband once out of the way; finds in him, with misgiving, a sort of forwardness, as she thinks, on this one matter, as if he understood her craft and despised it. He met her questions in truth with scarce so much as contempt, with laughing counter-queries, why people needed wedding at all? They might have *found* the children in the temples, or bought them, as you could buy flowers in Athens.

Meantime Phædra's young children draw from the seemingly unconscious finger the marriage-ring, set it spinning on the floor at his feet, and the staid youth places it for a moment on his own finger for safety. As it settles there, his step-mother, aware all the while, suddenly presses his hand over it. He found the ring there that night as he lay; left his bed in the darkness, and again, for safety, put it on the finger of the image, wedding once for all that so kindly mystical mother. And still, even amid his earthly mother's terrible misgivings, he seems to foresee a charming career marked out before him in friendly Athens, to the height of his desire. Grateful that he is here at all, sharing at last so freely life's banquet, he puts himself for a moment in his old place, recalling his old enjoyment of the pleasure of others; feels, just then, no different. Yet never had life seemed so sufficing as at this moment—the meat, the drink, the drives, the popularity as he comes and goes, even his step-mother's false, selfish, ostentatious gifts. But she, too, begins to feel something of the jealousy of that other divine, would-be mistress, and by way of a last effort to bring him to a better mind in regard to them both, conducts him (immeasurable privilege!) to her own private chapel.

You could hardly tell where the apartments of the adulteress ended and that of the divine courtesan began. Haunts of her long, indolent, self-pleasing nights and days, they presented everywhere the impress of Phædra's luxurious humour. A peculiar glow, such as he had never before seen, like heady lamplight, or sunshine to some sleeper in a delirious dream, hung upon, clung to, the bold, naked, shameful imageries, as his step-mother trimmed the lamps, drew forth her sickly perfumes, clad afresh in piquant change of raiment the almost formless goddess crouching there in her unclean shrine or stye, set at last her foolish wheel in motion to a low chant, holding him by the wrist, keeping close all the while, as if to catch some germ of consent in his indifferent words.

And little by little he perceives that all this is for him—the incense, the dizzy wheel, the shreds of stuff cut secretly from his sleeve, the sweetened cup he drank at her offer, unavailingly; and yes! his own features surely, in pallid wax. With a gasp of flighty laughter she ventures to point the thing out to him, full as he is at last of visible, irrepressible dislike. Ah! it was that very reluctance that chiefly stirred her. Healthily white and red, he had a marvelous air of discretion about him, as of one never to be caught unaware, as if he never could be anything but like water from the rock, or the wild flowers of the morning, or the beams of the morning star

turned to human flesh. It was the self-possession of this happy
mind, the purity of this virgin body, she would fain have
perturbed, as a pledge to herself of her own gaudy claim
to supremacy. King Theseus, as she knew, had had at
least two earlier loves; for once she would be a first love; felt
at moments that with this one passion once indulged, it might
be happiness thereafter to remain chaste for ever. And then,
by accident, yet surely reading indifference in his manner of
accepting her gifts, she is ready again for contemptuous, open
battle. Is he indeed but a child still, this nursling of the for-
bidding Amazon, of that Amazonian goddess—to be a child
always? or a wily priest rather, skilfully circumventing her
sorceries, with mystic precautions of his own? In truth, there
is something of the priestly character in this impassible discretion, reminding her of his alleged intimacy with the rival
goddess, and redoubling her curiosity, her fondness. Phædra,
love-sick, feverish, in bodily sickness at last, raves of the cool
woods, the chase, the steeds of Hippolytus, her thoughts running madly on what she fancies to be his secret business;
with a storm of abject tears, foreseeing in one moment of
recoil the weary tale of years to come, star-stricken as she
declares, she dared at last to confess her longing to already
half-suspicious attendants; and, awake one morning to find
Hippolytus there kindly at her bidding, drove him openly
forth in a tempest of insulting speech. There was a mordant
there, like the menace of misfortune to come, in which the
injured goddess also was invited to concur. What words! what
terrible words! following, clinging to him, like acrid fire upon
his bare flesh, as he hasted from Phædra's house, thrust out
at last, his vesture remaining in her hands. The husband
returning suddenly, she tells him a false story of violence to
her bed, and is believed.

King Theseus, all his accumulated store of suspicion and
dislike turning now to active hatred, flung away readily upon
him, bewildered, unheard, one of three precious curses (some
mystery of wasting sickness therein) with which Poseidon had
indulged him.[83] It seemed sad that one so young must call
for justice, precariously, upon the gods, the dead, the very
walls! Admiring youth dared hardly bid farewell to their late
comrade; are generous, at most, in stolen, sympathetic
glances towards the fallen star. At home, veiled once again in
that ancient twilight world, his mother, fearing solely for what
he may suffer by the departure of that so brief prosperity,

enlarged as it had been, even so, by his grateful taking of it, is reassured, delighted, happy once more at the visible proof of his happiness, his invincible happiness. Duly he returned to Athens, early astir, for the last time, to restore the forfeited gifts, drove back his gaily painted chariot to leave there behind him, actually enjoying the drive, going home on foot poorer than ever. He takes again to his former modes of life, a little less to the horses, a little more to the old studies, the strange, secret history of his favourite goddess,—wronged surely! somehow, she too, as powerless to help him; till he lay sick at last, battling one morning, unaware of his mother's presence, with the feverish creations of the brain; the giddy, foolish wheel, the foolish song, of Phædra's chapel, spinning there with his heart bound thereto. "The curses of my progenitors are come upon me!" he cries. "And yet, why so? guiltless as I am of evil." His wholesome religion seeming to turn against him now, the trees, the streams, the very rocks, swoon into living creatures, swarming around the goddess who has lost her grave quietness. He finds solicitation, and recoils, in the wind, in the sounds of the rain; till at length delirium itself finds a note of returning health. The feverish wood-ways of his fancy open unexpectedly upon wide currents of air, lulling him to sleep; and the conflict ending suddenly altogether at its sharpest, he lay in the early light motionless among the pillows, his mother standing by, as she thought, to see him die. As if for the last time, she presses on him the things he had liked best in that eating and drinking she had found so beautiful. The eyes, the eyelids are big with sorrow; and, as he understands again, making an effort for her sake, the healthy light returns into his; a hand seizes hers gratefully, and a slow convalescence begins, the happiest period in the wild mother's life. When he longed for flowers for the goddess, she went a toilsome journey to seek them, growing close, after long neglect, wholesome and firm on their tall stalks. The singing she had longed for so despairingly hovers gaily once more within the chapel and around the house.

At the crisis of that strange illness she had supposed her long forebodings about to be realised at last; but upon his recovery feared no more, assured herself that the curses of the father, the step-mother, the concurrent ill-will of that angry goddess, have done their utmost; he will outlive her; a few years hence put her to a rest surely welcome. Her misgivings, arising always out of the actual spectacle of his pro-

found happiness, seemed at an end in this meek bliss, the
more as she observed that it was a shade less unconscious
than of old. And almost suddenly he found the strength, the
heart, in him, to try his fortune again with the old chariot;
and those still unsatisfied curses, in truth, going on either
side of him like living creatures unseen, legend tells briefly
how, a competitor for pity with Adonis, and Icarus, and
Hyacinth, and other doomed creatures of immature radiance
in all story to come,[84] he set forth joyously for the chariot-
races, not of Athens, but of Trœzen, her rival. Once more he
wins the prize; he says good-bye to admiring friends anxious
to entertain him, and by night starts off homewards, as of
old, like a child, returning quickly through the solitude in
which he had never lacked company, and was now to die.
Through all the perils of darkness he had guided the chariot
safely along the curved shore; the dawn was come, and a
little breeze astir, as the grey level spaces parted delicately
into white and blue, when in a moment an earthquake, or
Poseidon the earth-shaker himself, or angry Aphrodite awake
from the deep betimes, rent the tranquil surface; a great wave
leapt suddenly into the placid distance of the Attic shore, and
was surging here to the very necks of the plunging horses, a
moment since enjoying so pleasantly with him the caress of
the morning air, but now, wholly forgetful of their old affectionate habit of obedience, dragging their leader headlong over
the rough pavements. Evening and the dawn might seem to
have met on that hapless day through which they drew him
home entangled in the trappings of the chariot that had been
his ruin, till he lay at length, grey and haggard, at the rest he
had longed for dimly amid the buffeting of those murderous
stones, his mother watching impassibly, sunk at once into the
condition she had so long anticipated.

Later legend breaks a supernatural light over that great
desolation, and would fain relieve the reader by introducing
the kindly Asclepius,[85] who presently restores the youth to
life, not, however, in the old form or under familiar conditions. To her, surely, counting the wounds, the disfigure-
ments, telling over the pains which had shot through that
dear head now insensible to her touch among the pillows
under the harsh broad daylight, that would have been no
more of a solace than if, according to the fancy of Ovid,[86]
he flourished still, a little deity, but under a new name and

veiled now in old age, in the haunted grove of Aricia,[37] far from his old Attic home, in a land which had never seen him as he was.

NOTES

1. Euripides (480–406 B.C.), whose tragic drama *Hippolytus* is Pater's prime source here.
2. Pausanias was a topographer of the second century B.C., whose *Description of Greece* contains a version of the story of Hippolytus.
3. The references are to Joseph Addison's *Remarks on Italy* (1705) and J. C. Eustace's *Tour Through Italy* (1813).
4. An instance, serio-comic, of Pater's historicized Romanticism. He asks for a Pausanias who would have written a kind of *Marius the Epicurean* set in ancient Greece, a Pausanias-Pater who would have added strangeness to beauty, curiosity to the picturesque.
5. Attica was divided into one hundred demes (townships) *circa* 500 B.C.
6. The Peloponnesian War (431–404 B.C.) was fought between Athens and Sparta, each at the head of a coalition of city-states.
7. This is the English-Scottish border, in the later medieval period.
8. Lucian (125-190 A.D.), Greek satirical author.
9. *In situ:* "in position."
10. The quotation is from Pausanius. Demeter or Ceres was the harvest-goddess; *sordes* is Latin for "filth."
11. Again from Pausanias; the satyr Silenus taught the young god Dionysus; the mysteries were performed at the temple of Demeter in Eleusis.
12. The quotation again is from Pausanias. The Amazons, fighting-women of Scythia, by legend perpetually fought against the Greeks. The purple-haired Nisus was King of Megara, a city magically safeguarded by his hair. Deucalion, the Green version of Noah, survived the floods brought down by Zeus, to beget a new race of men upon his wife Pyrrha.
13. The source is still Pausanias; Poseidon was god of ocean.
14. Fiesole, small city near Florence.
15. Johannes Adolf Overbeck (1826–1895), author of *Ancient Manuscript Sources for the History of Greek Arts* (1868).
16. The "invincible armada" of the Persians menaced Athens in 480 B.C.
17. *Hoplite:* soldier in Greek heavy infantry.

18. Marathon: mountain-pass north of Athens; site of Persian debacle at hands of the Greeks, 490 B.C.
19. *Paraloi:* sea-coast dwellers; *Diacrioi:* mountain-people; names given by Aristotle for two of the three Athenian political parties.
20. Theseus, mythological national hero of Athens; Pater's source here is from Plutarch's *Lives.*
21. Plutarch says that a wild woman robber chieftain of Crommyon, known as Phaea or the wild sow, was slain by Theseus.
22. Mausaleum: great tomb of King Mausalus of Caria, built around 350 B.C.
23. One of the dozen quests or "labors" of Hercules was to capture the girdle of the Amazon queen.
24. Delos: sacred isle of Apollo.
25. Minotaur: Cretan monster with head of human and body of a bull; slain by Theseus.
26. "This other god": other form of Artemis.
27. Hymettus marble came from Mt. Hymettus in Attica.
28. Hippolytus was the son of Theseus by Antiope.
29. Persephone: Roman name for Proserpina, seized by Dis (Pluto) and carried off to Hades as his queen. In Pater's highly characteristic myth-making, Hippolytus does not distinguish betwen Artemis and Persephone, both daughters of Demeter.
30. Hecate is identified here with Persephone as Queen of Hades, and thus identified also with Artemis.
31. Aphrodite, goddess of love.
32. "Sprightly goddess": Aphrodite.
33. Poseidon, his father, granted Theseus the power of three effectual curses, but no more.
34. Adonis, loved by Aphrodite, was killed by a wild boar he hunted, despite her warnings. Icarus and his father Daedalus, the great artificer, escaped Crete on wings, but Icarus drowned when he flew too near the sun, despite his father's warning. Hyacinth, youth loved by Apollo, died when struck accidentally by a discus thrown by the god in play.
35. Asclepius: god of medicine.
36. Ovid, *Metamorphoses,* XV, 470 ff.
37. In Ovid's version, Hippolytus survived as a woodland quasi-god under the name of Virbius, follower of Diana (Artemis) in Aricia, a valley in Italy.

from *Sketches and Reviews*

A Novel by Mr. Oscar Wilde

("THE PICTURE OF DORIAN GRAY.")

There is always something of an excellent talker about the writing of Mr. Oscar Wilde; and in his hands, as happens so rarely with those who practise it, the form of dialogue is justified by its being really alive. His genial, laughter-loving sense of life and its enjoyable intercourse, goes far to obviate any crudity there may be in the paradox, with which, as with the bright and shining truth which often underlies it, Mr. Wilde, startling his "countrymen," carries on, more perhaps than any other writer, the brilliant critical work of Matthew Arnold. *The Decay of Lying*, for instance, is all but unique in its half-humorous, yet wholly convinced, presentment of certain valuable truths of criticism. Conversational ease, the fluidity of life, felicitous expression, are qualities which have a natural alliance to the successful writing of fiction; and side by side with Mr. Wilde's *Intentions* (so he entitles his critical efforts) comes a novel, certainly original, and affording the reader a fair opportunity of comparing his practise as a creative artist with many a precept he has enounced as critic concerning it.

A wholesome dislike of the common-place, rightly or wrongly identified by him with the *bourgeois*, with our middle-class—its habits and tastes—leads him to protest emphatically against so-called "realism" in art; life, as he argues, with much plausibility, as a matter of fact, when it is really awake, following art—the fashion an effective artist sets; while art, on the other hand, influential and effective art, has never taken its cue from actual life. In *Dorian Gray* he is true certainly, on the whole, to the æsthetic philosophy of his *Intentions*; yet not infallibly, even on this point: there is a certain amount of the intrusion of real life and its sordid aspects—the low theatre, the pleasures and griefs, the faces of some very unrefined people, managed, of course, cleverly enough. The interlude of Jim Vane, his half-sullen but wholly faithful care for his sister's honour, is as good as perhaps anything of the kind, marked by a homely but real pathos, sufficiently proving a versatility in the writer's talent, which should make his books popular. Clever always, this book, however, seems to set forth anything but a homely philosophy of life for the middle-class—a kind of dainty Epicurean theory, rather—yet fails, to some degree, in this; and one can see why. A true Epicureanism aims at a complete though harmonious development of man's entire organism. To lose the moral sense therefore, for instance, the sense of sin and righteousness, as Mr. Wilde's heroes are bent on doing as speedily, as completely as they can, is to lose, or lower, organisation, to become less complex, to pass from a higher to a lower degree of development. As a story, however, a partly supernatural story, it is first-rate in artistic management; those Epicurean niceties only adding to the decorative colour of its central figure, like so many exotic flowers, like the charming scenery and the perpetual, epigrammatic, surprising, yet so natural, conversations, like an atmosphere all about it. All that pleasant accessory detail, taken straight from culture, the intellectual and social interests, the conventionalities, of the moment, have, in fact, after all, the effect of the better sort of realism, throwing into relief the adroitly-devised supernatural element after the manner of Poe, but with a grace he never reached, which supersedes that earlier didactic purpose, and makes the quite sufficing interest of an excellent story.

We like the hero, and in spite of his somewhat unsociable devotion to his art, Hallward, better than Lord Henry Wotton. He has too much of a not very really refined world in and about him, and his somewhat cynical opinions, which seem sometimes to be those of the writer, who may, however, have intended Lord Henry as a satiric sketch. Mr. Wilde can hardly have intended him, with his cynic amity of mind and temper, any more than the miserable end of Dorian himself, to figure the motive and tendency of a true Cyrenaic or Epicurean doctrine of life. In contrast with Hallward, the artist, whose sensibilities idealise the world around him, the personality of Dorian Gray, above all, into something magnificent and strange, we might say that Lord Henry, and even more the, from the first, suicidal hero, loses too much in life to be a true Epicurean—loses so much in the way of impressions, of pleasant memories, and subsequent hopes, which Hallward, by a really Epicurean economy, manages to secure. It should be said however, in fairness, that the writer is impersonal: seems not to have identified himself entirely with any one of his characters: and Wotton's cynicism, or whatever it may be, at least makes a very clever story possible. He becomes the spoiler of the fair young man, whose bodily form remains un-aged; while his picture, the *chef d'oeuvre*[1] of the artist Hallward, changes miraculously with the gradual corruption of his soul. How true, what a light on the artistic nature, is the following on actual personalities and their revealing influence in art. We quote it as an example of Mr. Wilde's more serious style.

"I sometimes think that there are only two eras of any importance in the world's history. The first is the appearance of a new medium for art, and the second is the appearance of new personality for art also. What the invention of oil-painting was to the Venetians, the face of Antinous was to late Greek sculpture, and the face of Dorian Gray will some day be to me. It is not merely that I paint from him, draw from him, sketch from him. Of course I have done all that. But he is much more to me than a model or a sitter. I won't tell you that I am dissatisfied with what I have done of him, or that his beauty is such that art cannot express it. There is nothing that art cannot express, and I know that the work I have done, since I met Dorian Gray, is good work, is the best work of my life. But in some curious way his personality has suggested to me an entirely new manner in art, an entirely new mode of style. I see things differently, I think of them differently. I can now recreate life in a way that was hidden from me before."

Dorian himself, though certainly a quite unsuccessful experiment in Epicureanism, in life as a fine art, is (till his inward spoiling takes visible effect suddenly, and in a moment, at the end of his story) a beautiful creation. But his story is also a vivid, though carefully considered, exposure of the corruption of a soul, with a very plain moral, pushed home, to the effect that vice and crime make people coarse and ugly.

General readers, nevertheless, will probably care less for this moral, less for the fine, varied, largely appreciative culture of the writer, in evidence from page to page, than for the story itself, with its adroitly managed supernatural incidents, its almost equally wonderful applications of natural science; impossible, surely, in fact, but plausible enough in fiction. Its interest turns on that very old theme, old because based on some inherent experience or fancy of the human brain, of a double life: of Döppelgänger[2]—not of two *persons*, in this case, but of the man and his portrait; the latter of which, as we hinted above, changes, decays, is spoiled, while the former, through a long course of corruption, remains, to the outward eye, unchanged, still in all the beauty of a seemingly immaculate youth—"the devil's bargain." But it would be a pity to spoil the reader's enjoyment by further detail. We need only emphasise, once more, the skill, the real sublety of art, the ease and fluidity withal of one telling a story by word of mouth, with which the consciousness of the supernatural is introduced into, and maintained amid, the elaborately conventional, sophisticated, disabused world Mr. Wilde depicts so cleverly, so mercilessly. The special fascination of the piece is, of course, just there—at that point of contrast. Mr. Wilde's work may fairly claim to go with that of Edgar Poe,[3] and with some good French work of the same kind, done, probably, in more or less conscious imitation of it.

NOTES

1. *Chef d'oeuvre:* "masterwork."
2. *Döppelgänger:* "a double, or shadow-self."
3. Presumably Pater is thinking of Poe's story of a *döppelgänger*, "William Wilson."

WITHDRAWN

WITHDRAWN